POEMS

AND

SELECTED

LETTERS

THE OTHER VOICE IN EARLY MODERN EUROPE

A Series Edited by
Margaret L. King and
Albert Rabil, Jr.

Veronica Franco

POEMS
AND
SELECTED
LETTERS

༄

Edited and Translated
by
Ann Rosalind Jones
and Margaret F. Rosenthal

THE UNIVERSITY OF CHICAGO PRESS
Chicago & London

Ann Rosalind Jones is Esther Cloudman Dunn Professor of Comparative Literature at Smith College. She is the author of *The Currency of Eros: Women's Love Lyric in Europe, 1540–1620.*
Margaret F. Rosenthal is associate professor of Italian at the University of Southern California. She is the author of *The Honest Courtesan: Veronica Franco, Citizen and Writer in Sixteenth-Century Venice,* published by the University of Chicago Press.

The University of Chicago Press, Chicago 60637
The University of Chicago Press, Ltd., London
© 1998 by The University of Chicago
All rights reserved. Published 1998
07 06 05 04 03 02 01 00 99 98   1 2 3 4 5

ISBN: 0-226-25986-2 (cloth)
ISBN: 0-226-25987-0 (paper)

The Italian text of Franco's poetry is reproduced from *Rime,* by Veronica Franco, edited by Stefano Bianchi (Milan: Gruppo Ugo Mursia, 1995) with the permission of the publisher.

This translation was supported by generous grants from the National Endowment for the Humanities and from the Mellon Foundation.

Library of Congress Cataloging-in-Publication Data
Franco, Veronica, 1546–1591.
    [Selections. English & Italian. 1998]
    Poems and selected letters / Veronica Franco ; edited and translated by Ann Rosalind Jones and Margaret F. Rosenthal.
        p.   cm. — (The other voice in early modern Europe)
    Includes bibliographical references and index.
    ISBN 0-226-25986-2 (cloth : alk. paper). — ISBN 0-226-25987-0 (pbk. : alk. paper)
        I. Jones, Ann Rosalind.   II. Rosenthal, Margaret F.   III. Title.
    IV. Series.
PQ4623.F6A613   1998
851'.4—dc21   98-25551
                                                                CIP

For our daughters, Anne and Anna

CONTENTS

THE OTHER VOICE
IN EARLY MODERN EUROPE
INTRODUCTION TO THE SERIES
Margaret L. King and Albert Rabil, Jr.

THE OLD VOICE AND THE OTHER VOICE

In western Europe and the United States women are nearing equality in the professions, in business, and in politics. Most enjoy access to education, reproductive rights, and autonomy in financial affairs. Issues vital to women are on the public agenda: equal pay, child care, domestic abuse, breast cancer research, and curricular revision with an eye to the inclusion of women.

These recent achievements have their origins in things women (and some male supporters) said for the first time about six hundred years ago. Theirs is the "other voice," in contradistinction to the "first voice," the voice of the educated men who created Western culture. Coincident with a general reshaping of European culture in the period 1300 to 1700 (called the Renaissance or early modern period), questions of female equality and opportunity ere raised that still resound and are still unresolved.

The "other voice" emerged against the backdrop of a three-thousand-year history of misogyny—the hatred of women—rooted in the civilizations related to Western culture: Hebrew, Greek, Roman, and Christian. Misogyny inherited from these traditions pervaded the intellectual, medical, legal, religious, and social systems that developed during the European Middle Ages.

The following pages describe the misogynistic tradition inherited by early modern Europeans, and the new tradition which the "other voice" called into being to challenge reigning assumptions. This review should serve as a framework for the understanding of the texts published in the series "The Other Voice in Early Modern Europe." Introductions specific to each text and author follow this essay in all the volumes of the series.

ix

THE MISOGYNIST TRADITION, 500 B.C.E.–1500 C.E.

Embedded in the philosophical and medical theories of the ancient Greeks were perceptions of the female as inferior to the male in both mind and body. Similarly, the structure of civil legislation inherited from the ancient Romans was biased against women, and the views on women developed by Christian thinkers out of the Hebrew Bible and the Christian New Testament were negative and disabling. Literary works composed in the vernacular language of ordinary people, and widely recited or read, conveyed these negative assumptions. The social networks within which most women lived—those of the family and the institutions of the Roman Catholic church—were shaped by this misogynist tradition and sharply limited the areas in which women might act in and upon the world.

GREEK PHILOSOPHY AND FEMALE NATURE. Greek biology assumed that women were inferior to men and defined them merely as childbearers and housekeepers. This view was authoritatively expressed in the works of the philosopher Aristotle.

Aristotle thought in dualities. He considered action superior to inaction, form (the inner design or structure of any object) superior to matter, completion to incompletion, possession to deprivation. In each of these dualities, he associated the male principle with the superior quality and the female with the inferior. "The male principle in nature," he argued, "is associated with active, formative and perfected characteristics, while the female is passive, material and deprived, desiring the male in order to become complete."[1] Men are always identified with virile qualities, such as judgment, courage, and stamina; women with their opposites—irrationality, cowardice, and weakness.

The masculine principle was considered to be superior even in the womb. Man's semen, Aristotle believed, created the form of a new human creature, while the female body contributed only matter. (The existence of the ovum, and the other facts of human embryology, were not established until the seventeenth century.) Although the later Greek physician Galen believed that there was a female component in generation, contributed by "female semen," the followers of both Aristotle and Galen saw the male role in human generation as more active and more important.

In the Aristotelian view, the male principle sought always to reproduce itself. The creation of a female was always a mistake, therefore, resulting from an imperfect act of generation. Every female born was considered a "defective" or "mutilated" male (as Aristotle's terminology has variously been translated), a "monstrosity" of nature.[2]

1. Aristotle, *Physics,* 1.9 192a20–4, in *The Complete Works of Aristotle,* ed. Jonathan Barnes, rev. Oxford translation, 2 vols. (Princeton, 1984), 1:328.

2. Aristotle, *Generation of Animals,* 2.3 737a27–8 (Barnes, 1:1144).

For Greek theorists, the biology of males and females was the key to their psychology. The female was softer and more docile, more apt to be despondent, querulous, and deceitful. Being incomplete, moreover, she craved sexual fulfillment in intercourse with a male. The male was intellectual, active, and in control of his passions.

These psychological polarities derived from the theory that the universe consisted of four elements (earth, fire, air, and water), expressed in human bodies as four "humors" (black bile, yellow bile, blood, and phlegm) considered respectively dry, hot, damp, and cold, and corresponding to mental states ("melancholic," "choleric," "sanguine," "phlegmatic"). In this schematization, the male, sharing the principles of earth and fire, was dry and hot; the female, sharing the principles of air and water, was cold and damp.

Female psychology was further affected by her dominant organ, the uterus (womb), *hystera* in Greek. The passions generated by the womb made women lustful, deceitful, talkative, irrational, indeed—when these affects were in excess—"hysterical."

Aristotle's biology also had social and political consequences. If the male principle was superior and the female inferior, then in the household, as in the state, men should rule and women must be subordinate. That hierarchy did not rule out the companionship of husband and wife, whose cooperation was necessary for the welfare of children and the preservation of property. Such mutuality supported male preeminence.

Aristotle's teacher, Plato, suggested a different possibility: that men and women might possess the same virtues. The setting for this proposal is the imaginary and ideal Republic that Plato sketches in his dialogue of that name. Here, for a privileged elite capable of leading wisely, all distinctions of class and wealth dissolve, as do consequently those of gender. Without households or property, as Plato constructs his ideal society, there is no need for the subordination of women. Women may, therefore, be educated to the same level as men to assume leadership responsibilities. Plato's Republic remained imaginary, however. In real societies, the subordination of women remained the norm and the prescription.

The views of women inherited from the Greek philosophical tradition became the basis for medieval thought. In the thirteenth century, the supreme scholastic philosopher Thomas Aquinas, among others, still echoed Aristotle's views of human reproduction, of male and female personalities, and of the preeminent male role in the social hierarchy.

ROMAN LAW AND THE FEMALE CONDITION. Roman law, like Greek philosophy, underlay medieval thought and shaped medieval society. The ancient belief that adult, property-owning men should administer households and make decisions affecting the community at large is the very fulcrum of Roman law.

Around 450 B.C.E., during Rome's Republican era, the community's customary law was recorded (legendarily) on the Twelve Tables, erected in the city's central forum. It was later elaborated by professional jurists whose activity increased in the imperial era, when much new legislation, especially on issues affecting family and inheritance, was passed. This growing, changing body of laws was eventually codified in the *Corpus of Civil Law* under the direction of the emperor Justinian, generations after the empire ceased to be ruled from Rome. That *Corpus,* read and commented upon by medieval scholars from the eleventh century on, inspired the legal systems of most of the cities and kingdoms of Europe.

Laws regarding dowries, divorce, and inheritance most pertain to women. Since those laws aimed to maintain and preserve property, the women concerned were those from the property-owning minority. Their subordination to male family members points to the even greater subordination of lower-class and slave women, about whom the laws speak little.

In the early Republic, the *paterfamilias,* "father of the family," possessed *patria potestas,* "paternal power." The term *pater,* "father," in both these cases does not necessarily mean biological father, but householder. The father was the person who owned the household's property and, indeed, its human members. The *paterfamilias* had absolute power—including the power, rarely exercised, of life or death—over his wife, his children, and his slaves, as much as over his cattle.

Male children could be "emancipated," an act that granted legal autonomy and the right to own property. Males over the age of fourteen could be emancipated by a special grant from the father, or automatically by their father's death. But females never could be emancipated; instead, they passed from the authority of their father to a husband or, if widowed or orphaned while still unmarried, to a guardian or tutor.

Marriage under its traditional form placed the woman under her husband's authority, or *manus.* He could divorce her on grounds of adultery, drinking wine, or stealing from the household, but she could not divorce him. She could possess no property in her own right, nor bequeath any to her children upon her death. When her husband died, the household property passed not to her but to his male heirs. And when her father died, she had no claim to any family inheritance, which was directed to her brothers or more remote male relatives. The effect of these laws was to exclude women from civil society, itself based on property ownership.

In the later Republican and Imperial periods, these rules were significantly modified. Women rarely married according to the traditional form, but according to the form of "free" marriage. That practice allowed a woman to remain under her father's authority, to possess property given her by her father (most frequently the "dowry," recoverable from the husband's household in the event of his death), and to inherit from her father.

She could also bequeath property to her own children and divorce her husband, just as he could divorce her.

Despite this greater freedom, women still suffered enormous disability under Roman law. Heirs could belong only to the father's side, never the mother's. Moreover, although she could bequeath her property to her children, she could not establish a line of succession in doing so. A woman was "the beginning and end of her own family," growled the jurist Ulpian. Moreover, women could play no public role. They could not hold public office, represent anyone in a legal case, or even witness a will. Women had only a private existence, and no public personality.

The dowry system, the guardian, women's limited ability to transmit wealth, and their total political disability are all features of Roman law adopted, although modified according to local customary laws, by the medieval communities of western Europe.

CHRISTIAN DOCTRINE AND WOMEN'S PLACE. The Hebrew Bible and the Christian New Testament authorized later writers to limit women to the realm of the family and to burden them with the guilt of original sin. The passages most fruitful for this purpose were the creation narratives in Genesis and sentences from the Epistles defining women's role within the Christian family and community.

Each of the first two chapters of Genesis contains a creation narrative. In the first "God created man in his own image, in the image of God he created him; male and female he created them" (NRSV, Genesis 1:27). In the second, God created Eve from Adam's rib (2:21–23). Christian theologians relied principally on Genesis 2 for their understanding of the relation between man and woman, interpreting the creation of Eve from Adam as proof of her subordination to him.

The creation story in Genesis 2 leads to that of the temptations in Genesis 3: of Eve by the wily serpent, and of Adam by Eve. As read by Christian theologians from Tertullian to Thomas Aquinas, the narrative made Eve responsible for the Fall and its consequences. She instigated the act; she deceived her husband; she suffered the greater punishment. Her disobedience made it necessary for Jesus to be incarnated and to die on the cross. From the pulpit, moralists and preachers for centuries conveyed to women the guilt that they bore for original sin.

The Epistles offered advice to early Christians on building communities of the faithful. Among the matters to be regulated was the place of women. Paul offered views favorable to women in Galatians 3:28: "There is neither Jew nor Greek, there is neither slave nor free, there is neither male nor female; for you are all one in Christ Jesus." Paul also referred to women as his coworkers and placed them on a par with himself and his male coworkers (Philippians 4:2–3; Romans 16: 1–3; 1 Corinthians 16:19). Elsewhere Paul limited women's possibilities: "But I want you to understand that the head of every man is Christ, the head of a woman is her husband, and the head of Christ is God" (1 Corinthians 11:3).

Biblical passages by later writers (though attributed to Paul) enjoined women to forego jewels, expensive clothes, and elaborate coiffures; and they forbade women to "teach or have authority over men," telling them to "learn in silence with all submissiveness" as is proper for one responsible for sin, consoling them however with the thought that they would be saved through childbearing (1 Timothy 2:9–15). Other texts among the later Epistles defined women as the weaker sex, and emphasized their subordination to their husbands (1 Peter 3:7; Colossians 3:18; Ephesians 5:22–23).

These passages from the New Testament became the arsenal employed by theologians of the early church to transmit negative attitudes toward women to medieval Christian culture—above all, Tertullian ("On the Apparel of Women"), Jerome (*Against Jovinian*), and Augustine (*The Literal Meaning of Genesis*).

THE IMAGE OF WOMEN IN MEDIEVAL LITERATURE. The philosophical, legal, and religious traditions born in antiquity formed the basis of the medieval intellectual synthesis wrought by trained thinkers, mostly clerics, writing in Latin and based largely in universities. The vernacular literary tradition that developed alongside the learned tradition also spoke about female nature and women's roles. Medieval stories, poems, and epics were infused with misogyny. They portrayed most women as lustful and deceitful, while praising good housekeepers and loyal wives, or replicas of the Virgin Mary, or the female saints and martyrs.

There is an exception in the movement of "courtly love" that evolved in southern France from the twelfth century. Courtly love was the erotic love between a nobleman and noblewoman, the latter usually superior in social rank. It was always adulterous. From the conventions of courtly love derive modern Western notions of romantic love. The phenomenon has had an impact disproportionate to its size, for it affected only a tiny elite, and very few women. The exaltation of the female lover probably does not reflect a higher evaluation of women, or a step toward their sexual liberation. More likely it gives expression to the social and sexual tensions besetting the knightly class at a specific historical juncture.

The literary fashion of courtly love was on the wane by the thirteenth century, when the widely read *Romance of the Rose* was composed in French by two authors of significantly different dispositions. Guillaume de Lorris composed the initial four thousand verses around 1235, and Jean de Meun added about seventeen thousand verses—more than four times the original—around 1265.

The fragment composed by Guillaume de Lorris stands squarely in the courtly love tradition. Here the poet, in a dream, is admitted into a walled garden where he finds a magic fountain in which a rosebush is reflected.

He longs to pick one rose but the thorns around it prevent his doing so, even as he is wounded by arrows from the God of Love, whose commands he agrees to obey. The remainder of this part of the poem recounts the poet's unsuccessful efforts to pluck the rose.

The longer part of the *Romance* by Jean de Meun also describes a dream. But here allegorical characters give long didactic speeches, providing a social satire on a variety of themes, including those pertaining to women. Love is an anxious and tormented state, the poem explains, women are greedy and manipulative, marriage is miserable, beautiful women are lustful, ugly ones cease to please, and a chaste woman is as rare as a black swan.

Shortly after Jean de Meun completed *The Romance of the Rose,* Mathéolus penned his *Lamentations,* a long Latin diatribe against marriage translated into French about a century later. The *Lamentations* sum up medieval attitudes toward women, and they provoked the important response by Christine de Pizan in her *Book of the City of Ladies.*

In 1355, Giovanni Boccaccio wrote *Il Corbaccio,* another antifeminist manifesto, though ironically by an author whose other works pioneered new directions in Renaissance thought. The former husband of his lover appears to Boccaccio, condemning his unmoderated lust and detailing the defects of women. Boccaccio concedes at the end "how much men naturally surpass women in nobility"[3] and is cured of his desires.

WOMEN'S ROLES: THE FAMILY. The negative perceptions of women expressed in the intellectual tradition are also implicit in the actual roles that women played in European society. Assigned to subordinate positions in the household and the church, they were barred from significant participation in public life.

Medieval European households, like those in antiquity and in non-Western civilizations, were headed by males. It was the male serf, or peasant, feudal lord, town merchant, or citizen who was polled or taxed or who succeeded to an inheritance or had any acknowledged public role, although his wife or widow could stand on a temporary basis as a surrogate for him. From about 1100, the position of property-holding males was enhanced further. Inheritance was confined to the male, or agnate, line—with depressing consequences for women.

A wife never fully belonged to her husband's family or a daughter to her father's family. She left her father's house young to marry whomever her parents chose. Her dowry was managed by her husband and normally passed to her children by him at her death.

A married woman's life was occupied nearly constantly with cycles of

3. Giovanni Boccaccio, *The Corbaccio or The Labyrinth of Love,* trans. and ed. Anthony K. Cassell (Binghamton, N.Y.; rev. paper ed., 1993), 71.

pregnancy, childbearing, and lactation. Women bore children through all the years of their fertility, and many died in childbirth before the end of that term. They also bore responsibility for raising young children up to six or seven. That responsibility was shared in the propertied classes, since it was common for a wet nurse to take over the job of breastfeeding, and servants took over other chores.

Women trained their daughters in the household responsibilities appropriate to their status, nearly always in tasks associated with textiles: spinning, weaving, sewing, embroidering. Their sons were sent out of the house as apprentices or students, or their training was assumed by fathers in later childhood and adolescence. On the death of her husband, a woman's children became the responsibility of his family. She generally did not take "his" children with her to a new marriage or back to her father's house, except sometimes in artisan classes.

Women also worked. Rural peasants performed farm chores, merchant wives often practiced their husbands' trades, the unmarried daughters of the urban poor worked as servants or prostitutes. All wives produced or embellished textiles and did the housekeeping, while wealthy ones managed servants. These labors were unpaid or poorly paid, but often contributed substantially to family wealth.

WOMEN'S ROLES: THE CHURCH. Membership in a household, whether a father's or a husband's, meant for women a lifelong subordination to others. In western Europe, the Roman Catholic church offered an alternative to the career of wife and mother. A woman could enter a convent parallel in function to the monasteries for men that evolved in the early Christian centuries.

In the convent, a woman pledged herself to a celibate life, lived according to strict community rules, and worshiped daily. Often the convent offered training in Latin, allowing some women to become considerable scholars and authors, as well as scribes, artists, and musicians. For women who chose the conventual life, the benefits could be enormous, but for numerous others placed in convents by paternal choice, the life could be restrictive and burdensome.

The conventual life declined as an alternative for women as the modern age approached. Reformed monastic institutions resisted responsibility for related female orders. The church increasingly restricted female institutional life by insisting on closer male supervision.

Women often sought other options. Some joined the communities of laywomen that sprang up spontaneously in the thirteenth century in the urban zones of western Europe, especially in Flanders and Italy. Some joined the heretical movements flourishing in late medieval Christendom, whose anticlerical and often antifamily positions particularly appealed to women. In these communities, some women were acclaimed as "holy women" or "saints," while others often were condemned as frauds or heretics.

Though the options offered to women by the church were sometimes less than satisfactory, sometimes they were richly rewarding. After 1520, the convent remained an option only in Roman Catholic territories. Protestantism engendered an ideal of marriage as a heroic endeavor, and appeared to place husband and wife on a more equal footing. Sermons and treatises, however, still called for female subordination and obedience.

THE OTHER VOICE, 1300–1700

Misogyny was so long established in European culture when the modern era opened that to dismantle it was a monumental labor. The process began as part of a larger cultural movement that entailed the critical reexamination of ideas inherited from the ancient and medieval past. The humanists launched that critical reexamination.

THE HUMANIST FOUNDATION. Originating in Italy in the fourteenth century, humanism quickly became the dominant intellectual movement in Europe. Spreading in the sixteenth century from Italy to the rest of Europe, it fueled the literary, scientific, and philosophical movements of the era, and laid the basis for the eighteenth-century Enlightenment.

Humanists regarded the scholastic philosophy of medieval universities as out of touch with the realities of urban life. They found in the rhetorical discourse of classical Rome a language adapted to civic life and public speech. They learned to read, speak, and write classical Latin, and eventually classical Greek. They founded schools to teach others to do so, establishing the pattern for elementary and secondary education for the next three hundred years.

In the service of complex government bureaucracies, humanists employed their skills to write eloquent letters, deliver public orations, and formulate public policy. They developed new scripts for copying manuscripts and used the new printing press for the dissemination of texts, for which they created methods of critical editing.

Humanism was a movement led by men who accepted the evaluation of women in ancient texts and generally shared the misogynist perceptions of their culture. (Female humanists, as will be seen, did not.) Yet humanism also opened the door to the critique of the misogynist tradition. By calling authors, texts, and ideas into question, it made possible the fundamental rereading of the whole intellectual tradition that was required in order to free women from cultural prejudice and social subordination.

A DIFFERENT CITY. The other voice first appeared when, after so many centuries, the accumulation of misogynist concepts evoked a response from a capable female defender, Christine de Pizan. Introducing her *Book of the City of Ladies* (1405), she described how she was affected by reading Mathéolus's *Lamentations:* "Just the sight of this book . . . made me wonder how it happened that so many different men . . . are so inclined to express both in speaking and in their treatises and writings so many wicked insults about women and their behavior."[4] These statements impelled her to detest herself "and the entire feminine sex, as though we were monstrosities in nature."[5]

The remainder of the *Book of the City of Ladies* presents a justification of the female sex and a vision of an ideal community of women. A pioneer, she has not only received the misogynist message, but she rejects it. From the fourteenth to seventeenth century, a huge body of literature accumulated that responded to the dominant tradition.

The result was a literary explosion consisting of works by both men and women, in Latin and in vernacular languages: works enumerating the achievements of notable women; works rebutting the main accusations made against women; works arguing for the equal education of men and women; works defining and redefining women's proper role in the family, at court, and in public; and works describing women's lives and experiences. Recent monographs and articles have begun to hint at the great range of this phenomenon, involving probably several thousand titles. The protofeminism of these "other voices" constitute a significant fraction of the literary product of the early modern era.

THE CATALOGUES. Around 1365, the same Boccaccio whose *Corbaccio* rehearses the usual charges against female nature wrote another work, *Concerning Famous Women.* A humanist treatise drawing on classical texts, it praised 106 notable women—100 of them from pagan Greek and Roman antiquity, and 6 from the religious and cultural tradition since antiquity—and helped make all readers aware of a sex normally condemned or forgotten. Boccaccio's outlook, nevertheless, was misogynist, for it singled out for praise those women who possessed the traditional virtues of chastity, silence, and obedience. Women who were active in the public realm, for example, rulers and warriors, were depicted as suffering terrible punishments for entering into the masculine sphere. Women were his subject, but Boccaccio's standard remained male.

Christine de Pizan's *Book of the City of Ladies* contains a second catalogue, one responding specifically to Boccaccio's. Where Boccaccio portrays female virtue as exceptional, she depicts it as universal. Many women in history were leaders, or remained chaste despite the lascivious approaches of men, or were visionaries and brave martyrs.

---

4. Christine de Pizan, *The Book of the City of Ladies,* trans. Earl Jeffrey Richards; foreword by Marina Warner (New York, 1982), 1.1.1., pp. 3–4.

5. Ibid., 1.1.1–2, p. 5.

The work of Boccaccio inspired a series of catalogues of illustrious women of the biblical, classical, Christian, and local past: works by Alvaro de Luna, Jacopo Filippo Foresti (1497), Brantôme, Pierre Le Moyne, Pietro Paolo de Ribera (who listed 845 figures), and many others. Whatever their embedded prejudices, these catalogues of illustrious women drove home to the public the possibility of female excellence.

THE DEBATE. At the same time, many questions remained: Could a woman be virtuous? Could she perform noteworthy deeds? Was she even, strictly speaking, of the same human species as men? These questions were debated over four centuries, in French, German, Italian, Spanish, and English, by authors male and female, among Catholics, Protestants, and Jews, in ponderous volumes and breezy pamphlets. The whole literary phenomenon has been called the *querelle des femmes,* the "woman question."

The opening volley of this battle occurred in the first years of the fifteenth century, in a literary debate sparked by Christine de Pizan. She exchanged letters critical of Jean de Meun's contribution to the *Romance of the Rose* with two French humanists and royal secretaries, Jean de Montreuil and Gontier Col. When the matter became public, Jean Gerson, one of Europe's leading theologians, supported de Pizan's arguments against de Meun, for the moment silencing the opposition.

The debate resurfaced repeatedly over the next two hundred years. *The Triumph of Women* (1438) by Juan Rodríguez de la Camara (or Juan Rodríguez del Padron) struck a new note by presenting arguments for the superiority of women to men. *The Champion of Women* (1440–42) by Martin Le Franc addresses once again the misogynist claims of *The Romance of the Rose,* and offers counterevidence of female virtue and achievement.

A cameo of the debate on women is included in *The Courtier,* one of the most read books of the era, published by the Italian Baldassare Castiglione in 1528 and immediately translated into other European vernaculars. *The Courtier* depicts a series of evenings at the court of the Duke of Urbino in which many men and some women of the highest social stratum amuse themselves by discussing a range of literary and social issues. The "woman question" is a pervasive theme throughout, and the third of its four books is devoted entirely to that issue.

In a verbal duel, Gasparo Pallavicino and Giuliano de' Medici present the main claims of the two traditions—the prevailing misogynist one, and the newly emerging alternative one. Gasparo argues the innate inferiority of women and their inclination to vice. Only in bearing children do they profit the world. Giuliano counters that women share the same spiritual and mental capacities as men and may excel in wisdom and action. Men and women are of the same essence: just as no stone can be more perfectly a stone than another, so no human being can be more perfectly human than others, whether male or female. It was an astonishing assertion, boldly made to an audience as large as all Europe.

THE TREATISES. Humanism provided the materials for a positive counterconcept to the misogyny embedded in scholastic philosophy and law, and inherited from the Greek, Roman, and Christian pasts. A series of humanist treatises on marriage and family, on education and deportment, and on the nature of women helped construct these new perspectives.

The works by Francesco Barbaro and Leon Battista Alberti, respectively *On Marriage* (1415) and *On the Family* (1434–37), far from defending female equality, reasserted women's responsibilities for rearing children and managing the housekeeping while being obedient, chaste, and silent. Nevertheless, they served the cause of reexamining the issue of women's nature by placing domestic issues at the center of scholarly concern and reopening the pertinent classical texts. In addition, Barbaro emphasized the companionate nature of marriage and the importance of a wife's spiritual and mental qualities for the well-being of the family.

These themes reappear in later humanist works on marriage and the education of women by Juan Luis Vives and Erasmus. Both were moderately sympathetic to the condition of women, without reaching beyond the usual masculine prescriptions for female behavior.

An outlook more favorable to women characterizes the nearly unknown work *In Praise of Women* (ca. 1487) by the Italian humanist Bartolommeo Goggio. In addition to providing a catalogue of illustrious women, Goggio argued that male and female are the same in essence, but that women (reworking from quite a new angle the Adam and Eve narrative) are actually superior. In the same vein, the Italian humanist Mario Equicola asserted the spiritual equality of men and women in *On Women* (1501). In 1525, Galeazzo Flavio Capra (or Capella) published his work *On the Excellence and Dignity of Women*. This humanist tradition of treatises defending the worthiness of women culminates in the work of Henricus Cornelius Agrippa, *On the Nobility and Preeminence of the Female Sex*. No work by a male humanist more succinctly or explicitly presents the case for female dignity.

THE WITCH BOOKS. While humanists grappled with the issues pertaining to women and family, other learned men turned their attention to what they perceived as a very great problem: witches. Witch-hunting manuals, explorations of the witch phenomenon, and even defenses of witches are not at first glance pertinent to the tradition of the other voice. But they do relate in this way: most accused witches were women. The hostility aroused by supposed witch activity is comparable to the hostility aroused by women. The evil deeds the victims of the hunt were charged with were exaggerations of the vices to which, many believed, all women were prone.

The connection between the witch accusation and the hatred of women is explicit in the notorious witch-hunting manual, *The Hammer of Witches* (1486), by two Dominican inquisitors, Heinrich Krämer and Jacob Sprenger. Here the inconstancy, deceitfulness, and lustfulness traditionally associated with women are depicted in exaggerated form as the core features of witch behavior. These inclined women to make a bargain with the devil—sealed by sexual intercourse—by which they acquired unholy powers. Such bizarre claims, far from being re-jected by rational men, were broadcast by intellectuals. The German Ulrich Molitur, the Frenchman Nicolas Rémy, the Italian Stefano Guazzo coolly informed the public of sinister orgies and midnight pacts with the devil. The celebrated French jurist, historian, and political philosopher Jean Bodin argued that, because women were especially prone to diabolism, regular legal procedures could properly be suspended in order to try those accused of this "exceptional crime."

A few experts, such as the physician Johann Weyer, a student of Agrippa's, raised their voices in protest. In 1563, Weyer explained the witch phenomenon thus, without discarding belief in diabolism: the devil deluded foolish old women afflicted by melancholia, causing them to believe that they had magical powers. His rational skepticism, which had good credibility in the community of the learned, worked to revise the conventional views of women and witchcraft.

WOMEN'S WORKS. To the many categories of works produced on the question of women's worth must be added nearly all works written by women. A woman writing was in herself a statement of women's claim to dignity.

Only a few women wrote anything prior to the dawn of the modern era, for three reasons. First, they rarely received the education that would enable them to write. Second, they were not admitted to the public roles— as administrator, bureaucrat, lawyer or notary, university professor—in which they might gain knowledge of the kinds of things the literate public thought worth writing about. Third, the culture imposed silence upon women, considering speaking out a form of unchastity. Given these conditions, it is remarkable that any women wrote. Those who did before the fourteenth century were almost always nuns or religious women whose isolation made their pronouncements more acceptable.

From the fourteenth century on, the volume of women's writings increased. Women continued to write devotional literature, although not always as cloistered nuns. They also wrote diaries, often intended as keepsakes for their children; books of advice to their sons and daughters; letters to family members and friends; and family memoirs, in a few cases elaborate enough to be considered histories.

A few women wrote works directly concerning the "woman question," and some of these, such as the humanists Isotta Nogarola, Cassandra

Fedele, Laura Cereta, and Olimpia Morata, were highly trained. A few were professional writers, living by the income of their pen: the very first among them Christine de Pizan, noteworthy in this context as in so many others. In addition to *The Book of the City of Ladies* and her critiques of *The Romance of the Rose,* she wrote *The Treasure of the City of Ladies* (a guide to social decorum for women), an advice book for her son, much courtly verse, and a full-scale history of the reign of King Charles V of France.

WOMEN PATRONS. Women who did not themselves write but encouraged others to do so boosted the development of an alternative tradition. Highly placed women patrons supported authors, artists, musicians, poets, and learned men. Such patrons, drawn mostly from the Italian elites and the courts of northern Europe, figure disproportionately as the dedicatees of the important works of early feminism.

For a start, it might be noted that the catalogues of Boccaccio and Alvaro de Luna were dedicated to the Florentine noblewoman Andrea Acciaiuoli and to Doña María, first wife of King Juan II of Castile, while the French translation of Boccaccio's work was commissioned by Anne of Brittany, wife of King Charles VIII of France. The humanist treatises of Goggio, Equicola, Vives, and Agrippa were dedicated, respectively, to Eleanora of Aragon, wife of Ercole I d'Este, duke of Ferrara; to Margherita Cantelma of Mantua; to Catherine of Aragon, wife of King Henry VIII of England; and to Margaret, duchess of Austria and regent of the Netherlands. As late as 1696, Mary Astell's *Serious Proposal to the Ladies, for the Advancement of Their True and Greatest Interest* was dedicated to Princess Ann of Denmark.

These authors presumed that their efforts would be welcome to female patrons, or they may have written at the bidding of those patrons. Silent themselves, perhaps even unresponsive, these loftily placed women helped shape the tradition of the other voice.

THE ISSUES. The literary forms and patterns in which the tradition of the other voice presented itself have now been sketched. It remains to highlight the major issues about which this tradition crystallizes. In brief, there are four problems to which our authors return again and again, in plays and catalogues, in verse and in letters, in treatises and dialogues, in every language: the problem of chastity, the problem of power, the problem of speech, and the problem of knowledge. Of these the greatest, preconditioning the others, is the problem of chastity.

THE PROBLEM OF CHASTITY. In traditional European culture, as in those of antiquity and others around the globe, chastity was perceived as woman's quintessential virtue—in contrast to courage, or generosity, or leadership, or rationality, seen as virtues characteristic of men. Opponents of women charged them with insatiable lust. Women themselves and their defenders—without disputing the validity of the standard—responded that women were capable of chastity.

The requirement of chastity kept women at home, silenced them, isolated them, left them in ignorance. It was the source of all other impediments. Why was it so important to the society of men, of whom chastity was not required, and who, more often than not, considered it their right to violate the chastity of any woman they encountered?

Female chastity ensured the continuity of the male-headed household. If a man's wife was not chaste, he could not be sure of the legitimacy of his offspring. If they were not his, and they acquired his property, it was not his household, but some other man's, that had endured. If his daughter was not chaste, she could not be transferred to another man's household as his wife, and he was dishonored.

The whole system of the integrity of the household and the transmission of property was bound up in female chastity. Such a requirement pertained only to property-owning classes, of course. Poor women could not expect to maintain their chastity, least of all if they were in contact with high-status men to whom all women but those of their own household were prey.

In Catholic Europe, the requirement of chastity was further buttressed by moral and religious imperatives. Original sin was inextricably linked with the sexual act. Virginity was seen as heroic virtue, far more impressive than, say, the avoidance of idleness or greed. Monasticism, the cultural institution that dominated medieval Europe for centuries, was grounded in the renunciation of the flesh. The Catholic reform of the eleventh century imposed a similar standard on all the clergy, and a heightened awareness of sexual requirements on all the laity. Although men were asked to be chaste, female unchastity was much worse: it led to the devil, as Eve had led mankind to sin.

To such requirements, women and their defenders protested their innocence. Following the example of holy women who had escaped the requirements of family and sought the religious life, some women began to conceive of female communities as alternatives both to family and to the cloister. Christine de Pizan's city of ladies was such a community. Moderata Fonte and Mary Astell envisioned others. The luxurious salons of the French *précieuses* of the seventeenth century, or the comfortable English drawing rooms of the next, may have been born of the same impulse. Here women might not only escape, if briefly, the subordinate position that life in the family entailed, but they might make claims to power, exercise their capacity for speech, and display their knowledge.

THE PROBLEM OF POWER. Women were excluded from power: the whole cultural tradition insisted upon it. Only men were citizens, only men bore arms, only men could be chiefs or lords or kings. There were exceptions that did not disprove the rule, when wives or widows or mothers took the place of men, awaiting their return or the maturation of a male heir. A woman who attempted to rule in her own right was perceived as an anomaly, a monster, at once a deformed woman and an insufficient male, sexually confused and, consequently, unsafe.

The association of such images with women who held or sought power explains some otherwise odd features of early modern culture. Queen Elizabeth I of England, one of the few women to hold full regal authority in European history, played with such male/ female images—positive ones, of course—in representing herself to her subjects. She was a prince, and manly, even though she was female. She was also (she claimed) virginal, a condition absolutely essential if she was to avoid the attacks of her opponents. Catherine de' Medici, who ruled France as widow and regent for her sons, also adopted such imagery in defining her position. She chose as one symbol the figure of Artemisia, an androgynous ancient warrior-heroine, who combined a female persona with masculine powers.

Power in a woman, without such sexual imagery, seems to have been indigestible by the culture. A rare note was struck by the Englishman Sir Thomas Elyot in his *Defence of Good Women* (1540), justifying both women's participation in civic life and their prowess in arms. The old tune was sung by the Scots reformer John Knox in his *First Blast of the Trumpet against the Monstrous Regiment of Women* (1558), for whom rule by women, defects in nature, was a hideous contradiction in terms.

The confused sexuality of the imagery of female potency was not reserved for rulers. Any woman who excelled was likely to be called an Amazon, recalling the self-mutilated warrior women of antiquity who repudiated all men, gave up their sons, and raised only their daughters. She was often said to have "exceeded her sex," or to have possessed "masculine virtue"—as the very fact of conspicuous excellence conferred masculinity, even on the female subject. The catalogues of notable women often showed those female heroes dressed in armor, armed to the teeth, like men. Amazonian heroines romp through the epics of the age—Ariosto's *Orlando Furioso* (1532), Spenser's *Faerie Queene* (1590–1609). Excellence in a woman was perceived as a claim for power, and power was reserved for the masculine realm. A woman who possessed either was masculinized, and lost title to her own female identity.

THE PROBLEM OF SPEECH. Just as power had a sexual dimension when it was claimed by women, so did speech. A good woman spoke little. Excessive speech was an indication of unchastity. By speech women seduced men. Eve had lured Adam into sin by her speech. Accused witches were commonly accused of having spoken abusively, or irrationally, or simply too much. As enlightened a figure as Francesco Barbaro insisted on silence in a woman, which he linked to her perfect unanimity with her husband's will and her unblemished virtue (her chastity). Another Italian humanist, Leonardo Bruni, in advising a noblewoman on her studies, barred her not from speech, but from public speaking. That was reserved for men.

Related to the problem of speech was that of costume, another, if silent, form of self-expression. Assigned the task of pleasing men as their primary occupation, elite women often tended to elaborate costume, hair-dressing, and the use of cosmetics. Clergy and secular moralists alike condemned these practices. The appropriate function of costume and adornment was to announce the status of a woman's husband or father. Any further indulgence in adornment was akin to unchastity.

THE PROBLEM OF KNOWLEDGE. When the Italian noblewoman Isotta Nogarola had begun to attain a reputation as a humanist, she was accused of incest—a telling instance of the association of learning in women with unchastity. That chilling association inclined any woman who was educated to deny that she was, or to make exaggerated claims of heroic chastity.

If educated women were pursued with suspicions of sexual misconduct, women seeking an education faced an even more daunting obstacle: the assumption that women were by nature incapable of learning, that reason was a particularly masculine ability. Just as they proclaimed their chastity, women and their defenders insisted upon their capacity for learning. The major work by a male writer on female education—*On the Education of a Christian Woman,* by Juan Luis Vives (1523)—granted female capacity for intellection, but argued still that a woman's whole education was to be shaped around the requirement of chastity and a future within the household. Female writers of the following generations—Marie de Gournay in France, Anna Maria van Schurman in Holland, Mary Astell in England—began to envision other possibilities.

The pioneers of female education were the Italian women humanists who managed to attain a Latin literacy and knowledge of classical and Christian literature equivalent to that of prominent men. Their works implicitly and explicitly raise questions about women's social roles, defining problems that beset women attempting to break out of the cultural limits that had bound them. Like Christine de Pizan, who achieved an advanced education through her father's tutoring and her own devices, their bold questioning makes clear the importance of training. Only when women were educated to the same standard as male leaders would they be able to raise that other voice and insist on their dignity as human beings morally, intellectually, and legally equal to men.

THE OTHER VOICE. The other voice, a voice of protest, was mostly female, but also male. It spoke in the vernaculars and in Latin, in treatises and dialogues, plays and poetry, letters and diaries and pamphlets. It battered at the wall of misogynist beliefs that encircled women and raised a banner announcing its claims. The female was equal (or even superior) to the male in essential nature—moral, spiritual, intellectual. Women were capable of higher education, of holding positions of power and influence in the public realm, and of speaking and writing persuasively. The last bastion of masculine supremacy, centered on the notions of a woman's primary domestic responsibility and the requirement of female chastity, was not as yet assaulted—although visions of productive female communities as alternatives to the family indicated an awareness of the problem.

During the period 1300 to 1700, the other voice remained only a voice, and one only dimly heard. It did not result—yet—in an alteration of social patterns. Indeed, to this day, they have not entirely been altered. Yet the call for justice issued as long as six centuries ago by those writing in the tradition of the other voice must be recognized as the source and origin of the mature feminist tradition and of the realignment of social institutions accomplished in the modern age.

W e would like to thank the volume editors in this series, who responded with many suggestions to an earlier draft of this introduction, making it a collaborative enterprise. Many of their suggestions and criticisms have resulted in revisions of this introduction, though we remain responsible for the final product.

PROJECTED TITLES IN THE SERIES

Cassandra Fedele, *Letters and Orations,* edited and translated by Diana Robin

Lucrezia Marinella, *The Nobility and Excellence of Women,* edited and translated by Anne Dunhill

Arcangela Tarabotti, *Paternal Tyranny,* edited and translated by Letizia Panizza

INTRODUCTION:
THE HONORED COURTESAN

THE OTHER VOICE

Veronica Franco was a poet who articulated her pro-woman views in poems and letters usually written in a tactful, courteous style. She was not an explicitly feminist essayist or polemicist. But her frank eroticism and her impressive eloquence set her apart from the chaste, silent woman prescribed in Renaissance gender ideology, and her sympathy for women, individually and collectively, links her to two of her Venetian contemporaries, Lucrezia Marinella and Moderata Fonte. In contrast to the prose works of these two writers, Franco's *Terze rime* (*Poems in Terza Rima,* 1575) dramatize her connections with men and her skill in sexual and rhetorical contests with them. It is in this context that she presents protofeminist arguments in sometimes oblique, sometimes openly defiant language.

All of Franco's literary production was inflected by her position as a *cortigiana onesta,* an "honored courtesan." She made her living by arranging to have sexual relations, for a high fee, with the elite of Venice and the many kinds of travelers—merchants, ambassadors, even kings—who passed through the city. To succeed as a courtesan, a woman needed to be beautiful, sophisticated in her dress and manners, and an elegant, cultivated conversationalist. If she demonstrated her intellectual powers by writing and publishing poetry and prose, so much the better. Franco became a writer by allying herself with distinguished men at the center of her city's culture, particularly in the informal meetings of a literary salon at the home of Domenico Venier, the oldest member of a distinguished patrician family and a former Venetian senator, in the 1570s and 1580s.[1] Through

---

1. On Venier's salon, see Margaret F. Rosenthal, *The Honest Courtesan: Veronica Franco, Citizen and Writer in Sixteenth-Century Venice* (Chicago: University of Chicago Press, 1992), 89–94, 150–60, 177–80; and Martha Feldman, *City Culture and the Madrigal at Venice* (Berkeley: University of California Press, 1995), 83–106.

Venier's protection and her own determination, Franco published texts in which she defended herself individually against attacks by a male poet of Venice. But, in a genuinely feminist mode, she also wrote to protect fellow courtesans against mistreatment by men and to criticize the subordination of women in general.

To understand Franco's feminism, her reader needs to see it operating in her life and to see her filtering and shaping that life in her writing. In both spheres, she was an energetic champion of women, concerned about the welfare of her fellow courtesans and of women in general in the *Serenissima* (most serene Republic). In the introductory biography that follows, we indicate specific letters and poems by Franco that illuminate her social life and aspirations.

BIOGRAPHY

Veronica Franco was born in 1546 in Venice into a family who were *cittadini originari*, native-born citizens who belonged by hereditary right to a professional caste that made up the government bureaucracy and were also members of the powerful confraternities, religious societies that organized private charities and commissioned opulent *scuole* (schools) in which they met to pray, socialize, and make decisions.[2] We know the names of Veronica's immediate family: her father was Francesco Franco and her mother Paola Fracassa. Paola had been a courtesan herself and her name appears together with Veronica's in the *Catalogue of All the Principal and most Honored Courtesans of Venice* (1565), a listing of the names, addresses, and fees of well-known prostitutes in the city.[3] Paola is listed as a go-between for her daughter, which meant that it was to her that Veronica's clients were expected to pay the fee her daughter charged.

What exactly was a courtesan? The most neutral word in mid-sixteenth-century Italy for a woman who made her living by selling her sexual services was *meretrice*, for which an English equivalent would be "prosti-

2. For the earliest biography of Veronica Franco, see Giuseppe Tassini, *Veronica Franco: Celebre poetessa e cortigiana del secolo XVI* (Venice: Fontana, 1874; reprinted Venice: Alfieri, 1969). More recent biographical information is available in Alvise Zorzi, *Cortigiana veneziana: Veronica Franco e i suoi poeti* (Milan: Camunia, 1986); Marcella Diberti Leigh, *Veronica Franco: Donna, poetessa e cortigiana del Rinascimento* (Ivrea: Priuli and Verlucca, 1988). On the *cittadini originari* of Venice, see Brian Pullan, *Rich and Poor in Renaissance Venice: The Social Institution of a Catholic State, 1580 to 1620* (Cambridge: Harvard University Press, 1971), 100–105; Robert Finlay, *Politics in Renaissance Venice* (New Brunswick: Rutgers University Press, 1980), 45–47.

3. *Il Catalogo di tutte le principali et più honorate cortigiane di Venezia* (1565), reproduced in Rita Casagrande di Villaviera, *Le Cortigiane veneziane del Cinquecento* (Milan: Longanesi, 1968).

tute." A word used to insult such women, because it described the poorest class and most morally condemned category of sex worker, was *puttana,* in English, "whore." *Cortigiana*—"courtesan"—had a different meaning. It was derived from *cortigiano,* meaning a man who served at court, so it had connotations of splendor and technical or at least bureaucratic expertise. The addition of *onesta* meant "honored" rather than "honest," that is, privileged, wealthy, recognized. At times, especially in Rome, *cortigiana* was used simply to mean "prostitute," while the Venetian authorities, publishing edicts to control the costume and public behavior of courtesans, often used the term *meretrice sumptuosa* (luxury prostitute).[4] The categories blur. But it was in the interest of a woman aiming for the heights of this profession to insist on the high-cultural accomplishments that separated her from poorer, less educated, more vulnerable women in the sex trade. The *cortigiana* lived splendidly, she had an intellectual life, she played music and knew the literature of Greece and Rome as well as of the present, she mingled with thinkers, writers, and artists. Franco was remarkably successful at advertising these accomplishments, intended to attract elite clients and to raise her above less educated women selling sex. But what makes her interesting is that although she was by necessity an individualist making her own way, she also thought in a "we plural" mode about women. As a courtesan, she wrote about the situation of women who shared her profession, and beyond that, she wrote about the situation of women in general.

Following women's common practice of making wills when they became pregnant to provide against the possibility of death in childbirth, Franco left two wills. Both show a practical economic concern for women like herself. The first, from 1564, when she was eighteen, indicates that she was pregnant for the first time that year: "retrovandomi maxime graveda" (being in the final term of my pregnancy).[5] In this will she left money for a dowry for the child should she be a girl, to her women servants, and to poor, unmarried Venetian girls eligible for the charitable system run by the confraternities, through which they could be chosen as recipients of dowries.[6] In her second will, dated 1570, Franco showed the same concern for the women of her city. She left money for the marriages of two Venetian girls otherwise unprovided for, but added the condition that if her executors found two prostitutes who wanted "to leave their wicked life by

4. For the Roman vocabulary, see Elizabeth Cohen, "'Courtesans' and 'Whores': Words and Behavior in Roman Streets," *Women's Studies* 19, no. 2 (1991), 201–8.

5. For a transcription of Franco's two testaments and for a discussion of their content, see Rosenthal, *The Honest Courtesan,* 111–15 (transcription) and 74–84.

6. On the dowry balloting system, see Pullan, *Rich and Poor in Renaissance Venice,* 85, 169, 184–86, and 189–92.

marrying or entering a convent,"[7] they should be the beneficiaries of this money.

Veronica was the only daughter among the family's three sons, to whom her wills show she was very attached. Sometime in the early 1560s she entered into what was probably an arranged marriage with a doctor, Paolo Panizza, but she separated from him not long afterward. In her 1564 will she asked for the return of her dowry, which suggests that she was already living apart from her husband. Of her six children, three of whom died in infancy, none were Paolo's, as her wills make clear. One of the fathers was a Venetian nobleman, Andrea Tron, and another was Jacomo di Baballi, a wealthy merchant of Ragusa (Dubrovnik). For most of her life, she supported herself and a large household of children, tutors, and servants.

Franco's *Lettere familiari a diversi* (*Familiar Letters to Various People,* 1580) reveal very little about her last years, but two legal documents and a petition clarify her economic situation in her middle and late thirties. The record of her 1580 trial by the Venetian Inquisition shows that she was accused of practicing magical incantations. Her own defense, the help of Venier, and the predisposition of the Inquisitor freed her from the charges.[8] But the episode must have damaged her reputation, adding to the financial difficulties she mentions in her draft petition to the Venetian council. In this request, she explains her poverty as the result of her flight from Venice during the plague years of 1575–77, her ensuing loss of many possessions through theft, and her decision to take on the additional burden of raising her nephews. Her tax declaration for 1582, when she was in her middle thirties, states that she was living in the neighborhood of Venice near the church of San Samuele, where the poorest Venetian prostitutes had their homes.[9]

Even in these lean years, however, she was still concerned about the welfare and honor of women of the city. She offered her help to the mother of a young woman whom she wanted to see marry properly rather than become a courtesan (*Familiar Letters,* 22). And in her draft to the Venetian council (1577) she proposed that the government found a new kind of home for women who, because they were already married or the mothers

---

7. For a transcription of the second testament, see Rosenthal, *The Honest Courtesan*, 113–15.

8. On the Inquisition trial and Alberto Bolognetti, the Inquisitor presiding in the case against Veronica Franco, see Rosenthal, *The Honest Courtesan*, 168–77. See also Alessandra Schiavon, "Per la biografia di Veronica Franco: Nuovi documenti," *Atti dell'Istituto Veneto di Scienze, Lettere ed Arti* 137 (1978–79): 243–56; Alvise Zorzi, *Cortigiana veneziana,* 145–53; Marisa Milani, "'L'incanto' di Veronica Franco," *Giornale storico della letteratura italiana* 262, no. 518 (1985): 250–63.

9. For a transcription of Veronica Franco's tax declaration, see Rosenthal, *The Honest Courtesan,* 115.

of children, were ineligible for the shelters already in place, the Casa delle Zitelle (House for Unmarried Maidens), which accepted only unmarried girls, and the Convertite (Home for Women Penitents), which required a vow of chastity.[10] Although Franco also hoped for a substantial state salary for administering this home, her recognition that women needed a different kind of refuge was practical and compassionate. Her death at forty-five ended a life that had included a decade of sumptuous wealth but also many difficulties, dangers, and losses.

Franco's intellectual life began with sharing her brothers' education by private tutors, an unusual opportunity for girls unless there was a father in the household actively encouraging his daughters to study. (Fewer than 4 percent of Venetian women had any public schooling in the 1580s and only 10 to 12 percent were literate, in contrast to men, of whom 30 percent were basically literate.)[11] She continued her education, as her letters show, by mixing with learned men, writers, and painters, whom she met in various social circumstances (Letters 17, 21). In the 1570s, she captured the interest of Domenico Venier, an adviser to many women writers, including Tullia d'Aragona and Moderata Fonte, and a generous reader and protector to Franco, and she became a frequent visitor to the literary salon at Ca Venier, the Venier palace (Letters 6, 31, 41, 47, 49). By her mid-twenties, she was known as a poet, writing sonnets and requesting them from other poets for anthologies assembled to commemorate men of the Venetian elite. For example, after the death in 1575 of the military hero Estore Martinengo, she wrote a letter (39) asking a fellow Venetian, probably Venier, to compose tributes in sonnet form for a collection of poems she had been asked to put together in Martinengo's honor. In the 1570s she was receiving intellectuals and artists at her own house in informal get-togethers (Letters 9 and 13).

Franco both represents and transforms her life in the poems she collected for her first book, *Poems in Terza Rima.* Her engagement with male patrons, both as a courtesan and a member of the Venier circle, is dramatized by the fact that she always addresses her poems to a particular man, from whom she requests a response. Franco is extremely forthright about her profession. From her first poem in the collection (*Capitolo* 2), she celebrates her sexual expertise, promises to satisfy her interlocutor's desires, and affirms the erotic pleasure that courtesans bring to their clients. This

10. On the Casa, see Monica Chojnacka, "Women, Charity, and Community in Early Modern Venice: The Casa delle Zitelle," *Renaissance Quarterly* 51 (Spring 1998): 68–91. For Franco's petition for the Casa del Soccorso, see Giuseppe Ellero, *Archivio I.R.E.: Inventari di fondi antichi degli ospedali e luoghi pii di Venezia* (Venice: 1984–87), 225–26.

11. For these figures and for female literacy in general in this period, see Paul F. Grendler, *Schooling in Renaissance Italy: Literacy and Learning, 1300–1600* (Baltimore: Johns Hopkins University Press, 1989), 87–102.

frankness justifies her in challenging the literary poses adopted by male poets who repeat the idealizing clichés of Petrarchan poetry: its praises of a reserved, unattainable woman, rarely represented as speaking in her own voice. The public literary self Franco created by offering alternatives to masculine discourse is most fully and dramatically staged in *Capitolo* 16, in which she defends herself against insults penned by Maffio Venier, a nephew of Domenico Venier. The literary context of this duel gave Franco a rhetorical power of which she took full advantage: her mock-military challenge to Maffio's authority and her triumphant dismissal of his capacities as poet and decency as a man were more possible in the pages of a poetic collection than they could have been in the everyday interactions between a courtesan and her more socially powerful clients.

Franco's *Familiar Letters* likewise use literary form to shape a representation of the courtesan's life for a public audience. The letters have biographical value; they show her in a variety of daily activities—playing music, sitting for a portrait, organizing a dinner party (Letters 9, 21, 13), even asking for the loan of a wheelchair after a domestic accident (44). She writes as a mother on two occasions, congratulating a noblewoman on the birth of her son (16) and apologizing for not writing to a friend because her own sons have been sick with smallpox (39). The letters also comment on events and situations represented in the poems, so that reading the two together is highly informative. But at the same time, these letters inform us about Franco's public literary activities and the image she wished to project. She sends her poems to a writer she admires, probably Domenico Venier, to request help in revising them (6, 41, 49), as many male writers of the period also did. In letters to a fellow Venetian and to the painter Tintoretto (17, 21), she declares her enthusiasm for the intellectual discussions that occur in "the academies of talented men." And her longer, most polished letters show her writing as an exemplary moralist, giving advice to a patrician male friend (4, 17) and to a woman friend who is thinking of making her daughter into a courtesan (22). In this way, as in her poems, Franco adopts a position of public authority that calls attention to her education, her rhetorical skill, and the solidarity she feels with women.

SOURCES

Franco shaped her poetry and prose in response to the literary experimentation in which the writers of the Venier *ridotto* (salon) were engaged. One of their great interests was the recovery and analysis of medieval vernacular poetry, which had been more or less banished in Pietro Bembo's influential treatise, *Essays on the Common Language* (1525). Bembo had praised the Petrarchan sonnet as a model verse form and recommended a dignified, emotionally restrained style based on ancient Roman rhetoric and the

Tuscan writers of the fourteenth century. Rather than follow these norms exclusively, the Venier group also focused on the *capitolo*, a verse form used by thirteenth-century Provençal poets for literary debate. This was a poem of variable length, written in eleven-syllable verse. It had been resuscitated by early-sixteenth-century satirists such as Francesco Berni, Luigi Grazzini (Il Lasca), and Giovanni Gelli, who had given it a colloquial force and informality very different from the decorous norm recommended by Bembo. One use of the *capitolo* was the *tenzone*, a poetic debate in which one poet answers another's poem in a combative dialogue. This *proposta/risposta* (challenge/response) pattern was of particular interest to Domenico Venier, who, although he never appears by name in Franco's *capitoli*, is often invoked as a literary counselor in them (5, 18, 23, 24). Franco sharpens and foregrounds the *proposta/risposta* element of the *tenzone* in the outrageously amusing *capitoli* in which she equates her sexual prowess as a courtesan and her verbal prowess as a poet with the armed battle of a duel (13, 16), a playful use of the form that is unique to her. But her *Capitolo* 16 also picks up the potential seriousness of the debate implicit in the *tenzone*. In this poem, a fierce and persuasive response to three obscene poems written against her in Venetian dialect by Maffio Venier, the quality of direct address, that is, the dramatization of speech from the poet to an interlocutor, is evidence of her engagement with actual rather than imagined readers: with the person to whom the *capitolo* is written (Maffio Venier), with the Ca Venier audience, and with Venetian readers beyond the Venier circle. The *tenzone* form was designed precisely for this kind of public debate, and Franco used its traditional subject matter—the attack on specific people and on poetic practice—to defend herself against Maffio's attempt to humiliate her in public.

In addition to Dante's *Commedia (Divine Comedy)* and the myths collected in Ovid's *Metamorphoses*, a major source for Franco's *capitoli* was the Venier group's project of translating and writing commentary on the themes, figures of speech, and rhetoric of ancient Roman elegy—that is, love poetry. First, the return to the Latin elegists Catullus, Ovid, Propertius, and Tibullus provided the basis for Franco's adaptation to a female voice of their first-person laments about infidelity, jealousy, and loss. Second, Ovid's *Heroides*, letters attributed to such classical heroines as Sappho and Dido in which the male author ventriloquizes the complaints of abandoned women to their lovers, provided Franco with an epistolary model, while the poems Ovid wrote after he was exiled from Rome, the *Epistulae ex Ponto*, dealt with physical separation from a beloved country, a theme Franco adapted to her own absences from Venice. Elegiac themes were seen by the Venier literary theoreticians as well suited to the *capitolo* as a form. In treatises on the writing of poetry, members of the group argued that the *capitolo*'s chain of interlocking rhymes, creating a suspended yet controlled sense of uncertainty, was a good vehicle for the dramatization of conflicting and shifting emotions, especially the emotions of love.[12]

Franco picks up two different strands from the Roman poets in her *capitoli.* Like Ovid, she writes some in the painful present tense of exile (3, 9, 11, 17, 20); like the elegists, she describes the effects of the betrayal, indifference, or cruelty that have led to her flight (21, 22). Although most of the themes of the Roman poets are easily adaptable to a woman's text, Franco's elegiac *capitoli* transform the male-gendered voice of Latin love poetry through a shift in the position of the speaker. Whereas the Roman poets present themselves as helpless victims of courtesans (Lesbia, Cynthia, Corinna), whom they represent as powerful, talkative, and frankly sexual, Franco, as a courtesan herself, enacts those qualities—unavailable to either decorous Roman or Venetian women—in the forthright, active voice of her poems.

A third literary model that Franco took from the past was the familiar letter, a letter written to a friend but intended for eventual publication. Familiar letters had a complex origin: Cicero's and Seneca's letters, ancient Roman debates about oratorical practice, and Renaissance reworkings of the epistolary genre. When Franco writes in Letter 37 that she will imitate her correspondent by using a style that is *laconica* rather than *asiatica,* she is referring to (though not, in fact, using) the brevity and plain speech of Cicero's letters, as opposed to the highly stylized, intricate prose style condemned by Quintilian in his book on the ideal orator, in which he equated a man using such elaborate style to "a dressed-up whore." [13] Pietro Aretino, who claimed to be the first to bring classical epistolary writing into Italian, similarly denounced the artifice and reverence for classical style of his contemporaries, claiming that his own energetic, convoluted syntax was closer to nature than their decorative refinements.[14] The members of Venier's academy translated a number of volumes of Latin letters, including those of Seneca and Pliny, in the 1540s, and handbooks on letter-writing multiplied rapidly after Francesco Sansovino's 1565 guide to epistolary models, *Il Segretario* (The Secretary).[15] By the end of the 1560s, in the

12. On the uses of the *capitolo* in *terza rima* for love poetry, see Rosenthal, *The Honest Courtesan*, 204–13.

13. Quintilian, *Institutio oratoria*, translated into Italian by Orazio Toscanella and dedicated to Domenico Venier in 1566. On the equation of a man who uses an elaborate rhetorical style and a "dressed-up whore," see Jacqueline Lichtenstein, "Making Up Representation: The Risks of Femininity," *Representations* 20 (1987): 77–87, especially 79–80. See also Rosenthal, *The Honest Courtesan*, 314 nn. 36, 37.

14. Pietro Aretino, *Lettere, il primo e il secondo libro*, in *Tutte le opere*, ed. Francesco Flora and Alessandro del Vita (Milan: Mondadori, 1960). See Letter 1: 156 (Venice, 25 June 1537), 193–94.

15. On volumes of letters printed in Venice in the mid-to-late sixteenth century, see Amedeo

midst of a heated debate about the proper style and topics for letters—should they be formal and full of wise sayings or direct and down to earth?—floods of collected letters by one author or many hands were being published in Italy, including those of Andrea Calmo, Annibale Caro, and Pietro Bembo.[16] But by the 1580s, far fewer epistolary volumes were being printed for the first time.

The ending of the vogue of the genre invites us to ask why the familiar letter was still so attractive to Franco. One reason was that the familiar letter shifted private life into the public sphere; it permitted Franco to comment in print on the behavior of men. That is, the genre enabled her to position herself as a judge and advisor, writing as a courtesan-secretary to advise patricians who had been led astray by passion unmoderated by reason. Given that the standard accusation against the courtesan was that she led a chaotic, dissolute private life, the familiar letter made it possible for Franco to turn the tables in a kind of moral one-upsmanship, acting as an expert in virtue more able to resist the temptations of the world and the flesh than the men to whom she wrote. Her tone of restraint and wisdom is reinforced by the fact that she added neither dates nor names to her letters. By creating a certain indeterminacy of person and place in this way, she achieves a universalizing effect: this is advice for all reasonable beings, not simply a word of wisdom tailored for a particular friend in a particular crisis. Finally, in contrast to the polemical mode of the *capitolo,* the familiar letter establishes the appearance of a certain equality and intimacy between writer and recipient. At the same time, because it requires a grasp of the proper rhetorical forms advocated by classical authors and reinterpreted by the Venier circle, the letter demonstrates the learning and the savoir-faire of its writer.

SUMMARY/ANALYSIS

In the critical analysis of Franco's writing that follows, we begin with her *Familiar Letters* because, although she published them in 1580, five years after her *Poems*, she probably wrote and assembled them throughout the 1570s. We have chosen fifteen out of the fifty she collected because they illustrate her social life, her literary projects, and above all, her use of this literary form to comment philosophically on the behavior of her contemporaries in ways that could raise her status as courtesan-writer.

In fact, the framing of Franco's *Letters* suggests that she was publishing them to establish her reputation firmly as a courtesan to the elite. Her

Quondam, *Le 'carte messaggiere': Retorica e modelli di communicazione epistolare per un indice dei libri di lettere del Cinquecento* (Rome: Bulzoni, 1981), 255–76, 279–316.

16. On this point, see Rosenthal, *The Honest Courtesan*, 122–23, 312 nn. 25–26.

extremely ornate, conventional dedication to Luigi d'Este, Cardinal of Ferrara, is followed by a second dedication and two sonnets intended to advertise a triumph of her early career: her encounter with Henri III, about to become the king of France, when he visited Venice in 1574. Among spectacular civic festivities that lasted ten days, Henri spent a night secretly in her house. In her letter and her two sonnets to Henri, she makes the secret public. In spite of the contrast she sets up between his high status and her lowly one, to record his visit as these texts do was, in fact, to elevate herself in the eyes of her fellow citizens.

In more or less subtle ways, all of Franco's *Letters* contribute to an impression not only of charm and social ease but of literary cultivation and wisdom. In Letter 13, in which she invites the recipient to dine with her and another man, she calls attention to her familiarity with classical epistles. To describe the relaxed, unpretentious occasion she has in mind, she quotes from a letter of Cicero but revises the citation to suit her purpose. In his first letter to Atticus, Cicero had written that his political competitor P. Galba had been refused the position he sought "sine fuco ac fallaciis more maiorum" (without falsity or deceit, in the fashion of our ancestors).[17] Franco retains most of this Latin phrase but applies it, instead, to the informal get-together she is offering to her two men friends: "We can partake, *sine fuco et caerimoniis more maiorum* [without falsity or pomp, in the fashion of our ancestors], of whatever food there will be."

This witty revision of a classical citation stands at the lighter end of the spectrum of Franco's uses of the familiar letter. In others, she adopts the position of serious moral advisor to fellow Venetians. In Letter 4, for example, reminding an unnamed male correspondent that he has given her wise advice on how to face adversity, she tells him that she is going to give that advice back to him. The friendly yet serious counsel here, typical of the familiar letter, is crucial to Franco's feminist position because it allows her to use her exemplary behavior as a letter-writer to undercut the stereotype of the greedy, immoral prostitute. In the third paragraph of the letter, she seems to accept the second-class status of women when she reminds her interlocutor, who is lamenting his misfortune, of his privileged social position. God, she points out, "though capable of making you born from the filthiest and lowest species of all the beasts, . . . gave you birth in the most perfect, the human species, and of that species he gave you the male sex, and not, as to me, the female one." But if this sounds like an acknowledgment of male superiority, Franco's insistence on the absolute reciprocity between the man's advice to her and hers to him establishes a parity between them that contradicts any assumption of men's greater wisdom or

17. Cicero, *Letters to Atticus*, I.1, trans. E. D. Winstedt (Cambridge: Harvard University Press, 1928), 2–3.

authority: "And be aware that in paying you what I owe you, I am paying you in exactly the same coin you gave me; for the fair repayment of virtue demands that I proceed not only in a way similar to yours but in exactly the same way." In this metaphor, too, Franco departs from the role of a venal courtesan: she insists that this is an exchange of virtuous counsel, not of sex for cash, and she emphasizes that she is giving as much as she has received.

In fact, Franco presents herself as having learned more than the man who taught her. Reminding him of his privileges as a nobleman and a Venetian citizen, she praises the city as a miracle of freedom and tranquillity. In the third paragraph of her letter, she invokes the myth of Venice, a much repeated formula celebrating the Republic as a city founded by God and protected throughout its existence from internal political takeover and attack by rival powers. The feminine gender of "Venezia," allegorized as an imperial virgin by writers and as a sumptuous blonde beauty by official state painters,[18] gives the myth particular resonance when it is repeated by a woman writer and a courtesan. Franco identifies herself through citizenship with a personified figure who combines the autonomy she claims for herself in her writing and the public admiration on which she and the city both actually depended, as spectacular beauties commodified for visitors (the visit of Henri III to the city, whose patrician officials most likely guided him to Franco, typifies the parallel between both feminine "attractions"). To invoke this myth in her letter is to draw on a pool of positive associations with the feminized city-state and to raise her status as a courtesan by demonstrating her participation in a patriotic discourse to which distinguished male writers from Petrarch and Aretino to Domenico Venier had contributed.

In addition to presenting herself as more appreciative of the benefits of Venetian citizenship than the man she addresses in Letter 4, Franco presents herself as his superior in moral wisdom. She instructs him to live according to his principles: if he cannot put the Christian Stoicism he has recommended to her—that is, the focus on spiritual rather than worldly wealth—into practice in his "hour of need," he is revealing the shallowness of his own teaching: "When it comes to the values that you have so often taught me, you will show that you no longer understand them if you do not apply them." As in many of the texts she addresses to men, she distinguishes sharply between high-sounding moral claims and actual behavior.

This position of moral superiority, combined with a sense of serious duty to a friend, also characterizes Franco's letter to a woman friend who has decided to turn her daughter into a courtesan (22). But the striking difference between 4 and 22 is that the mother of Letter 22 has none of the privileges the man addressed in 4 enjoys. She is poor, unprotected, and

18. One painter's typically lush allegory of Venezia is Paolo Veronese's *Triumph of Venice,* for the Ducal Palace. Rosenthal discusses this painting in *The Honest Courtesan,* 261–62 n. 12.

forced by her circumstances to think about profit rather than virtue. In this letter, Franco makes very clear the difference between the opportunities that her city makes available to a wealthy man and a poor woman. She reminds her friend that she has promised to help place her daughter in one of the few refuges the city offered unmarried girls at risk of losing their virginity: the Casa delle Zitelle, where, after a period of residence, girls became eligible for respectable marriages. Franco's generous, even insistent offer of assistance makes this a familiar letter with an urgent, practical motive: she wants to protect not only the daughter but the mother, who will ruin her own reputation and lose her daughter's love if she becomes her go-between. Yet the woman to whom the letter is addressed appears to have rejected Franco's help. As a result, Franco composes an eloquent warning against the dangers of the prostitute's life to which poor women in the city could be driven. She stresses the risk of physical violence and disease as much, if not more, than spiritual damnation, and she insists on the financial instability of such a life and the practical requirements for succeeding in it.

Readers of this letter often ask, "Is this Franco's despairing denunciation of her own life as a courtesan?" We think not. She never names herself specifically as the victim of the dangers she describes, and she never mentions her own mother as a go-between or declares any intention of leaving her profession. Indeed, her practical comments on the girl's lack of what it takes to succeed as a courtesan—beauty, "grace and wit in conversation," and "style, good judgment, and proficiency in many skills"—suggest that she is distinguishing herself from the lower ranks of sex workers which this daughter is likely to join. Rather, Franco is constructing a portrait of herself as a realistic, honest advisor to her friend. She does refer to the religious catastrophe of a prostitute's life, but her principle concern is pragmatic: the predictable social consequences of the decision this mother is about to make.

In addition, Franco is revising literary portraits of prostitution written by men. Pietro Aretino, for example, in his *Dialogues* (1556), had presented conversations between an aged prostitute, Nanna, and her daughter, Pippa, in which, with a certain sympathy, he ventriloquized the older woman's complaint about the lack of freedom that such a woman suffers. Nanna says, "She must, whether she likes it or not, sit with someone else's buttocks, walk with someone else's feet, sleep with someone else's eyes, and eat with someone else's mouth."[19] But a main reason for Aretino's hatred of this lack of freedom was that he saw it as an analogy to the strict social requirements confronted by male courtiers; to him, these physical con-

19. Pietro Aretino, *Dialogues*, trans. Raymond Rosenthal (New York: Marsilio, 1994), as cited in the epilogue by Margaret Rosenthal, 396.

straints were partly a metaphor for the dynamic between men at court and their powerful patrons. When Franco writes a series of verbs illustrating the actions a courtesan was obliged to perform according to the wishes of her clients, she is speaking literally for women who have experienced the actual enslavement of their bodies and their daily activities to their client's desires: "to eat with another's mouth, sleep with another's eyes." She also emphasizes the involuntary quality of such actions over their physicality ("to move according *to another's will*"), just as she adds, at several points in the letter, references to the lack of mental and spiritual autonomy in a prostitute's life: "the shipwreck" of the "mind" (*facoltà*, that is, mental capacities), the danger to "the soul." Franco's project in her *Poems*, as we show in the analysis that follows, is to overcome this actual lack of freedom by constructing a poetic realm in which she dramatizes the mind and soul of the courtesan interacting in forceful, even triumphant ways with her male critics and patrons.

THE POEMS

Franco's *Poems* consists of twenty-five examples of the *capitolo*, written in the *terza rima* that Dante had used in *The Divine Comedy*. This meter and rhyme scheme consists of eleven-syllable lines arranged in interlocking tercets (aba, bcb, cdc) The length of the *capitolo* is variable: Franco's shortest *capitolo* is 39 lines long, her longest 565. Her collection may be divided into two parts. The first, containing poems written by men as well as by Franco, consists of fourteen poems arranged in pairs: a *capitolo* from a man followed by a response from Franco, or a poem by Franco followed by one by a man. This mixed authorship may seem surprising in a book published under Franco's name. But another courtesan-poet, Tullia d'Aragona, compiled a similar collection: her *Rime* contain many sonnets from well-known men. Courtesans, rather than conceal their connections to famous men, advertised them. Like Tullia, Franco presents herself as a poet engaged in intellectual exchanges with literary men by including their work in her pages. *Capitolo* 1 was composed by Marco Venier, the nephew of Domenico Venier, whose name appears at the head of the poem in one of the original copies of the book but is replaced with "Incerto autore" (unknown author) in other copies. The authors of the other poems in men's voices are not identified. In these pairs of poems, the first writer sets a theme and the second responds to it.

This pattern of poems paired in dialogue changes in the second part of the collection. From *Capitolo* 15 on, all the poems are by Franco. She continues to address her eleven final *capitoli* to male readers, but she also produces more meditative, elegiac poems—laments over love or separation from her city—and she ends with a long *capitolo* dedicated to a Veronese churchman, Marc'antonio della Torre, in praise of his country estate. Two groups of poems tell a story that spans both sections of the collection. A trio of Franco's poems (3, 17, 20) deals with jealousy and separation in terms clearly drawn from Roman elegy. And two poems crucial to her defense of herself and of women in general against a male attacker begin in the first section (13) and continue into the second (16).

The story of the collection is always the story of Franco as a poet. The pair of poems with which she opens the collection emphasize her fame as a writer, exceptional among Venetian women and among courtesans as a literary "star." In *Capitolo* 1, Marco Venier presents himself as the traditional woeful Petrarchan lover, displaying a "pale / and mournful look" in his "solitary wandering" (49–50), and he praises the features that Petrarch had celebrated in Laura: bright eyes, golden hair, a white hand. But Venier also refers directly to Franco as a poet: *her* lovely hand holds a pen. He acknowledges her inspiration by Apollo, who "breathes his benign knowledge into you" (72); he encourages her to go on composing "graceful and pleasant rhymes" (77); and he praises her for writing in the spirit of the ancients (85–86). These compliments are part of an argument of seduction through which he links his praise of her poetry to his request that she satisfy his desire: "Let Venus be no less pleased by your beauty; / you must put to good use the many gifts she bestowed upon you" (152–55). In Franco's response, she follows his logic, wittily assuring him that the skills she has learned from Venus will make him find her "dearer still" (51). But she proposes a bargain to him in which she insists on intellectual collaboration as a precondition for erotic fulfillment. Rather than simply demand "silver or . . . gold" as proof of his love, she asks repeatedly for "deeds" (28, 37, 181–82), and to describe these deeds, she uses a word, *opre,* that means literary works (181). When she tells him that what she really values are actions that prove a man's "virtues" (which in the Venier group meant intellectual skill) and his "wisdom" (106, 108), she is using the same vocabulary in which she describes her enthusiasm for "the academies of talented men" (Letter 17). Rejecting Marco Venier's compliments as "fictions" (40), she invites him, we believe, into an exchange of written texts that she can use as proof of a relationship extending beyond the private sexual liaison of courtesan and client. Her publication of his poem as the first in her book confirms this conjecture. Franco admits and celebrates the sexual prowess with which she can reward Venier: critics have been astonished and delighted by the frankness with which she speaks of her expertise in "the delights of love" (149–50). What we see as new, in addition to this courtesan's openly erotic rejection of the high-minded poses of Petrarchan poetry, is her insistence that her lover interact with her as an intellectual, complying with her demand for proof of their literary connection.

Franco's interest in presenting herself as a serious participant in intellectual life comes through clearly again in an exchange with a man whose poetic compliments she rejects even more forcefully than the "fictions" of Marco Venier. In *Capitolo* 11, an unnamed man pleads with her to return to Venice from Verona, which, he claims, by way of extravagant praise, has been gloriously embellished by Franco's presence there: "Lovely Verona, you are one of a kind, / now that my gentle Veronica / beautifies you." In *Capitolo* 12 Franco devastatingly rejects this man's practice as a poet, accusing him of "wandering in vain versifying" (14) and using lying exaggerations (17–18). She criticizes not only his style but his subject, telling him that if he wanted to praise her, he should have praised her native city rather than praising Verona. Here again, as in Letter 17 (and at length in *Capitolo* 22, 154–95), by invoking traditional celebrations of Venice, she identifies herself as a loyal citizen, establishes her superiority to her interlocutor, who has forgotten the honor the city bestows on its inhabitants, and identifies herself with a figure of feminine allure and power.[20] Indeed, in her description of the city (20–48), Franco expands her prose version of the civic myth to stress the city's visual beauty, the highest possible in heaven and on earth. In *Capitolo* 12, Franco writes as a confident master and critic of poetic style and claims the authority to define appropriate ways in which male poets should speak of her.

By far the most serious critique of poetry in which Franco engaged, however, was her debate with Maffio Venier (1550–86), which led her to defend not only herself but her sex in general against mockery and hatred from men. The history of her debate with this erring member of the Venier clan, who was famous for his poems in Venetian dialect, can be summed up as follows. Sometime in the 1570s, Maffio circulated in manuscript three poems specifically targeting Franco: a *capitolo* beginning "Franca, credéme che per San Maffio" (Franco, believe me, in the name of Saint Maffio), another beginning "An, fia, cuomuodo? A che muodo zioghémo?" (What suits you, girl? How shall we play?), and a sonnet beginning, "Veronica, ver unica puttana" (Veronica, a verily unique whore; see figure 1).[21]

Maffio was attacking not only Franco but the men who had written poems praising her by means of a similar but positively intended pun on her name. In *Capitolo* 7, an unnamed author praises her as "vera, unica al mondo eccelsa dea" (true and unique goddess, supreme on earth, 173), and, as we have seen, the man writing to her in Verona (*Capitolo* 11) opens by using the same words to link the city's name to hers ("Truly, lovely Verona, you are one of a kind, / now that my gentle Veronica / beautifies you with

20. On the myth of Venice, see Edward Muir, *Civic Ritual in Renaissance Venice* (Princeton: Princeton University Press, 1981), especially chap. 1, "The Myth of Venice."

21. For the texts of Maffio Venier's dialect poems directed to Franco, see Manlio Dazzi, *Il fiore della lirica veneziana: Il libro segreto (chiuso)*, vol. 2 (Vicenza: Neri Pozza, 1956). See also Armando Balduino, "Restauri e ricuperi per Maffio Venier," in *Medioevo e Rinascimento veneto: Con altri studi in onore di Lino Lazzarino* (Padua: Antenore, 1979), 2: 231–63.

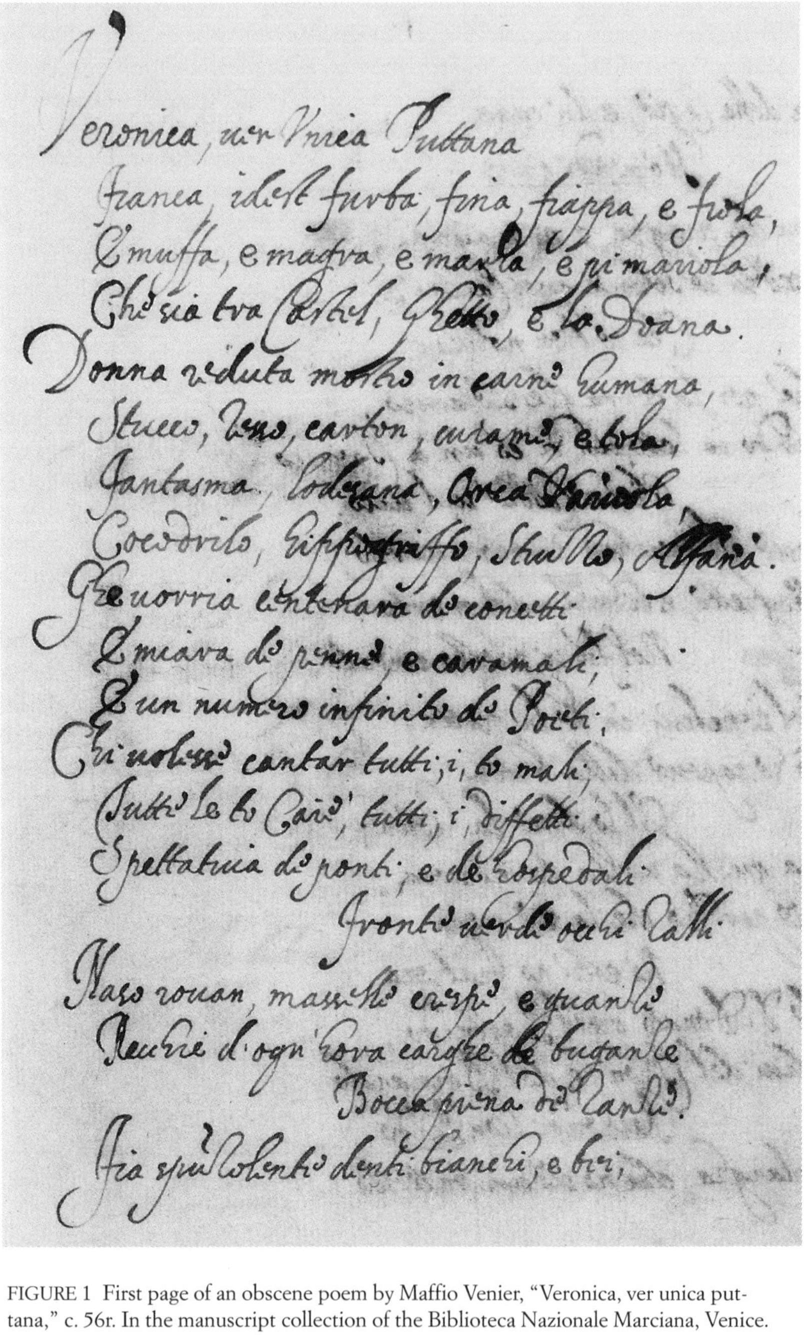

FIGURE 1 First page of an obscene poem by Maffio Venier, "Veronica, ver unica puttana," c. 56r. In the manuscript collection of the Biblioteca Nazionale Marciana, Venice. MSS it. IX 217 (= 7091).

her unique beauty"). It may well be that Franco saw this attack on male poets as well as herself as a justification for asking for advice, in *Capitolo 23*, from a man expert in the language of dueling, possibly Domenico Venier, as she prepared to respond to her enemy. She is not alone in having been satirized by the man who has defamed her, so she invites her interlocutor to counsel her on the shared project of taking up arms against Maffio, the parodist of poetry written by several men in her honor.

Franco was not certain at first of the identity of the man who had written against her. *Capitolo 13*, in which she reproaches a lover for "merciless mistreatment" in an unexpected betrayal, shows that she believes that a man with whom she has had happy sexual encounters (34–36), probably Marco Venier, has turned on her with lies. She adopts a vocabulary of dueling to respond to the man's lies, but the poem works toward a witty revelation: the battle Franco has been proposing is a sexual contest in bed. Certainly, she would not offer such a sexual invitation to an enemy like Maffio. The man's response in the next poem likewise suggests that Franco has mistaken him for the man who betrayed her. He protests his innocence and conjectures that someone else, disapproving of their living together, has "scattered his poison over their sweetness" (64–66). Finally, one of Franco's letters confirms that she has confused a man she admired with the author of the satirical verses against her. In Letter 47 she apologizes to a man she respectfully calls "your Lordship." She now sees that the poems written against her were not good enough to have come from his pen, and she explains that she sent her response to him under the mistaken impression that he had been the author of these insults.

To come now to *Capitolo 16* itself: Franco's maneuvers in this clearly focused counterattack show that her confusion has been cleared up. She has seen Maffio's poems (she quotes one specifically) and she knows who her detractor is (she identifies him as using Venetian dialect). Accordingly, she sets out to expose him, his inept sonnet, and his hostility to women. Here, as in 13, she adopts the vocabulary of dueling—more precisely, chivalrous warfare. But she is no longer jokingly making erotic puns. By dueling here, she means writing: the hidden weapons with which Maffio ambushed her are the insults in his sonnet, which she criticizes and rewrites. Quoting the beginning of his sonnet, "Veronica, ver unica puttana," she ignores the term of sexual insult and focuses instead on the word "unique." This cannot have a negative meaning, she informs him; her dictionary and the practice of better writers than Maffio affirm the positive connotation of the word (142, 154–55). She even turns his semantic error into a compliment to prostitutes in general: his *unica* either means that she is not a prostitute or it applies to her "whatever good prostitutes have," which she specifies as some degree of "grace and nobility of soul" (178–82).

This light touch, through which she aligns herself with other women who make their living through sex, is linked to a move that Franco makes much more emphatically earlier in the poem: she turns her defense of herself against Maffio into a defense of all women. At first, she criticizes Maffio for his lack of chivalry in a way that appears to concede a great deal to conventional ideas about women's nature and social role: because they are weak and timid, they deserve men's protection, not their abuse (10–16). But she revises her apparent acceptance of women as the weaker sex as the poem goes on. The man's attack has forced her to toughen up, to become as capable of battle as he is. Although Franco first presents this capacity for transformation as hers alone—Maffio's attack has spurred her to train herself—she moves from this individual claim to a feminist focus on women as a group. She takes her personal experience as proof that women in general "are no less agile than men" (36) in warfare—and, as the rest of the poem shows, in verbal combat.

She expands her argument for women's equality to men by insisting that training, not innate essence, determines women's abilities. As Lucrezia Marinella would do in her *La nobiltà e l'eccellenza delle donne*, citing a 1581 poem by Moderata Fonte, Franco imagines a situation in which women enjoy the same opportunities as men and therefore demonstrate the same physical and mental strength ("hands and feet and hearts like yours," 66).[22] She rejects gender fixity more radically by pointing out that masculinity itself is not a unified given. Men vary in physical strength; further, their diversity proves that there is no necessary connection between body types and mental qualities: "some men who are delicate are also strong, / and some, though coarse and rough, are cowards" (68–69). She also suggests that it is ideology that prevents women from discovering their capabilities. If they were not kept ignorant of their potential, they would reveal it in triumphant encounters with men (70–72).

Franco concludes her defense of women with a neat combination of the two roles she has claimed as Maffio's challenger: poetic virtuosa and member of the female sex. She declares herself the champion of women: she is the first to write against Maffio, their common enemy, but she intends that others will follow in her footsteps: "Among so many women, I will be the first to act, / setting an example for all of them to follow" (74–75). Franco's verve and eloquence in this *capitolo* would indeed reappear in the

---

22. In *La nobiltà e l'eccellenza delle donne* (Venice: Giovanni Battista Ciotti, 1600; 2d ed., 1601), Lucrezia Marinella raises training above fixed gender capacity as follows: "Let them train a boy and a girl of the same age, both well born and with good minds, in letters and in arms; . . . they would see in how short a time the girl would be more expertly accomplished than the boy" (33). She cites in support a passage from Moderata Fonte's 1581 epic, *Il Floridoro*: "If when a daughter is born to a father, / He set her to the same work as his son, / In solemn or gay tasks, she'd hold her own, / Neither less than her brother nor unequal to him, / Whether he placed her in fiercely armed squadrons / Or assigned her to learn any liberal art" (11, canto 4).

work of women prose writers, if not poets, in the late 1500s. But her decla-
ration that she represents what all women are potentially able to do broad-
ens the field of combat, shifting her response to Maffio from a one-on-one
duel to a display of feminine competence in general: "I will show you how
much the female sex / excels your own" (94–95).

In other *capitoli*, too, Franco looks sympathetically at the situation of
women, although she is never again as fierce in her confrontation with a
male interlocutor. In one of her elegiac poems— *Capitolo* 22, a lament on
her absence from Venice and the miseries of love—she seems again to be
conceding the truth of misogynist cliché: women suffer more in love than
men because they are less rational: "the slightest breeze disturbs the female
mind, / and our simple souls are set ablaze / . . . by even a tepid fire"
(76–78). But she explains this surface phenomenon as the result of social
oppression, not female nature, echoing arguments (for example, Boc-
caccio's in the opening of *The Decameron*)[23] that confining women against
their will makes them more, not less, susceptible to passion: "The less free-
dom we possess, / the more blind desire . . . / will find a way to penetrate
our hearts" (79–81). Limited autonomy, "our shared constraint," she sug-
gests, rather than moral frailty, leads women to two equally grim alterna-
tives: dying of love or going "astray because of a slight mistake" (82–84).

Franco's longest and most inventive defense of women—of a fellow
courtesan and of the female sex in general—occurs toward the end of her
Poems, in *Capitolo* 24. She speaks with elaborate courtesy to a man who has
not only insulted a woman verbally but threatened to scar her permanently
by slashing her face (35)—a form of violence through which angry clients
attempted to end the careers of courtesans of whom they were jealous.
Franco's intention here is gently persuasive rather than openly polemical:
she wants to bring the man back into an orbit of gentlemanly chivalry so
that he will make peace with the woman. But in the course of her tactful
suggestions to him, she fills nearly sixty lines with a variety of claims in de-
fense of the female sex.

Some of her arguments are playful and lighthearted, as when she argues
from observable social facts to their underlying cause: men's gratitude for
women's courtesy and admiration of their wisdom is proved by the fact that
they dress women richly, give them the right of way indoors and out, and

---

23. Giovanni Boccaccio, *Tutte le opere di Giovanni Boccaccio*, vol. 4 (*Il Decamerone*), ed. Vit-
tore Branca (Milan: Mondadori, 1976). Boccaccio writes in his preface that women are more
prone to uncontrollable passions because they are sheltered from the public, social world and
cannot free themselves, as do men, of the intense feelings of love: "It is women who timorously
and bashfully conceal Love's flame within their tender breasts; and those who have had ex-
perience of it know well enough how much harder it is to control the suppressed than the
open flame. Moreover, circumscribed as women are, . . . they brood on all manner of things"
(trans. Guido Waldman [Oxford: Oxford University Press, 1993], 4).

even wear hats in order to take them off in women's honor (97–108).[24] But she also writes in a passionately serious tone about women's disempowerment, as when she describes the entire sex as "always subjected and without freedom" (56–57) and complains of the injustice of their subordination, given that they have minds and souls equal or superior to men's (61–66). She claims, in fact, that women combine rationality with virtues such as modesty and flexibility in a mixture that preserves the social fabric.

This claim leads her into her most sustained argument, in which she rewrites the social relations between the sexes to define men not as the lords and masters of creation but as the beneficiaries of feminine intelligence and patience. In her counter-myth to the Fall caused by Eve, she proposes that the continuation of the human race has resulted from women's willingness to lay aside the fierce resistance that men deserve. Rather, to preserve the world, "so beautiful through our species," women are strategically silent and submissive (85–90). Ignorant men glory in the power they thereby gain over women, but wiser men recognize this voluntary vassalage as a reason for gratitude and respectful treatment of the female sex.

This view of gender relations is less radical than the critique of male injustice to which Lucrezia Marinella would devote the second half of her *Nobiltà delle donne* or the freedom from men that Moderata Fonte celebrates in her *Merito delle donne* through the unmarried Corinna and the financially independent widow Leonora.[25] But Franco's position as a courtesan, in this case protecting another woman who shares her profession, accounts for the particular inflection she gives her view of women's superiority to men. For their forbearance, she insists, women deserve respectful treatment from men. This logic serves all courtesans, whose interest lay in managing the realities of their lives—men's ownership of the cash they needed, their potential violence, and their ability to destroy women's reputations—by encouraging their clients to follow the code of chivalry. Franco clearly models this code in the gentle tact with which she opens

24. Here, with the exception of her remark about men's hats, Franco appears to be drawing on Livy, or, more likely, on Agrippa's summary, in his *De nobilitate et praecellentia foeminei sexus*, of Livy's history of Coriolanus. Agrippa, following Livy, explains that to reward the women of Rome, through whose intervention Coriolanus was diverted from attacking the city, the Roman senate gave them "the privilege of walking on the high side of the street, and men rising to render homage to them and ceding their place to them." The senate also permitted them to wear "purple garments with golden fringes, even ornaments of precious stones," a list similar to Franco's in the preceding tercets (lines 97–100). See Henricus Cornelius Agrippa, *Declamation on the Nobility and Preeminence of the Female Sex* (1509), trans. Albert Rabil (Chicago: University of Chicago Press, 1996), 90. Rabil identifies two Italian translations of Agrippa's defense of women, both published in Venice, the first by Francesco Coccio (Gabriele Giolito, 1554), the second by Alessandro Piccolomini or Ludovico Domenichi in 1545 and 1549 (27 n. 48).

25. These two characters are the principal speakers in Moderata Fonte's *Il merito delle*

Capitolo 24. She imagines not a world in which women live without men (given her profession, this was an unlikely fantasy) but one in which they can coexist in safe reciprocity with men. This poem, by arguing for women's merit in a tone and logic that call on men to keep their real social power in check, typifies the delicate balance the courtesan poet needed to maintain between her sense of her own worth and her need to win and keep the support of men. Franco's *Letters* and *Poems* dramatize her search for autonomy and her solidarity with women at the same time that they record her skillful courtship of the male-dominated cultural elite on whom she depended for security and fame.

THE AFTERLIFE OF FRANCO'S TEXTS

Franco's reputation during her life and after her death is not easy to re-construct. We know that she was recognized in Venice in her lifetime be-cause she was asked to participate in the anthology of poems for Marti-nengo, among others, and her sonnets appear in collections that include poems by noblewomen of the Republic. She was also known outside Italy; the courtier Muzio Manfredi wrote her a letter from France in 1591 (not knowing she had died three months before), thanking her for her sonnet in praise of his tragedy *Semiramis* and saying that he had heard of her am-bition to write an epic. But however widely her poems circulated in manu-script in or beyond the Venier circle, her two books are unlikely to have been read very widely in her lifetime, because few copies of either one were printed. Neither book identifies a publisher on its title-page, which sug-gests that they were published privately, probably at Franco's expense. Pri-vate editions were usually small, as the very few extant copies of *The Poems* (four) and *The Letters* (two) confirm.[26]

Franco is not mentioned by her contemporaries Moderata Fonte and Lucrezia Marinella, possibly because they belonged to a wealthy profes-

donne (Venice: Domenico Umberti, 1600), ed. Adriana Chemello (Mirano: Eidos, 1988). See also Moderata Fonte, *The Worth of Women: Wherein Is Clearly Revealed Their Nobility and Their Superiority to Men,* ed. and trans. Virginia Cox (Chicago: University of Chicago Press, 1997).

26. Stefano Bianchi mentions two Italian copies of the *Terze rime,* one in Florence, the other in Venice, in *Veronica Franco: Rime* (Milan: Mursia, 1995), "Nota al testo," 41. A third copy belongs to the Special Collections of Van Pelt Library at the University of Pennsylvania, and Marilyn Migiel writes that she has seen a fourth; see "Veronica Franco (1546-1591)," in *Ital-ian Women Writers: A Bio-bibliographic Sourcebook,* ed. Rinaldina Russell (Westport, Conn.: Greenwood Press, 1994), 142. Croce describes the volume of the *Letters* that he used as *raris-simo* (xxvii), but two copies of *Lettere familiari* exist, one at the Marciana in Venice and one at the University of Pennsylvania. Through the University of Pennsylvania's Van Pelt Library, Special Collections, an electronic facsimile of both the *Terze rime* and *Lettere familiari* is avail-able through e-mail: ceti@pobox. upenn.edu.

sional class very different from the elevated but far more precarious status of the *cortigiana onesta*.[27] But two of her *capitoli* (12 and 24) were reprinted in an anthology of women poets edited by Luisa Bergalli in the eighteenth century (1726), and M. Tobia published *Capitolo* 5 in an 1850 anthology of women poets. More general interest in Franco revived in the late nineteenth century when the Venetian scholar Giuseppe Tassini wrote a first biography (1874); Arturo Graf published an appreciative study of her in 1888. In the twentieth century, three modern editions of the *Poems* have been published, G. Beccari's in 1912, Abdelkader Salza's in 1913, and Stefano Bianchi's excellent *Rime* in 1995. Benedetto Croce published the *Letters* in 1949, accompanied by the engraved title page intended for Franco's *Rime*. In 1997, Laura Anna Stortoni edited a dual-language anthology, *Women Poets of the Italian Renaissance: Courtly Ladies and Courtesans,* which includes her translations of three of Franco's poems and one letter. These editions, combined with the rise of feminist literary studies, have produced a number of recent studies focusing on Franco as a woman writer, and, in addition, an imaginative reconstruction of her life, Dacia Maraini's play *Veronica, meretrice e scrittora.* It is possible that further research will show that she was read by women poets in her own time and later. But for now, Marco Venier's prediction in *Capitolo* 1 that she would be "a true ornament to every age" (line 26) seems less true of the three hundred years following her death than of the twentieth century.

A note on the translation: In the *Familiar Letters,* we have maintained the elaborate syntax of Franco's dedications but have given a slightly less formal character to the epistles themselves. To help readers understand the ideas and images in her *capitoli,* we have produced a fairly literal rendering of the *Poems,* without attempting to reproduce her *terza rima.* Rather than imitate her eleven-syllable lines, we have aimed for a four-beat line in English. The prose summaries of each *capitolo* are ours. We are indebted throughout to Stefano Bianchi's edition of the *Rime,* including his notes. We have omitted the prose summaries he reproduces from Abdelkader Salza's edition, but we include his line numbers as well as Salza's. We are also indebted to four readers of our translation, the first Elissa Weaver, the second from the University of Chicago Press, the third the eagle-eyed Elena Maclachlan, and the fourth Marilyn Migiel.

27. On the social positions of Veronica Franco and Moderata Fonte, who were contemporaries, see Margaret Rosenthal, "Venetian Women Writers and Their Discontents," in *Sexuality and Gender in Early Modern Europe: Institutions, Texts, Images,* ed. James Granthem Turner (Cambridge: Cambridge University Press, 1992).

VERONICA FRANCO,
FAMILIAR LETTERS TO VARIOUS
PEOPLE (1580)

To the most illustrious and revered Monsignor Luigi d'Este, Cardinal

Because anyone, even though Fortune has set her in the lowest
place, can honor and glorify almighty God with offerings and
prayers in equal proportion to the wealthiest men, richly endowed
with all good things; indeed, because people who make the smallest
offerings often excel those who build temples and perform other
lavish rites, since God, King of the universe, considers the spiritual
eagerness and the ability of a donor rather than the particular qual-
ity of the gift; so in your divine presence, without hesitation, a per-
son desiring to show you her soul's devotion finds some way or
another to prove it in outward deeds, hoping through a small and
feeble tribute that nonetheless includes matchless yearning and an
enlightened, eager will to surpass the honor of whoever, unable to
show signs of such reverent feeling, offers far more expensive things
out of respect for your most excellent judgment—which, with the
kindliness of God, whose deserving and famous minister you are on
earth, valuing the intention of the heart more than the pretension of
things, cannot fail to accept a tiny sign of devotion more willingly
than an endless effort toward some final, unattainable declaration of
respect. This truth, which I have clearly understood in the light of
your famous virtue and encountered directly in the match and fit
between your fame and the dignity of your person, along with your
blessed and divine intelligence, has so enflamed me that amidst the
competition of many men famous for their learning, constantly
addressing their wonderful works of science and elegant studies to
you and also their compliments, in which the writer's judgment is
more to be honored the more that he lacks the ability to praise you,
I have not hesitated, though a woman untrained in the disciplines   *23*

and poor in invention and language, to dedicate to you this volume of letters written in my youth, which, with the help of your amazing courtesy and my deepest respect, ought to have that place in the blessedly fortunate shelter of your superhuman kindness, among the wealth of large and brilliant lights burning in the temple, that a well-trimmed and filled oil lamp used to have in heaven. Perhaps at a more propitious time, in better fortune and a more practiced style, with the help of your divine kindness, I will dare to try a greater undertaking, expressing more fully my soul and my gratitude than laying this little book at the feet of your high valor, through which you, holding out the arms of your courtesy from the lofty throne of your immense grace to accept and receive this little display, derived from my most fervent desire to acknowledge the duty I owe you, will win esteem for your kindness, all the greater the farther I am from deserving anything from your illustrious Lordship. Your kindness will lay upon me that command which, eagerly sought, is never without effect in the mind of someone who wants to work in pleasing and skillful ways.

> *May our Lord bless your most illustrious person.*
> *From Venice, the second of August, 1580.*
> *Your most illustrious and most reverend Lordship's*
> *humblest and most devoted servant,*
>
> *Veronica Franca*[1]

To the Most Unvanquished and Christian King, Henri III of France and Poland

To the immensely high favor that Your Majesty deigned to show me, coming to my humble house, by taking my portrait away with you in exchange for the living image of your heroic virtues and divine valor that you left deep in my heart—an exchange all too fortunate and happy on my side—I am unable to reciprocate, even in thought or desire; for what can be born from me worthy of the supreme height of your heavenly soul and your fate? Nor can I compensate even partly with any form of thanks for the infinite merit of the kindly and gracious offers you made to me on the subject of this book, which I am about to dedicate to you, offers more fitting to your greatness and most serene kingly splendor than to any talent of mine. And even so, as the whole world can be drawn in the small space of the narrowest page, I have, in these few verses which I send

---

1. Writing a woman's surname with a feminine ending was common practice in Franco's time.

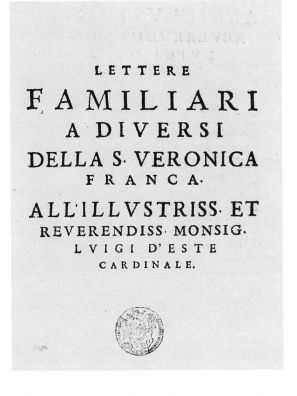

LETTERE
F AMILIARI
A DIVERSI
DELLA S· VERONICA
F R A N C A·
ALL'ILLVSTRISS· ET
REVERENDISS· MONSIG·
L V I G I D' E S T E
C A R D I N A L E.

FIGURE 2
Frontispiece for
Veronica Franco's
Lettere familiari a diversi
(1580), dedicated to
Cardinal Luigi d'Este
and Henri III, king of
France.

with all respect to Your Majesty, set down a sketch, however cramped and rough, of my gratitude and my immense, burning desire to celebrate beyond the limits of any earthly hope the innumerable and superhuman gifts lodged, to their good fortune, in your generous breast. And with devoted and deep affection I bow down reverently to embrace your sacred knees.

Your Majesty's most humble and devoted servant,

Veronica Franca

SONNETS TO HENRI III

1

Come talor dal ciel sotto umil tetto
Giove tra noi qua giù benigno scende,
e, perch' occhio terren dall' alt' oggetto
non resti vinto, umana forma prende:

OME tal'hor dal Ciel sotto hu-
mil tetto
Gioue trà noi quà giù benigno
scende,
Et perche occhio terren dall'
alt'oggetto
Non resti uinto humana for-
ma prende:

Cosi uenne al mio pouero ricetto
Senza pompa real, ch'abbaglia, e splende
Dal fato Henrico à tal dominio eletto,
Ch'un sol mondo no'l cape, & nol comprende.

Benche si sconosciuto, anc'al mio core
Tal raggio impresse del diuin suo merto,
Che'n me s'estinse il natural uigore.

Di ch'ei di tant'affetto non incerto,
L'imagin mia di smalt', e di colore
Prese al partir con grat'animo aperto.

Rendi, Re per uirtù sommo,
& perfetto,
Quel che la mano à porger-
ti si stende:
Questo scolpito, & colorato
aspetto,
In cui'l mio uiuo, & natu-
ral s'intende.

E, s'à essempio si basso, & sì imperfetto
La tua uista beata non s'attende;
Risguarda à la cagion, non à l'effetto.
Poca fauilla ancor gran fiamma accende.

E come'l tuo immortal diuin ualore,
In armi, è in pace, à mille proue esperto
M'empio l'alma di nobile stupore,

Cosi'l desio di donna in cor sofferto
D'alzarti sopra'l Ciel dal mondo fore
Mira in quel mio sembiante espresso, & certo.

FIGURE 3
Two dedicatory sonnets by
Veronica Franco for Henri
III, king of France, after his
entry into Venice in 1574, in
Franco's *Lettere familiari a
diversi* (1580), Biblioteca
Nazionale Marciana, Venice.
Rari V. 494

così venne al mio povero ricetto
senza pompa real, ch'abbaglia e splende,
dal fato Enrico a tal dominio eletto,
ch'un sol mondo nol cape e nol comprende.
   Benché sì sconosciuto, anch'al mio core
tal raggio impresse del divin suo merto,
ch'in me s'estinse il natural vigore.
   Di ch'ei, di tanto affetto non incerto,
l'imagin mia di smalto e di colore
prese al partir con grat'animo aperto.

As from heaven down to a humble roof
Beneficent Jove descends to us here below,
and to avoid blinding mortal eyes
with such a noble sight, takes human shape:
   so to my poor dwelling came Henri,
without royal show, which blinds and dazzles—
Henri, whom fate chose for such an empire
that one world alone cannot contain it.
   Even so disguised, into my heart
he shone such a ray of his divine virtue
that my innate strength completely failed me.
   So, assured of the depth of my affection,
he took my image, in enamel and paint,
away with him in a gracious, open spirit.

2

   Prendi, re per virtù sommo et perfetto,
quel che la mano a porgerti si stende:
questo scolpito e colorato aspetto,
in cui 'l mio vivo e natural s'intende.
   E, s'a esempio si basso e si imperfetto
la tua vista beata non s'attende,
risguarda a la cagion, non a l'effetto.
Poca favilla ancor gran fiamma accende.
   E come 'l tuo immortal divin valore,
in armi e in pace a mille prove esperto,
m'empío l'alma di nobile stupore,
   così 'l desio, di donna in cor sofferto,
d'alzarti sopra 'l ciel dal mondo fore,
mira in quel mio sembiante espresso e certo.

Take, king, sum of virtue and perfection,
what my hand reaches out to give you:
this carved and colored countenance,
in which my living, real self is represented.
    And if such a lowly and imperfect image
is not what your blessed gaze expects,
Consider my motive rather than the result.
A small spark can still kindle a great flame.
    And because your undying, celestial valor,
tested by a thousand trials in war and peace,
filled my soul with noble wonder,
    So the desire felt in a woman's heart
to raise you above heaven, beyond this world,
see, expressed and proved, in this likeness of me.

Letter 4

FRANCO RETURNS A FRIEND'S ADVICE TO HIM IN HIS ADVERSITY

The words you said to me the other evening made me realize that your soul is seriously troubled and shaken by mishaps arising from your bad luck—so much so that I was dumbfounded to recall the many occasions on which I've found you to be a man of prudence and quite capable of defending yourself with the powerful shield of virtue against the blows of hostile fate. And because I, too, once suffering, as we do in the world, found you ready and willing to comfort me with your good advice, from which I benefited so much that my trouble almost turned to gain as I followed your wise warnings, I mustn't fail to perform the same duty of consoling you in your crisis. Doing this, on one hand, will be harder for me than you because I have so little experience with the reasoning on which, with sound doctrine, you have based your position. On the other hand, it will be easy for me because I have nothing to tell you except exactly what you once told me. And if my memory serves me as it should, I'll talk to you in your own words and say your own speech back to you. And be aware that in paying you what I owe you, I am paying you back in exactly the same coin you gave me. For the fair repayment of virtue requires that I proceed not only in a way like yours but in exactly the same way.

    Vain and foolish is the man who thinks he can pass without troubles through this mortal life, into which we are first born crying, signifying that we have entered upon a demanding and difficult pilgrimage, full of miseries and afflictions, which is wrongly called life but actually leads to life or death, according to whether we lean to the right or the left. What's more, the world by its nature is so full of grief and unhappiness everywhere that the man's considered best off who is least badly off. There's no question of goodness in this worldly exile. But not only is there nothing good in earthly life, there's nothing worth paying any attention to at all. "Vanity of vanities, all is vanity," the wise man said.

But if through human imperfection and the illusory desires of the flesh, which last less than a minute compared to time's eternity, anything should be valued, along with the philosopher thank divine goodness. For though He could have made you be born from the filthiest and lowest species of all the beasts, He gave you birth in the most perfect species—humankind—and of that species He gave you the male sex and not, as to me, the female one. And among men from different countries He gave you as a homeland a city neither barbarous nor enslaved, but gracious, and not only free, but mistress of the sea and of the loveliest region of Europe. A truly maiden city, immaculate and never violated, free from the taint of injustice, never harmed by an enemy force through the fires of war or the world's conflagration, in every revolution uniquely, miraculously preserved, not only whole but untouched by hostile attack, as if founded alone by a miracle in the midst of the sea, and with marvelous tranquillity firmly established and constantly increased through endless time. A city full of marvels and surprises, and one that, described without being seen, can't be known or grasped by the human intellect.

And what if you'd been born in this city among the dregs of the people? The ancient annals are full of your ancestors' brave deeds, and your nobility down through an unbroken line is famous and pure. Do you by chance not have wealth? Look how little nature accepts as enough, to see how much she surpasses you. And if it seems to you that you are poor because another man is richer than you, if this is how wealth is measured, how many rich men must exist in the huge treasury of the whole world? And then tell me: would you exchange everything—fortune, material possessions, body, and soul—with anyone more powerful and more fortunate on earth? And if no man can be found who, however he complains about his situation, wants to exchange it all for another, what are you complaining about? But you want both to hold onto your wisdom and to change places with another man because of his good fortune. And if this can't be done, why not rejoice instead that you outdo him in the strength of your soul, thinking that he should envy you for this quality rather than envying him yourself for his wealth? Especially since anyone has only the wealth that he spends, and no more? And if it doesn't seem to you that you have money enough for the habits of a world corrupted by excessive spending, consider how much less you might have and how much worse off you could be, lowering your gaze to examples at your feet, of which there are infinite numbers.

But man is so arrogant that when he should be lifting his eyes to heaven so as to lower them to earth and disdain in it all the things that are empty and vain compared to the undying, holy lights and the infinite order of stars strewn throughout such a stupendous machine, he looks up as if to compete with these celestial intelligences, daring to envy their fortune. How much better it is, and closer to the rule of reason, to scorn entirely, in the knowledge of eternity, the frail, corruptible body, which lasts so few years that a deer or a crow lives ten times longer than a man arriving at decrepit old age! And if man, as long as he lives on earth, can't avoid being stained with earthly mud, may the one who has most strength of mind be least soiled by it.

And if you, through the influence of a benign planet, have attained a good intelligence and made it disciplined and skillful through practice, how could you use it better than by wisely judging fortune's gifts, which are worthless things compared to virtue? This teaches you to feed your abilities by starving desire, purging your soul of empty and always damaging lust. And virtue not only teaches you how to have plenty in the midst of poverty, it shows you as well that true wealth consists in peace of mind and contentment. And the contentment of our soul is nothing else but the possession of virtue, easily recognized by its effects, which have the power to make man happy in the face of every hostile attack of misfortune. From the worst disasters, virtue draws the strength to exert itself further and so in this way to bless whoever possesses it. And this is why many truly courageous men have defied fortune, rivaling and overcoming her greatest enmity with the effects of strength and other virtues, which give to the man who possesses them, in comparison to whoever lacks them, the appearance of a living man, compared to a painted corpse. Perhaps speaking to you this way is redundant and, as they say, like carrying water to the sea, to the extent that I talk to you about matters which you understand perfectly well and about which you've enlightened and advised me.

Nonetheless, a duty born of love and gratitude compels me further to tell you that virtue inheres more in practice than in pretense. So when it comes to the values that you have so often taught me, you'll show that you no longer understand them or possess them if you don't apply them in your hour of need, which is never so urgent that it surpasses the power of reason and prudence. With that, I cease to write to you, recommending myself—as always—most heartily to you.

Letter 6

**THANKS TO A FRIEND WHO HAS SENT HER SOME SONNETS,
TO WHOM SHE SENDS TWO OF HER OWN**

Since I can't praise enough your Lordship's divine writing and the sonnets you have composed, conforming so closely to the strictures of rhyme, or even find the words to thank you as I should for the many honors and favors I've received from you, I'll keep silently in the depth of my soul my admiration of your skill and the memory of what I owe you. And I'll let it pass that you begin with ennobling comparisons of the lowliest possible object that can be chosen for praise so that the light of your famous style burns all the more brightly, though it doesn't need such help at all, and you continue to enjoy the pleasure that every really noble heart feels at behaving courteously, especially toward ladies. May your gentle thought be happy as you turn over in your mind the generous favor and great liberality you have granted me. If I fail to deserve them in any other way, I do because I need the help of another's kind praises when I lack any of my own, even though such praise makes me uneasy because I so admire the skill of its makers, equal (if any equal can be found) to your Lordship.

To whom as a sign of my gratitude, though warned against it by my judgment, I send two sonnets written in the same rhymes as your four. I, too, would have written four, which, though they wouldn't be worth a single one of yours, would at least show that I'm eager to learn. For I work so hard at them, longing to reveal my soul, which corresponds in such writing neither to the desire nor the need to return such graces and favors. May your Lordship make up for my lack with your skill, and wherever I may be, I will still be yours. Do me the favor, as your servant, of making me worthy of your commands, which I'm sorry not to be able to fulfill by coming to you today, as I'd planned to do, taking the occasion to visit my aunt the nun. But something has come up that keeps me from it. So, against my will, I must stay in this city for the time being.

Letter 9

A REQUEST FOR THE LOAN OF A MUSICAL INSTRUMENT AND AN INVITATION TO A CONCERT

Trusting in Your Lordship's infinite courtesy and matching your noble soul with the ardent desire alive in me always to honor and serve you, I have summoned the courage to ask you a favor. Please grant me your harpsichord for several days, and if possible let me have it from eight o'clock tomorrow night, when I invite you to come and honor my house with your presence, at an occasion when I will be playing music. And please bring Messer Vincenzo with you. And if I am making trouble for you, may the blame for it fall upon the shoulders of your great kindness, which gives me confidence. Until then, I kiss your hands with all my heart.

Letter 13

AN INVITATION TO A MEAL AT HER HOUSE

Among the many favors I could receive through your kindness, the best of all will be that you do me the favor of enjoying some pleasant conversation today, along with your friend, who will be very eager to come. You see how this rainy weather invites all good folk to settle down inside by the fire, at least until evening. If you're willing to come, we can partake in mutual comfort, *sine fuco et caerimoniis more maiorum* [without pomp and ceremony, in the manner of our ancestors],[2] of whatever food there'll be. And if you'd be so kind as to add a little flask of that good malmsey of yours, I am content and ask nothing more. This evening, then, I'll obey your order, a delight to me, to go to your friend's house. And whatever you choose to do, for my part, I'll always behave most lovingly toward you.

Letter 16

A LETTER OF CONGRATULATIONS TO A NEW MOTHER

In the end, the fatigue and pain of childbirth have turned out to be a sweet blessing to you. Now you have borne such a beautiful baby boy, which delights me as much as the difficulties of your pregnancy saddened me, all the more since they're no sooner felt than forgot-

---

2. Franco cites but revises a line from Cicero's first letter to Atticus, "sine fuco et fallaciis more maiorum" [without pomp or pretense, in the manner of our ancestors].

ten, and joy increases hand in hand with the life of the child, who, as he grows in beauty, will doubtless grow as well in kindness and strength. And because he's the offshoot of a stock that can't degenerate or produce any less than perfect fruit and he's growing up in the care of people who won't neglect a single detail of his perfect upbringing, these signs of eternal beauty, flourishing and growing, are surely lights that, shining out from his inner being, predict the joyful news of his successful attainment of goodness. This goodness, I pray Our Lord, will increase in your admirable family without end or limit through the actions of such a noble boy, so that in addition to the glory won by your ancestors' high deeds, it may shine like a celestial sun on earth in the new accomplishments of such a well-born little son. May his years, along with those of your Ladyship and the lord your husband, be long and happy.

Letter 17

ADVISING A YOUNG MAN THAT INTELLECTUALS WIN HER AFFECTION

The things of this world, which are not ordered by an enduring law as is the fixed movement of the stars, are arranged so that, depending on chance, they can take various shapes and follow various patterns, according to whether they are directed well or badly, by caution or by lack of judgment. As a result they have various and contrasting outcomes. So something done one way would be delightful, which, done differently, would cause harm, and what, well handled, could be a shield and a defense, badly managed, wounds and kills. And without speaking of sword and fire, which are tools for good and ill depending on how they're used, or of wealth or beauty or high birth and other similar gifts, which take a good or bad form according to the ways they're used, but turning instead to our subject of love, there's no doubt that it acts as a stimulus in us, which, depending on how it's shaped by our feelings, is the source of opposite things. So while one man, carried away by the recklessness of his sex, ends in ruin and open shame, another, refraining from indecency so as not to offend his lady and setting his mind on virtue to win her favor, has accomplished impressive and memorable things.

And for this reason, the wise man said that to assemble an army that would be undefeated and always victorious, it should be made up of men who respect loving and being loved by each other.[3] And

---

3. This is one of Socrates' arguments, as recorded by Plato in *The Symposium*.

if this is the conclusion of Socrates, who can never be praised too much because, though he was totally dedicated to philosophical study in leisure and peace, performed wonders of bravery in warfare and on the battlefield, in the presence and for the defense of the person he so loved, who though he was a woman in his delicate complexion and timid soul, was a young man in his sturdy body and forceful spirit, think how much more this brave lover would have done if he'd seen a lady in danger, unable at all to act to save herself by resistance or flight, because of her panic in the noise and heat of battle. An infinite number of other examples could show you how many great actions have been caused by love, and if some of the worst actions have also been born of it, this doesn't mean that a man of your stature should be alarmed or lose courage. For the fault is the misuse of love, and not love itself.

Instead, calm and appease your over-intense and anxious imaginings. And if you must put on spurs, don't put on the kind that push you wildly out of your homeland into a shiftless and pointless exile, but rather the kind that lead you to win virtue befitting your true worth. In this way, a man fully succeeds in enjoying honest leisure in his own country, among fellow citizens and in the presence of his beloved lady, trying to rival his peers in the theater of public competition by acquiring merit greater than theirs and hoping for a reward equal to his brave service.

You know full well that of all the men who count on being able to win my love, the ones dearest to me are those who work in the practice of the liberal arts and disciplines, of which (though a woman of little knowledge, especially compared to my inclination and interest) I am so fond. And it's with great delight that I talk with those who know, so as to have further chances to learn, for if my fate allowed, I would happily spend my entire life and pass all my time in the academies of talented men. This could be a great advantage to you, being industrious, as you are, in fine writing and in the flower of your youth, which, if you nourish and cultivate it well, will bear fruit to your perpetual praise and fame in the opinion of every wise and experienced person. Take advantage of these capacities, attend to your studies, and (if you're as eager as you say for my love—I hesitate to say whether I have a good or bad opinion of you—I assure you that your frenzies and wandering and ranting by day and night, intent on besieging me with your service, make me consider you an idle and empty-headed young man, more inclined to be ruined by your appetites than edified by reason) by living a settled life in the tranquillity of study and showing me the profit you gain from honest learning rather than any of the world's goods, you could lead me to love and cherish you.

And if, through impatience, unwilling to spend your time winning my favor this way and unable to tolerate serving literature, you're determined to wander uselessly here and there, I warn you that if your love for me is not feigned, recourse to distance will do you harm—in the painful thoughts that will pursue you more closely the farther from me you go, renewing in your loving memory the pleasure that you could often have, almost as a lover, in seeing me and hearing me and sometimes being invited in to talk with me. And the farther you see yourself distanced from this, the more the desire to be near it will gnaw at you and consume you. And you'll discover through the bitter experience of sharp regret that the kind of love that at first can be conquered by flight before it really strikes, later, when you've fled with its iron still in your side, kills rather than comforts by flight. If you're really in love with me, what I've said about you will have the power to make you stay, if you think carefully; and if you leave, it will be clear proof that your love is false. And in that case, not only will I free myself from any duty to love you, but I'll be persuaded to laugh at you and make fun of you. I have nothing else to write to you. Think carefully about your situation and behave with good judgment and good sense. May our Lord protect you.

Letter 21

TO THE PAINTER JACOPO TINTORETTO

Signor Tintoretto, I can't bear to listen to people who praise ancient times so much and find such fault with our own, who claim that nature was a loving mother to men of antiquity but that she is a cruel stepmother to men today. How far this is from the truth I leave people of good judgment to decide, less biased, I think, than these. Among the other things they use to raise the ancients up to heaven is whichever art is most beautiful and noble, be it painting, sculpture, or bas relief, claiming that no one is found in the world today who matches the excellence of Apelles, Zeuxis, Phidias, Praxiteles, and other noble and famous painters and sculptors of those times— though on what basis, I don't know. I have heard gentlemen expert in antiquity and highly knowledgeable about these arts say that in our era and even today, there are painters and sculptors who must be acknowledged not only to equal but to surpass those of ancient times, as Michelangelo, Raphael, Titian, and others did, and as you do today

FIGURE 4 A portrait of Veronica Franco by Jacopo Tintoretto. Oil on canvas, sixteenth century (1575?). Worcester Art Museum, Worcester, Mass., Austin S. and Sarah C. Garver Fund.

I don't say this to flatter you, you know, because it's common knowledge. If it doesn't seem so to you, it's because you close your ears to praise and don't care to know what men think of you, as other artists—painters and others—do. I think this happens because, having reached the summit of your art and knowing that no one else has gone so far, like a man who refuses a guide who has never traveled his path before, you pay no attention to other people's judgments, whether they praise or blame. You concentrate entirely on methods of imitating—no, rather of outdoing—nature, not only in what can be imitated by modeling the human figure, nude or clothed, adding color, shading, contour, features, muscles, movements, actions, postures, curves, and structure conforming to nature, but by expressing emotional states as well. I don't think that Roscius[4] was able to act as many feelings on stage as your wonderful, immortal brush paints on panels, walls, canvas, and other surfaces.

I swear to you that when I saw my portrait, the work of your divine hand, I wondered for a while whether it was a painting or an apparition set before me by some trickery of the devil, not to make me fall in love with myself, as happened to Narcissus[5] (because, thank God, I don't consider myself so beautiful that I'm afraid to go mad over my own charms), but for some other reason unknown to me. So I say to you, and rest assured of this, that divine nature sees how skillfully you imitate, even surpass her, so much that what you gain in honor through your immortal works is her loss. So she will never dare grant to men of our time the high, bold intelligence required to explain in full the excellence of your art. In this way she hopes to avoid shame, in word and deed, in every age to come. And I, certain not to succeed in such a great enterprise myself, lay down my pen and pray to our blessed Lord for your happiness.

Letter 22

A WARNING TO A MOTHER CONSIDERING TURNING HER DAUGHTER INTO A COURTESAN

The fact that you go around complaining that I'm no longer willing for you to come to my house to see me, loving you as well as I do, bothers me less than the fact that I have a good reason for it. Since you see it as unfair and have complained about me endlessly, I would like to respond to you in this letter, making a last attempt to dissuade you from your evil intent, owing you greater friendship than ever before if you accept my truthful argument—or, if you don't, to take away any hope that you should ever speak to me again. I'm all the more eager to fulfill this duty toward you because

---

4. Roscius (d. 62 BC) was a famous comic actor in Rome, a friend to Cicero.

5. Narcissus, a beautiful young man, fell in love with his own reflection in a pool and died of starvation as a result (*Metamorphoses*, 3.407–510 ff.).

to the extent that I clear myself of your accusations, I also fulfill a humane obligation by showing you a steep precipice hidden in the distance and by shouting out before you reach it, so that you'll have time enough to steer clear of it. Although it's mainly a question of your daughter's well-being, I'm talking about you, as well, for her ruin cannot be separated from yours. And because you're her mother, if she should become a prostitute, you'd become her go-between and deserve the harshest punishment, while her error wouldn't perhaps be entirely inexcusable because it would have been caused by your wrongdoing.

You know how often I've begged and warned you to protect her virginity. And since this world is so full of dangers and so uncertain, and the houses of poor mothers are never safe from the amorous maneuvers of lustful young men, I showed you how to shelter her from danger and to help her by teaching her about life in such a way that you can marry her decently. I offered you all the help I could to assure that she'd be accepted into the Casa delle Zitelle,[6] and I also promised you, if you took her there, to help you with all the means at my disposal, as well. At first you thanked me and seemed to be listening to me and to be well disposed toward my affectionate offer. Together we agreed on what needed to be done so that she'd be accepted there, and we were about to carry out our plan when you underwent I don't know what change of heart. Where once you made her appear simply clothed and with her hair arranged in a style suitable for a chaste girl, with veils covering her breasts and other signs of modesty, suddenly you encouraged her to be vain, to bleach her hair and paint her face. And all at once, you let her show up with curls dangling around her brow and down her neck, with bare breasts spilling out of her dress, with a high, uncovered forehead, and every other embellishment people use to make their merchandise measure up to the competition.

I swear to you, by my faith, that when you first showed her so disguised to me, I could hardly recognize her, and I told you what friendship and charity required. But you, by taking my words as an insult, as though I'd spoken maliciously in my own interest, proved to me that I was right to be displeased—as, in fact, I've been ever since, so that I haven't made any effort to maintain the closeness we once shared. Rather, I've had you told that I wasn't at home or given you a chilly welcome. I've expressed my distress over you and your household to other people, thinking that complaining to them might

6. The Casa delle Zitelle was a charitable institution founded to shelter poor, unmarried girls, in order to prevent their loss of chastity and the ensuing loss of the possibility of marriage.

be some use to you if you heard about it and that if they repeated my words to you, they'd reproach you sharply. And I've been told that someone did carry out this duty, out of affection and the wish to do you good. But you, remaining stubborn and hardheaded, swore on one hand that your daughter was a saint while on the other you led people to believe that she has little concern for her honor through the gossip and scandal you, her mother, provoked.

Now, finally, I wanted to be sure to write you these lines, urging you again to beware of what you're doing and not to slaughter in one stroke your soul and your reputation, along with your daughter's—who, considered from the purely carnal point of view, is really not very beautiful (to say the least, for my eyes don't deceive me) and has so little grace and wit in conversation that you'll break her neck expecting her to do well in the courtesan's profession, which is hard enough to succeed in even if a woman has beauty, style, good judgment, and proficiency in many skills. And just imagine a young woman who lacks many of these qualities or has them only to an average degree! And because, persisting in your error, you might say that such matters depend on chance, I reply first that there's nothing worse that can be done in life than to let oneself become a plaything of fortune, which can as easily or more easily hand out evil as good. But anyone with good sense, to avoid being deceived in the end, builds her hopes on what she has inside her and on what she might be able to make of herself.

I'll add that even if fate should be completely favorable and kind to her, this is a life that always turns out to be a misery. It's a most wretched thing, contrary to human reason, to subject one's body and labor to a slavery terrifying even to think of. To make oneself prey to so many men, at the risk of being stripped, robbed, even killed, so that one man, one day, may snatch away from you everything you've acquired from many over such a long time, along with so many other dangers of injury and dreadful contagious diseases; to eat with another's mouth, sleep with another's eyes, move according to another's will, obviously rushing toward the shipwreck of your mind and your body—what greater misery? What wealth, what luxuries, what delights can outweigh all this? Believe me, among all the world's calamities, this is the worst. And if to worldly concerns you add those of the soul, what greater doom and certainty of damnation could there be?

Pay attention to what people say, and in matters crucial to life on earth and to the soul's salvation, don't follow examples set by others. Don't allow the flesh of your wretched daughter not only to be cut into pieces and sold but you yourself to become her butcher.

Consider the likely outcome; and if you want to observe other cases, look at what's happened and happens every day to the multitude of women in this occupation. If you can be convinced by reason, every argument about this world and all the more about heaven opposes you and urges you to avoid this fatal course. Turn your hopes to God and take advantage of the help your friends offer you.

As for me, besides the promises I've already made you, which I have every intention of keeping, ask me to do anything I can and I'll be ready immediately to help you in any way possible—as I now beg you, as much as I can, to avoid this dire possibility before it's too late. For once you've thrown the stone into the water, you'll find it very hard to get it out again. If you do this, I could be a closer friend to you than ever. By the same account, if you do otherwise, you'll have no cause to blame me for withdrawing from your friendship, for if you persist in such unfriendly behavior, the more chance and reason you give others to flee you the more they love you, because they can't bear to see you in such misfortune without being able to help you. It won't be long, perhaps, before your daughter herself, recognizing the great harm you've done her, will flee from you more than anyone else does—all the more because, as her mother, you should have helped her and you'll have exploited and ruined her instead. And this may be only the beginning of your torment. May Our Lord save you from your obvious intention to ruin and corrupt what you created from your own flesh and blood. However much I could say to you, I'd still have more to say on this subject. So I'll go no further but leave you to think carefully before you come to any decision.

Letter 31

THANKS TO A MAN FOR PRAISING HER IN HER ABSENCE TO COUNTER THE ATTACK MADE ON HER BY ANOTHER

My bad luck of rightly continuing to feel offended by that friend of mine was not as great as the much greater good luck of having your courteous protection on my side in my absence—protection that was not only a shield supplying me the surest defense against those insults, but also, because it sheltered me from the onslaught of hostile accusations rather than support my arguments, succeeded in making me the winner through praise. This praise, given me by your authority, was affirmed in the opinion and speech of everyone who was there, so I was assured by one person present at the scene, who told me that in this controversy my opponent had lost a great deal and I had come out well ahead. I attribute this entirely to your kindness, though my cause itself was so just that when the reckoning came, it could hardly have ended any other way.

Yet I am still pained by the error and stubbornness of that gentleman, on his account because I neither can nor want to make up my mind not to love him, and on my account because I've been not only deceived but also reproached by the judgment that led me to invent such a great fantasy about him. Though who wouldn't have made a mistake? But everyone can be wise after the fact. Still, who wouldn't have been moved and persuaded by those manners and by those words, adroitly spoken from the mouth of a gentleman of such rank and quality? And if, beyond that, you had heard the promises he not only made on faith but affirmed with the strongest oaths, I'm sure you'd have taken me for a woman of little spirit and less faith if I hadn't believed, on my side, that he'd keep the promises I'd also made, with less ceremony. And so sometimes, through Nature's kindness, someone is mocked and fooled, though the man who mocks and fools her this way mocks and fools himself more than anyone else. In the end these blows fall on the head of the man who deals them out, and as far as the person they're aimed at is concerned, they drift away into the air and the wind.

I prefer by far having been deceived by a gentleman to having anyone able to say that he's been deceived by me. And it isn't enough to avoid being deceptive only in order to avoid being deceived; good conduct is more praiseworthy the less it is aimed at a particular end but is contented in itself and exists for its own sake. Even so, I'll make an effort, based on these lessons, to be more careful in the future; and perhaps— I hope—this misfortune will be the source of countless benefits. That is, I hope through divine justice, as solace to me and shame to the man who's been unfaithful to me, that in well-deserved retribution he won't escape vain regret and a constant eating away at his heart, like Tityos's,[7] whose tale was told in antiquity to express the pain the soul feels when it recognizes its wrongdoing. And even if I'm unable to pay the debt I owe your Lordship, Heaven will make up for it, multiplying infinite favors toward you, as I fondly and devoutly pray.

---

7. Tityos, mentioned by the Greek poet Pindar, was a giant, killed by Apollo and Diana for attempting to rape their mother, Leto. Virgil puts him in Tartarus, the lower depth of the underworld, where his liver is constantly gnawed by a vulture (*Aeneid*, 6.789–96).

THANKS TO A GENTLEMAN FOR HIS LETTERS AND
FAVORS TO HER

In the letters that come from your Lordship, written laconically, I understand and consider more than asiatically the real extent of your wonderfully abundant courtesy, which, in the manner of a swollen torrent that breaks its banks and floods the countryside, refusing the narrow bed of such a short letter and leaping beyond its course, widens and surges forward in a way that leaves me overwhelmed and outdone. Lacking the strength to resist the power of such a flow, it's best that I retreat and make up with the fullness of my eagerness and desire for the lack in my attempts to respond to the generosity of such kind writing and for the lack, as well, of any words capable of thanking your Lordship sufficiently. On this subject, too, I will proceed with laconic reserve, for any degree of lavish eloquence would still be surpassed by the infinite quantity of your merit, valor, and noble amiability, through which you have obliged me to be so entirely yours that nothing is as deeply printed in my heart as the image of your courtesy, accompanied by a burning desire, living inextinguishably in me, always to please and serve you. Please command me and make use of my service, increasing your dignity through your honored demands and allowing me the more than infinite satisfaction of responding to your high worth. Nor can I say anything on this subject, overcome by emotion as I am, except that among all the signs I could have that my devotion is not unwelcome to you, the best would be always to see you, in loving confidence, freely making use of my accomplishments, considering them as thoroughly yours as I am myself, won over by your immeasurably precious qualities—on whose behalf, since I always think, speak, and write willingly of them, I beg your Lordship to remember my affection now and then and to write to me from time to time in your absence. During it, following you continually in my mind and all my thought, I shall make every effort to be with you physically as well, as occasion permits, intimately enjoying your sweet conversation, which at this distance I love and long for with all my soul. With which from here I bow and kiss your Lordship's most revered hands, begging you to give your most honored colleague the ever increasing best wishes of the lady left behind.

Letter 39

A REQUEST TO A FRIEND TO CONTRIBUTE POEMS TO THE MEMORIAL ANTHOLOGY FOR ESTORE MARTINENGO

Although I've let my pen lie idle from writing to your Lordship for a while, I deserve not only that you excuse me but that you defend and pity me, for I've neglected writing to you not by choice but against my will, since the misfortune has befallen me of my two young sons' illness these past days—one after the other has come down with fever and smallpox—along with other crises that have kept me busy and worried beyond all measure. Now that, by God's mercy, they're a good deal better, as soon as I could catch my breath in order to fulfill my duty to answer your very gracious letters, and to please myself in no small measure, I've taken pen in hand to write to you, if not as much as I would like, given my other occupations— which like a many-headed serpent, the more I cut them off, the more they multiply— at least enough to pay you the respect I owe.

And I beg you to indulge me by agreeing to use your most refined skills in the composition of whatever number of sonnets that time and my entreaties permit you, on the occasion of the death of the illustrious Count Estore Martinengo, whom I hold in great respect. And in addition to the sense of duty I feel to commemorate him and the surviving members of his whole family, I've been asked by a man whose wish is my command to compose some sonnets myself and to have all my friends and lords write on this subject. So, not dawdling at all in the task of commissioning such works, I've begged the favor of writing from many other noble spirits, and many whom I've asked have already written. So I want to move ahead quickly and do it well, if I can. You'll have these men, your Lordship, as your valiant companions in this undertaking. And you'll be doing me a very great favor. And the opportunity to request this of you has been almost a pleasure for me, by increasing your willingness to prevail upon me for anything I can and wish to do for you. I am always ready to serve your Lordship.

Letter 41

A REQUEST FOR HELP IN REVISING HER LETTERS

Trusting in your Lordship's kindness, on a par with the immense affection and respect I feel for you, I'm sending you this volume of my letters, which I've collected as best as I could, so that you may read it, and by compensating with your wisdom for my imperfections, you'll partly excuse and partly correct my mistakes. I also hope that you'll forgive my presumption not only in sending you these trifles of mine to look at, but also in wanting to see and talk to you in person, and that you'll set aside any consideration of the difference between your skill and my unworthiness. Still, given that this is caused by a most powerful love—for otherwise I wouldn't dare to request it of you—I beg you with all my heart to favor me with whatever sort of correspondence suits your kindness, by allowing me as soon as possible to spend two hours of whatever day suits you in talking to you in person and through good fortune enjoying pleasant conversation with your Lordship. To whom I affectionately send my regards.

Letter 44

A REQUEST TO DOMENICO VENIER FOR THE LOAN OF A WHEELCHAIR

Fortune favors me by giving me an ailment of the limbs similar to your Lordship's, having made me almost lose a leg, as if nature and art were opposed and unwilling to make me resemble you in spirit and intellect. May the wound to my body make up for the weakness of my spirit! A welcome offense, since in addition to imitating your Lordship's indisposition in this way, I'll also enjoy some of your esteemed cast-offs in my need—for example, one of those wheelchairs of yours, which I beg you to send me by the bearer of this letter, so that I may profit from it in the unlucky accident to my knee, whose muscle I've pierced, I don't know how, with a hair pin.[8] And this has kept me from coming to pay you my respects in person, which I constantly do in my heart.

Letter 47

AN APOLOGY TO A MAN FOR SUSPECTING HIM OF BEING THE AUTHOR OF THE SATIRIC VERSES WRITTEN BY ANOTHER

Rumor, which reports events with less concern for what is true than for what might seem true, made me believe with convincing reasons that your Lordship was the author of that satire, considering that men who have talent similar to yours try to prove themselves by discussing subjects void of any interest and to make up for their scant

---

8. *Ago da treccia* may also mean embroidery needle.

material with an abundance of good judgment and invention. This is exactly what was done by the man who has written those verses against me, for if I don't deserve great praise, neither certainly do I deserve blame so much that someone I've never harmed and who doesn't know me should write against me with such venom—proof, no doubt, of his great intellect, and greater than praising me would have been, given that I'm a woman and have always tried to please kind and valorous men, without ever displeasing anyone. And if I am not highly skilled myself, I'm at least a lover of skill in people who are gifted with it, as is your Lordship, for whom on this account I've always felt great affection and respect. And for this reason I was truly astonished to be paid back for my devotion with such defamatory libels. And I also didn't wholly want to believe that this was your doing, once I had seen the imperfection of the work, full of errors, and for other reasons, too, not a worthy offspring of your noble intellect. Still, I remained in doubt because of several accounts I had had of it, now leaning toward thinking yes, now no. And in this indecision, it occurred to me for my own amusement to write the *capitolo,* which has so pleased me, given that you have been willing to keep it, that I was even glad it was sent to you by mistake.

And in the certainty that it happened this way and that a gentleman as honorable as you are wouldn't say one thing and mean another, I no longer have a reason for a duel or a challenge. Rather, I thank you for your offer of acting as my second in the duel, which, coming to me from such a great patron, I accept as an extraordinary favor. And because I need it, I'll take advantage of it with the same confidence that I want you to have in me. And I'll avail myself of it especially against whoever wrote that composition attacking me, if he ever comes to light. In the meantime, so as not to abandon the training in arms that I need, I entreat your Lordship, as the perfect instructor, to teach me some secret stroke, or, rather, to take the sword into your own hand, not one with a sharp edge but one for play, and to engage with me in a duel as virtuoso as you like, challenging me to a response by sending me whatever opening lines are convenient for you, in whatever language suits you. And if you deign to do this, I'll be grateful to you and make every effort to answer as quickly as I read profitably what you send me. And let this be the answer to your highly appreciated letter, which I've read several times with the greatest pleasure at receiving your Lordship's courteous pledge of skill and favor. I entrust myself to you.

Letter 49

ACCOMPANYING A SET OF PAGES, A REQUEST
FOR REVISIONS

I thank your Lordship for your praise of my book, because more than from any merit of mine, it comes from the kind of affection I have wanted to repay in a similar way, an affection I feel in all reverence for your valor and many other virtues. Blessed be Our Lord God that in the hardest ice and the indestructible diamond of your reason, completely free and detached from the power of inflamed senses, you have still received the imprint and stamp of that image of charitable love with which I love your Lordship most sincerely, keeping carved in my heart the living likeness of that virtue and courtesy of yours, which gives me confidence in your favor and your beneficence. And if the fire of love, which conquers men and gods, of which you write at the end of your letter is the ardor of a courteous desire to assist me in my need and according to your promises, I praise you and give you infinite thanks for your kindness.

Now I send you the second set of ten pages in compliance with your request, so that it, too, may receive the favor of your stripping it down to its doublet, as did the first. I'd certainly be very happy if in your leisure, having taken off your clothes, you took the trouble to correct this work, which you need to do—because otherwise, just sitting there undressed and unoccupied, you might catch cold! And by doing so, you'd increase my will to arrange quickly for the transcription of other books of mine, so far only in the form of rough drafts, by sending them to you, making up in part for this way of keeping you busy, and getting even with you for your great idleness in all the time that you haven't written me, and also by pestering you with the annoying task of reading these lines!

VERONICA FRANCO,
POEMS IN TERZA RIMA (1575)

To the most serene prince, my lord and patron, the most reverend Duke of Mantua and of Monferrato,[1] from Veronica Franca

Although only the most remote parallel and almost total inequality exist between your Highness's world-famous virtue and my desire to honor and serve you as I should, so that anything I could do in this undertaking would be less than a shadow compared to the truth; even so, in this book, in which I have lacked the ability and the proper formulas to praise and exalt you, my eagerness to express the virtuous though unattainable desire to do so overcame my hesitation to the extent that I could not refrain from assuring you of it through the weak evidence of these few poems in *terza rima,* which I dedicate to you—not because they have any relation to the extraordinary merit of your great talents, for these cannot be a subject for my inept style—but so that by offering a slight taste of my lowly muse to your wise judgment, I may demonstrate my limited talent in this sample and so have a good excuse for not daring to raise my speech to the sky of your immeasurable valor, and so that the poems may come out at this time under the protection of your famous name and be openly introduced as depending in every way upon your Highness's will. Who, I am sure, seeing in them my longing, whose only goal is to show you my readiness to serve you, will accept in this modest gift my soul's infinite gratitude for your merit and the only tribute of which I am capable, since I cannot offer you the one you deserve. And as the clearest sign of my devotion, I present this volume of mine to you through my young son, sent to you to perform this duty. May he, expressing my own heart in his face and behavior and every

---

1. The Duke of Mantua at this time, Guglielmo Gonzaga (1538–87), famous as a protector of musicians, employed the poet Bernardo Tasso as his principal secretary (Bianchi, 181 n. 2).

kind of humble reverence in your most serene presence, win me the grace of your kind favor in exchange for my ardent homage, and compensating for my inability to match in deeds my powers to my will, by which I am bound by a permanent, insoluble tie of most humble service to your great Highness.

FIGURE 5 Frontispiece portrait of Veronica Franco, originally intended for her volume of poems, the *Terze rime* (1575). A detached anonymous engraving in the manuscript collections of the Biblioteca Nazionale Marciana, Venice. MSS it. IX 14 (= 6988).

Capitolo I

DEL MAGNIFICO MESSER MARCO VENIERO
ALLA SIGNORA VERONICA FRANCA

S'io v'amo al par de la mia propria vita,
donna crudel, e voi perché non date
in tanto amor al mio tormento aita?

E se invano mercé chieggio e pietate,
perch'almen con la morte quelle pene,   5
ch'io soffro per amarvi, non troncate?

So che remunerar non si conviene
mia fé cosí; ma quel mal, che ripara
a un maggior mal, vien riputato bene:

piú d'ogni morte è la mia doglia amara,   10
e morir di man vostra, in questo stato,
grazia mi fia desiderata e cara.

Ma com'esser può mai che, dentro al lato
molle, il bianco gentil vostro bel petto
chiuda sí duro cor e sí spietato?   15

Com'esser può che quel leggiadro aspetto
voglie e pensier cosí crudi ricopra,
che 'l servir umil prendano in dispetto?

La gran bellezza a voi data di sopra
spender in morte di chi v'ama e in doglia,   20
qual potete peggior far di quest'opra?

Ciò da l'uman desir vostro si toglia,
e 'n sua vece vi penetri a la mente,
conforme a la beltà, pietosa voglia.

Cosí dentro e di fuor chiara e splendente   25
sarete d'ogni età vero ornamento,
non pur di questo secolo presente.

Pria che de' be' crin l'òr si faccia argento,
da custodir è quel che poi si perde,
chi 'l lascia in man del tempo, in un momento: 30

e se ben sète d'età fresca e verde,
nulla degli anni è piú veloce cosa,

Capitolo 1

FROM THE MAGNIFICO MARCO VENIER TO VERONICA FRANCO

If I love you as much as my own life,
cruel lady, why do you offer no relief
for my suffering in such great love?

And if I ask in vain for grace and pity,   4
why do you not at least end with death
this pain I endure for love of you?

I know you are not right to reward   7
my faithfulness in this way; but a wrong
that rights a greater wrong is well received;

my suffering is more bitter than any death,   10
and to die by your hand in this condition
would be a boon I longed for and cherished.

But how ever can it be, in the tenderest part   13
of your body, that your fair, fine, white breast
can enclose a heart so hard and pitiless?

How can it be that such a gay appearance   16
conceals desires and thoughts so cruel
that they disdain my humble devotion?

To use the great beauty given you by heaven   19
for the death and grief of a man who loves you—
what deed worse than this could you commit?

Let your natural desire be freed from all this   22
and let compassion fitting to your beauty
make its way into your mind instead.

So, bright and resplendent inside and out,   25
you will be the true ornament of every age,
not only of this present century.

Before the gold of your lovely hair turns silver   28
you must take good care of what is lost
in a single moment, once left in the hands of time;

and though you're now in a fresh and flowering age, 31
nothing flies past so swiftly as the years,

sí ch'a tenervi dietro il pensier perde;
   e mentre di qua giú nessun ben posa,
nasce e spar la beltà piú che baleno,   35
non che qual nata e secca a un tempo rosa.
   Ma poi chi la pietà chiude nel seno,
col merto de la fama sua ravviva
le chiome bionde e 'l viso almo e sereno.
   Dunque, per farvi al mondo eterna e diva,   40
amica di pietà verso chi v'ama,
siate di crudeltà nemica e schiva.
   Oh, se vedeste in me l'ardente brama,
c'ho di servir voi sola a tutte l'ore,
con quel pensier ch'ognor vi chiede e brama;   45
   se mi vedeste in mezzo 'l petto il core,
a me son certo che null'altro amante
pareggereste nel portarvi amore!
   Ma guardatemi 'l cor fuor nel sembiante
pallido e mesto e nel mio venir solo,   50
dí e notte, con piè lasso e cor costante;
   e conoscendo il mio soverchio duolo,
e come in lui convien ch'ognor trabbocchi
di pene cinto da infinito stuolo,
   volgete a me pietosamente gli occhi,   55
a veder come presso e di lontano
quinci ognor empio Amor l'arco in me scocchi;
   stendete a me la bella e bianca mano
a rinovar il colpo, e che in tal guisa
il sen piú m'apre e insieme il rende sano.   60
   O beltà d'ogni essempio altro divisa,
di cui l'anima in farsi umil soggetta,
stando lieta, qua giú s'imparadisa!
   Amor da que' begli occhi in me saetta
con tal dolcezza, che 'l mio espresso danno   65
via piú sempre mi giova e mi diletta.
   Ben questi al chiaro sole invidia fanno,
ben ch'ancor Febo con diletto mira
le bellezze che tante in voi si stanno:

which outstrip even thought;
    and while here on earth no good thing lasts,   34
beauty is born and vanishes quick as a flash,
like the rose that blooms and withers all at once.

    But whoever harbors pity in her breast   37
by virtue of her fame brings back to life
her golden locks and her kind and serene face.

    So, to become eternal and divine on earth,   40
be hostile and averse to cruelty,
a friend to pity for the man who loves you.

    Oh, if you were to see my fiery longing   43
to serve only you at every hour of the day,
and my thought, which always seeks and longs for you,

    if you were to see my heart deep in my breast,   46
I know that you could compare no other lover
to me for the love he feels toward you.

    But behold my heart, revealed in my pale   49
and mournful look, and my solitary wandering,
day and night, with weary foot and constant heart;

    and, taking notice of my crushing pain,   52
and how at every moment it must overflow,
bound to an infinite throng of woes,

    turn your eyes toward me pitifully,   55
to see how, from near and far away,
cruel Love constantly aims his bow at me;

    reach out to me your fair white hand   58
to renew his blows, to let him pierce my breast
more deeply and heal it at the same time.

    Oh, beauty far surpassing any other,   61
through which the soul, delighted to humble itself,
becomes one with paradise here on earth![2]

    Love, through those lovely eyes, shoots me   64
so sweetly that the harm he's aimed at me alone
delights and rejoices me more and more.

    These eyes indeed make the bright sun envious, 67
and even Phoebus gazes in delight[3]
at the beauties which so abound in you;

---

2. A citation from Dante's *Paradiso* (canto 28.3), identified by Bianchi, 183 n. 63.

3. In Greek mythology, Phoebus and Apollo are both names of the god of light, Phoebus emphasizing his role as the sun.

di queste vago Apollo arde e sospira,   70
e per virtú di tai luci gioconde
il suo saper in voi benigno inspira;
    e mentre questo in gran copia v'infonde,
move la chiara voce al dolce canto,
ch'a' bei pensier de l'animo risponde.   75
    La penna e 'l foglio in man prendete intanto,
e scrivete soavi e grate rime,
ch'ai poeti maggior tolgono il vanto.
    O bella man, che con bell'arte esprime
sí leggiadri concetti, e le sue forme   80
dentro 'l mio cor felicemente imprime!
    De l'antico valor segnando l'orme
questa ne va sí candida e gentile,
svegliando la virtú dove piú dorme;
    né pur rinova il glorïoso stile   85
del poetar sí celebre trascorso,
che non ebbe fin qui par né simíle;
    ma de le menti afflitte alto soccorso
è quella man ne l'amorosa cura,
che quivi ha 'l suo rifugio e 'l suo ricorso.   90
    Di viva neve man candida e pura,
che dolcemente il cor m'ardi e consumi
per miracol d'amor fuor di natura,
    e voi, celesti e grazïosi lumi,
ch'ardor e refrigerio in un mi sète,   95
e parer gli altrui rai fate ombre e fumi,
    perch'a me 'l vostro aviso contendete?
e non piú tosto con pietosi modi
al mio soccorso, oimè, vi rivolgete?
    Né però chieggio che disciolga i nodi,   100
che 'ntorno al cor m'ordío, la man sí vaga,
né che in alcuna parte men m'annodi;
    non chiedo ch'entro al sen saldi la piaga
il bel guardo gentil, che in me l'impresse,
d'amor con arte lusinghiera e vaga: 105
    da quelle mani e da le braccia stesse

for these, longing Apollo burns and sighs,   70
and through the power of such merry eyes
he benignly breathes his knowledge into you,
   and, as he infuses it lavishly into you,   73
you turn your clear voice to sweet song,
which matches the lovely thoughts in your mind.
   Take pen and paper in hand, then,   76
and write pleasant and graceful rhymes,
which strip the glory from the greatest poets.
   Oh, lovely hand, which with lovely art   79
expresses such winning conceits, and happily
imprints its shape upon my heart!
   Following the footsteps of ancient valor,   82
it moves along, so pure and gentle, awakening
virtue where it sleeps most deeply;
   not only does it revive the splendid style   85
of the celebrated poetry of the past,
which so far has had no like or equal;
   but to suffering minds, that hand   88
is a great help in the suffering of love,
for here it finds its shelter and relief.
   Hand of living snow, white and pure,   91
which sweetly inflames and consumes my heart,
through a supernatural miracle of love,
   and you, heavenly and gracious eyes,   94
which to me are ardor and coolness all in one,
and make other glances seem mere smoke and shadow,
   why do you refuse me your counsel?   97
and why, instead, in pitiful fashion
do you not come, alas, to my rescue?
   Not that I ask you to untie the knots   100
that your lovely hand wove around my heart,
nor to loosen my bonds in any place;
   I do not ask that your lovely, gentle glance   103
should heal in my breast the wound it dealt me
through the sly, alluring art of love;
   by those hands and by those very arms   106

esser bramo raccolto in cortesia,
e che 'l mio laccio stringan piú sempre esse;
   bramo che quella vista umana e pia
si volga al mio diletto, e del bel viso   110
e de la bocca avara non mi sia.
   Oh che grato e felice paradiso,
dal goder le bellezze in voi sí rade
non si trovar giamai, donna, diviso:
   donna di vera ed unica beltade,   115
e di costumi adorna e di virtude,
con senil senno in giovenil etade!
   Oh che dolce mirar le membra ignude,
e piú dolce languir in grembo a loro,
ch'or a torto mi son sí scarse e crude!   120
   Prenderei con le mani il forbito oro
de le trecce, tirando de l'offesa,
pian piano, in mia vendetta il fin tesoro.
   Quando giacete ne le piume stesa,
che soave assalirvi! e in quella guisa   125
levarvi ogni riparo, ogni difesa!
   Venere in letto ai vezzi vi ravvisa,
a le delizie che 'n voi tante scopre
chi da pietà vi trova non divisa;
   sí come nel compor de le dotte opre,   130
de le nove Castalie in voi sorelle
l'arte e l'ingegno a l'altrui vista s'opre.
   E cosí 'l vanto avete tra le belle
di dotta, e tra le dotte di bellezza,
e d'ambo superate e queste e quelle;   135
   e mentre l'uno e l'altro in voi s'apprezza,
d'ambo sarebbe l'onor vostro in tutto,
se la beltà non guastasse l'asprezza.
   Ma se 'n voi la scïenzia è d'alto frutto,
perché de la bellezza il pregio tanto   140
vien da la vostra crudeltà distrutto?
   Accompagnate l'opra in ogni canto;
e come la virtú vostra ne giova,

I long to be embraced, in courtesy,
and to have them pull my ties tighter still.
    I long for that kind and gracious sight   109
to tend to my delight, and not to withhold
your lovely face and mouth from me.
    Oh, what a happy and blessed paradise   112
never to be parted from enjoying,
lady, your unparalleled charms;
    lady of true and unique beauty,[4]   115
and improved by fine manners and skill,
with mature wisdom in your early youth!
Oh, how sweet to gaze upon those naked limbs,   118
which now are so unfairly hard and cruel,
and sweeter still to lie languid in your lap!
    I would take in my hands the burnished gold   121
of your tresses, pulling that fine treasure
gently, in revenge for your offense.
    When you lie stretched out upon the pillows,   124
how sweet to fall upon you! and in that way
to strip you of any retreat or defense!
    The man who finds you not opposed to pity   127
sees you as Venus for your charms in bed
and the many delights discovered in you,
    just as when you compose learned verses,   130
the art and intellect of the nine Castalians,[5]
sisters to you, are revealed to one's eyes.
    And so among beauties you are famous for your learning, 133
and among learned women you are known for your beauty,
and in both you excel one group and the other;
    and while each of these qualities wins you admiration, 136
the honor for both would be yours altogether,
if only your harshness did not spoil your beauty.
    But if knowledge in you is so nobly fruitful,   139
why is it that beauty, also a treasure,
comes to ruin through your hard heart?
    Circulate your work, go with it everywhere,   142
and as your virtuosity gains from doing so,[6]

---

4. This is the first time in the *Poems* that a man puns on Veronica's name. Compare *capitolo* 7, line 173; 11, lines 1–3; and 16, lines 139–56.

5. The Castalians are the nine muses, so named for their proximity to Castalia, a spring on Mt. Parnassus.

6. *Virtù*, in the context of literary salons such as the Venier group, usually meant skill, technical brilliance, virtuosity rather than moral virtue.

la beltà non sia seme del mio pianto:
   in tanto amor tanto dolor vi mova,   145
sí che di riparar ai tristi affanni
entriate meco in lodevole prova.
   S'al tempo fa sí glorïosi inganni
la vostra musa, la beltà non faccia
a se medesma irreparabil danni.   150
   A Febo è degno che si sodisfaccia
dal vostro ingegno, ma da la beltate
a Venere non meno si compiaccia:
   le tante da lei grazie a voi donate
spender devete in buon uso, sí come   155
di quelle, che vi diede Apollo, fate:
   con queste eternerete il vostro nome,
non men che con gli inchiostri; e lento e infermo
farete il tempo, e le sue forze dome.
   Per la bocca di lei questo v'affermo: 160
non lasciate Ciprigna per seguire
Delio, né contra lei tentate schermo;
   ché Febo se le inchina ad obedire,
né può far altrimenti, se ben poi
gran piacer tragge in ciò dal suo servire.   165
   Cosí devete far ancora voi,
seguitando l'essempio di quel dio,
che v'infonde i concetti e i pensier suoi.
   La bellezza adornate col cor pio,
sí che con la virtú ben s'accompagne,   170
lontan da ogni crudel empio desio:
   queste in voi la pietà faccia compagne,
e in tanto vi rincresca, com'è degno,
d'un che de l'amor vostro ognora piagne.
   E son quell'io, che umile a voi ne vegno,   175
cercando di placar con dolci preghi
la vostra crudeltate e 'l vostro sdegno:
   mercé da voi, per Dio, non mi si nieghi,
donna bella e gentil, ma in tanta guerra
benigno il vostro aiuto a me si pieghi.   180
   Cosí sarete senza par in terra.

let not your beauty be the source of my tears;
 may so much sorrow in so much love move you, 145
so that, to relieve my heart-heavy grief,
you join me in a contest worthy of praise.
 If your muse vanquishes time 148
through such glory-winning tricks,
may your beauty not do itself unending harm.
 It is right that Phoebus should be satisfied 150
by your intellect; but let Venus
be no less pleased by your beauty.
 You must put to good use all the gifts 154
that she made you, as you do
with the gifts granted you by Apollo;
 you'll make your name immortal through Venus's gifts 157
no less than you will do with your ink;
and you'll slow down time and weaken its force.
 Through her mouth I assure you of this: 160
do not desert Cypris to follow after Delios,[7]
or attempt to defend yourself against her.
 For Phoebus himself bows down to obey her, 163
and he cannot do otherwise, though in the end
he takes great pleasure in service to her.
 So you, as well, must do the same, 166
imitating the example set by this god,
who inspires you with his ideas and thoughts.
 Adorn your beauty with a pitying heart; 169
so that it is properly accompanied by virtue,
far from every cruel, fierce desire;
 in you let these two join hands with pity 172
and make you feel as sorry as you should
for a man who weeps for your love every moment.
 And I am that man, who comes humbly to you, 175
hoping to placate with caressing entreaties
your rigor together with your disdain;
 do not, in God's name, refuse me your mercy, 178
fair, gentle lady, but in such great war
extend your kindly help to me.
 In this way you will be without equal on earth. 181

---

7. Venus was named for Cyprus, the island where she was born, as Apollo was named for his native island Delos.

Capitolo 2

ぷ

S'esser del vostro amor potessi certa
per quel che mostran le parole e 'l volto,
che spesso tengon varia alma coperta;
  se quel che tien la mente in sé raccolto
mostrasson le vestigie esterne in guisa   5
ch'altri non fosse spesso in frode còlto,
  quella téma da me fôra divisa,
di cui quando perciò m'assicurassi,
semplice e sciocca, ne sarei derisa:
  « a un luogo stesso per molte vie vassi »,   10
dice il proverbio; né sicuro è punto
rivolger dietro a l'apparenzie i passi.
  Dal battuto camin non sia disgiunto
chïunque cerca gir a buona stanza,
pria che sia da la notte sopragiunto.   15
  Non è dritto il sentier de la speranza,
che spesse volte, e le piú volte, falle
con falsi detti e con finta sembianza;
  quello della certezza è destro calle,
che sempre mena a riposato albergo,   20
e refugio ha dal lato e da le spalle:
  a questo gli occhi del mio pensier ergo,
e da parole e da vezzi delusa,
tutti i lor vani indizi lascio a tergo.
  Questa con voi sia legitima scusa,   25
con la qual di non creder a parole,
né a vostri gesti, fuori esca d'accusa.
  E se invero m'amate, assai mi duole
che con effetti non vi discopriate,
come chi veramente ama far suole: 30
  mi duol che da l'un canto voi patiate,
e da l'altro il desio, c'ho d'esser grata

Capitolo 2
FRANCO'S RESPONSE TO CAPITOLO 1

If I could be certain of your love,
from what your words and face display,
which often conceal a changing mind;
 if external signs revealed what the mind   4
conceals within, so that a person
were not so often entrapped by deceit,
 I would cast aside this fear, for which,   7
however I tried to protect myself,
I would be mocked as simple and unwise;
 "to the same place one can take many roads,"   10
the proverb says; and it is never safe
to change one's direction according to appearances.
 Let no one stray from the beaten path   13
who is trying to find safe shelter
before the night comes to catch up with him.
 The path of hope is not straightforward,   16
for more often than not, it leads astray
with lying words and false pretense;
 the path of certainty is the right way,   19
which always leads to peaceful rest
and is safe on both sides and from behind;
 to this path I raise up my eyes' thought   22
and, disappointed by words and charm,
I leave behind all their misleading lures.
 May you find this an acceptable excuse,   25
may it acquit me of the charge that I believe
neither your gestures nor your words.
 And if you truly love me, it grieves me very much 28
that you do not reveal yourself by deeds,
as a man who loves truly usually does:
 I am sorry, on one hand, that you feel pain,   31
and on the other, that you frustrate me

al vostro vero amor, m'interrompiate.
   Poi ch'io non crederò d'esser amata,
né 'l debbo creder, né ricompensarvi   35
per l'arra che fin qui m'avete data,
   dagli effetti, signor, fate stimarvi:
con questi in prova venite, s'anch'io
il mio amor con effetti ho da mostrarvi;
   ma s'avete di favole desio,   40
mentre anderete voi favoleggiando,
favoloso sarà l'accetto mio;
   e di favole stanco e sazio, quando
l'amor mi mostrerete con effetto,
non men del mio v'andrò certificando.   45
   Aperto il cor vi mostrerò nel petto,
allor che 'l vostro non mi celerete,
e sarà di piacervi il mio diletto;
   e s'a Febo sí grata mi tenete
per lo compor, ne l'opere amorose   50
grata a Venere piú mi troverete.
   Certe proprïetati in me nascose
vi scovrirò d'infinita dolcezza,
che prosa o verso altrui mai non espose,
   con questo, che mi diate la certezza   55
del vostro amor con altro che con lodi,
ch'esser da tai delusa io sono avezza:
   piú mi giovi con fatti, e men mi lodi,
e, dov'è in ciò la vostra cortesia
soverchia, si comparta in altri modi.   60
   Vi par che buono il mio discorso sia,
o ch'io m'inganni pur per aventura,
non bene esperta de la dritta via?
   Signor, l'esser beffato è cosa dura,
massime ne l'amor; e chi nol crede,   65
ei stesso la ragion metta in figura.
   Io son per caminar col vostro piede,
ed amerovvi indubitatamente,
sí com'al vostro merito richiede.

in my desire to satisfy your true love.
    Since I will not believe that I am loved,   34
nor should I believe it or reward you
for the pledge you have made me up to now,
    win my approval, sir, with deeds: 37
prove yourself through them, if I, too,
am expected to prove my love with deeds;
    but if instead you long for fictions,   40
as long as you persist in spinning out tales,
my welcome to you will be just as false;
    and, when, fatigued and annoyed by fictions,   43
you show me your love in deeds,
I will assure you of mine in the same way.
    I will show you my heart open in my breast,   46
once you no longer hide yours from me,
and my delight will be to please you;
    and if you think I am so dear to Phoebus   49
for composing poems, in the works of love
you'll find me dearer still to Venus.
    Certain qualities concealed within me,   52
I will reveal to you, infinitely sweetly,
which prose or verse has never shown another,
    on this condition: that you prove your love to me   55
by other means than compliments, for I
take care not to be fooled by them;
    please me more with deeds and praise me less,   58
and where your courtesy overflows into praise,
distribute it in some other way.
    Does what I say seem right to you,   61
or do you instead perhaps think I am wrong,
lacking experience to choose the right path?
    Sir, being mocked is a most painful thing,   64
especially in love; and let whoever
does not believe this show his reason why.
    I am ready to walk in step with you,   67
and I will love you beyond any doubt,
just as your merit requires I should.

Se foco avrete in sen d'amor cocente,   70
io 'l sentirò, perch'accostata a voi
d'ardermi il cor egli sarà possente:
    non si pònno schivar i colpi suoi,
e chi si sente amato da dovero
convien l'amante suo ridamar poi;   75
    ma 'l dimostrar il bianco per lo nero
è un certo non so che, che spiace a tutti,
a quei ch'anco han giudicio non intiero.
    Dunque da voi mi sian mostrati i frutti
del portatomi amor, ché de le fronde   80
dal piacer sono i vani uomini indutti.
    Ben per quanto or da me vi si risponde,
avara non vorrei che mi stimaste,
ché tal vizio nel sen non mi s'asconde;
    ma piaceríami che di me pensaste   85
che ne l'amar le mie voglie cortesi
si studian d'esser caute, se non caste:
    né cosí tosto d'alcun uom compresi
che fosse valoroso e che m'amasse,
che 'l cambio con usura ancor gli resi.   90
    Ma chi per questo poi s'argomentasse
di volermi ingannar, beffa se stesso;
e tale il potría dir, chi 'l domandasse.
    E però quel che da voi cerco adesso
non è che con argento over con oro   95
il vostro amor voi mi facciate espresso:
    perché si disconvien troppo al decoro
di chi non sia piú che venal far patto
con uom gentil per trarne anco un tesoro.
    Di mia professïon non è tal atto;   100
ma ben fuor di parole, io 'l dico chiaro,
voglio veder il vostro amor in fatto.
    Voi ben sapete quel che m'è piú caro:
seguite in ciò com'io v'ho detto ancora,
ché mi sarete amante unico e raro.   105
    De le virtuti il mio cor s'innamora,

If in your breast you have love's burning fire   70
I'll feel it by your side, for it will have
the power to set my heart aflame, too;
    it's not possible to escape its blows,   73
and whoever feels truly loved
is bound to love the lover in return;
    but attempting to make white pass for black   76
is something that everybody dislikes,
even those whose judgment is weak.
    So show me the fruits of your love for me,   79
for only foolish folk are deceived
by the lure of empty words.
    Despite what I now answer you,   82
I'd not want you to think me greedy for gain,
for that vice is not concealed in my breast;
    but I would like you to believe   85
that when I love, my courteous desires,
if not chaste, are decidedly chary;
    and as soon as I have understood   88
that a man is brave and that he loves me,
I've returned his principal with interest.
    But whoever, on this account, should decide   91
to try to fool me is himself a fool;
and anyone he asks could tell him so.
    And what I now request from you   94
is not that you express your love
for me with silver or with gold;
    for to make a deal with a gentleman   97
in order to extract a treasure from him
is most improper if one's not entirely venal.
    Such an act doesn't suit my profession,   100
but I want to see, I say it clearly,
your love in deeds instead of words.
    You know well what I most cherish: 103
behave in this as I've already told you,
and you'll be my special, matchless lover.
    My heart falls in love with virtues,   106

e voi, che possedete di lor tanto,
ch'ogni piú bel saver con voi dimora,
  non mi negate l'opra vostra intanto,
ché con tal mezzo vi vegga bramoso   110
d'acquistar meco d'amador il vanto:
  siate in ciò diligente e studïoso,
e per gradirmi ne la mia richiesta
non sia 'l gentil vostro ozio unqua ozioso.

  A voi poca fatica sarà questa,   115
perch'al vostro valor ciascuna impresa,
per difficil che sia, facil vi resta.
  E se sí picciol carico vi pesa,
pensate ch'alto vola il ferro e 'l sasso,
che sia sospinto da la fiamma accesa: 120
  quel che la sua natura inchina al basso,
piú che con altro, col furor del foco
rivolge in su dal centro al cerchio il passo;
  onde non ha 'l mio amor dentro a voi loco,
poi ch'ei non ha virtú di farvi fare   125
quel ch'anco senz'amor vi saría poco.
  E poi da me volete farvi amare?
quasi credendo che, cosí d'un salto,
di voi mi debba a un tratto innamorare?
  Per questo non mi glorio e non m'essalto;   130
ma, per contarvi il ver, volar senz'ale
vorreste, e in un momento andar troppo alto:
  a la possa il desir abbiate eguale,
benché potreste agevolmente alzarvi
dov'altri con fatica ancor non sale.   135
  Io bramo aver cagion vera d'amarvi,
e questa ne l'arbitrio vostro è posta,
sí che in ciò non potete lamentarvi.
  Dal merto la mercé non fia discosta,
se mi darete quel che, benché vaglia   140
al mio giudicio assai, nulla a voi costa:
  questo farà che voli e non pur saglia
il vostro premio meco a quell'altezza,

and you, who possess so many of them
that in you all the finest wisdom dwells,
   don't deny me your effort in such a great cause,[8]   109
let me see you longing in this way
to acquire a lover's claim upon me;
   be diligent and eager in this task   112
and in order to grant my wish,
do not be idle in your free time.
   This will be no burden to you   115
for to your prowess any undertaking,
however difficult, comes with ease.
   And if such a small task weighs you down,   118
think of how iron and stone fly aloft,
when set in motion by a burning flame;
   whatever by nature tends to sink downward   121
through the fury of fire, more than any other force,
turns to rise from the center to the rim;[9]
   so love for me has no place within you   124
since it lacks the power to make you do
what even without love would be a small thing.
   And do you then hope to make me love—   127
as if you believed that with one single leap
I should suddenly fall in love with you?
   I don't glory in this or exalt myself;   130
but, to tell you the truth, you want to fly
without wings and rise too high all at once;
   let your desire match your ability,   133
for you can easily reach a height
that others, with effort, cannot attain.
   I long to have a real reason to love you   136
and I leave it up to you to decide,
so that you have no right to complain.
   There'll be no gap between merit and reward   139
if you'll give me what, though in my opinion
it has great value, costs you not a thing;
   your reward from me will be   142
not only to fly but to soar so high

---

8. Salza's edition, following the original text, gives *in tanto* here (240, sig. B2v), which we prefer to Bianchi's amended *intanto.*

9. Franco here quotes from Dante's *Paradiso* (14.1), from the scene in which Dante, having listened to the speech of Thomas Aquinas, compares the outward and inward movement of water in a bowl to the loving understanding he is gaining of divine order (123, 187). See Elena

che la speranza col desire agguaglia.
   E qual ella si sia, la mia bellezza,   145
quella che di lodar non sète stanco,
spenderò poscia in vostra contentezza:
     dolcemente congiunta al vostro fianco,
le delizie d'amor farò gustarvi,
quand'egli è ben appreso al lato manco;   150
     e 'n ciò potrei tal diletto recarvi,
che chiamar vi potreste per contento,
e d'avantaggio appresso innamorarvi.
     Cosí dolce e gustevole divento,
quando mi trovo con persona in letto,   155
da cui amata e gradita mi sento,
     che quel mio piacer vince ogni diletto,
sí che quel, che strettissimo parea,
nodo de l'altrui amor divien piú stretto.
     Febo, che serve a l'amorosa dea,   160
e in dolce guiderdon da lei ottiene
quel che via piú che l'esser dio il bea,
     a rivelar nel mio pensier ne viene
quei modi che con lui Venere adopra,
mentre in soavi abbracciamenti il tiene;   165
     ond'io instrutta a questi so dar opra
sí ben nel letto, che d'Apollo a l'arte
questa ne va d'assai spazio di sopra,
     e 'l mio cantar e 'l mio scriver in carte
s'oblía da chi mi prova in quella guisa,   170
ch'a' suoi seguaci Venere comparte.
     S'avete del mio amor l'alma conquisa,
procurate d'avermi in dolce modo,
via piú che la mia penna non divisa.
     Il valor vostro è quel tenace nodo   175
che me vi può tirar nel grembo, unita
via piú ch'affisso in fermo legno chiodo:
     farvi signor vi può de la mia vita,
che tanto amar mostrate, la virtute,
che 'n voi per gran miracolo s'addita.   180

that your hope will match your desires.
    And my beauty, such as it is,   145
which you never tire of praising,
I'll then employ for your contentment;
    sweetly lying at your left side,   148
I will make you taste the delights of love
when they have been expertly learned;
    And doing this, I could give you such pleasure   151
that you could say you were fully content,
and at once fall more deeply in love.
    So sweet and delicious do I become,   154
when I am in bed with a man
who, I sense, loves and enjoys me,
    that the pleasure I bring excels all delight,   157
so the knot of love, however tight
it seemed before, is tied tighter still.
    Phoebus, who serves the goddess of love,   160
and obtains from her as a sweet reward
what blesses him far more than being a god,
    comes from her to reveal to my mind   163
the positions that Venus assumes with him
when she holds him in sweet embraces;
    so that I, well taught in such matters,   166
know how to perform so well in bed
that this art exceeds Apollo's by far,
    and my singing and writing are both forgotten   169
by the man who experiences me in this way,
which Venus reveals to people who serve her.
    If your soul is vanquished by love for me,   172
arrange to have me in far sweeter fashion
than anything my pen can declare.
    Your valor is the steadfast knot   175
that can pull me to your lap,
joined to you more tightly than a nail in hard wood;
    your skill can make you master of my life,   178
for which you show so much love—
that skill that miraculously stands out in you.

Urgnani, "Veronica Franco: Tracce di dantismi in una scrittura femminile," *Canadian Journal of Italian Studies* 14, no. 42–43 (1991): 1–10.

Fate che sian da me di lei vedute
quell'opre ch'io desío, ché poi saranno
le mie dolcezze a pien da voi godute;
    e le vostre da me si goderanno
per quello ch'un amor mutuo comporte,   185
dove i diletti senza noia s'hanno.
    Aver cagion d'amarvi io bramo forte:
prendete quel partito che vi piace,
poi che in vostro voler tutta è la sorte.
    Altro non voglio dir: restate in pace.   190

Let me see the works   181
I've asked for from you,
for then you'll enjoy my sweetness to the full;
    and I will also take pleasure in yours,   184
in the way that mutual love allows,
which provides delight free from all pain.
    I yearn and long to have a good reason   187
to love you: decide what you think best,
for every outcome depends on your will.
    I have no more to say; go in peace.   190

Capitolo 3

ᴥ

Questa la tua fedel Franca ti scrive,
dolce, gentil, suo valoroso amante;
la qual, lunge da te, misera vive.
  Non cosí tosto, oimè, volsi le piante
da la donzella d'Adria, ove 'l mio core   5
abita, ch'io mutai voglia e sembiante:
  perduto de la vita ogni vigore,
pallida e lagrimosa ne l'aspetto,
mi fei grave soggiorno di dolore;
  e, di languir lo spirito costretto,   10
de lo sparger gravosi afflitti lai,
e del pianger sol trassi alto diletto.
  Oimè, ch'io 'l dico e 'l dirò sempre mai,
che 'l viver senza voi m'è crudel morte,
e i piaceri mi son tormenti e guai.   15
  Spesso, chiamando il caro nome forte,
Eco, mossa a pietà del mio lamento,
con voci tronche mi rispose e corte;
  talor fermossi a mezzo corso intento
il sole e 'l cielo, e s'è la terra ancora   20
piegata al mio sí flebile concento;
  da le loro spelunche uscite fuora,
piansero fin le tigri del mio pianto
e del martír che m'ancide e m'accora;
  e Progne e Filomena il tristo canto   25
accompagnaron de le mie parole,
facendomi tenor dí e notte intanto.
  Le fresche rose, i gigli e le vïole
arse ha 'l vento de' caldi miei sospiri,
e impallidir pietoso ho visto il sole;   30
  nel mover gli occhi in lagrimosi giri
fermârsi i fiumi, e 'l mar depose l'ire

Capitolo 3

ELEGIAC VERSES WRITTEN BY FRANCO, AWAY
FROM VENICE

This your faithful Franca writes you,[10]
tender, well-bred, and gallant lover,
she who in misery lives far away from you.
   No sooner, alas, had I turned my steps   4
from the maiden of Adria, where my heart dwells,[11]
than I was transformed in will and appearance:
   my life bereft of any strength,   7
with my face turned pale and bathed in tears,
I passed a time weighed down with grief;
   and, with my spirit forced to languish,   10
my only real pleasure came from reciting
heavy, pain-filled lays and from weeping.
   Alas, I say now and will always say   13
that life is cruel death to me without you,
and pleasures to me are torments and woes.
   Often, as I cried aloud that dear name,   16
Echo, touched with pity by my lament,
answered me with brief and broken calls.[12]
   At times in mid-course the sun and the sky   19
stood still, intent, and even the earth
bent down to hear my pitiful tones.
   Coming out of their secret lairs,   22
even tigers wept at my weeping
and the mortal pain that stabs my heart.
   And Procne and Philomela joined in[13]   25
with my sad melody and words,
singing in harmony both day and night.
   The cool roses, lilies, and violets   28
were burnt by the wind of my hot sighs,
and I saw the sun turn pale with pity.
   Moving their eyes in tearful swirls,   31
the rivers stood still, and the sea quelled its rage,

10. The feminine ending of Franco's surname here is typical of sixteenth-century practice.

11. Venice was called Adria, a name derived from the Adriatic Sea, on which the city was built.

12. In Ovid's *Metamorphoses*, 3.356–401, Echo is a maiden transformed through Juno's vengeance into a bodiless spirit, unable to speak except to repeat what others, especially her beloved Narcissus, say.

13. In Ovid's *Metamorphoses* (6.424–674) Procne and Philomela are human sisters turned

per la dolce pietà de' miei martíri.
  Oh quante volte le mie pene dire
l'aura e le mobil foglie ad ascoltare   35
si fermâr queste e lasciò quella d'ire!
  E finalmente non m'avien passare
per luogo ov'io non veggia apertamente
del mio duol fin le pietre lagrimare.
  Vivo, se si può dir che quel ch'assente   40
da l'anima si trova viver possa;
vivo, ma in vita misera e dolente:
  e l'ora piango e 'l dí ch'io fui rimossa
da la mia patria e dal mio amato bene,
per cui riduco in cenere quest'ossa.   45
  Fortunato 'l mio nido, che ritiene
quello a cui sempre torno col pensiero,
da cui lunge mi vivo in tante pene!
  Ben prego il picciol dio, bendato arciero,
che m'ha ferito 'l cor, tolto la vita,   50
mostrargli quanto amandolo ne pèro.
  Oh quanto maledico la partita
ch'io feci, oimè, da voi, anima mia,
bench'a la mente ognor mi sète unita,
  ma poi congiunta con la gelosia,   55
che, da voi lontan, m'arde a poco a poco
con la gelida sua fiamma atra e ria!
  Le lagrime, ch'io verso, in parte il foco
spengono; e vivo sol de la speranza
di tosto rivedervi al dolce loco.   60
  Subito giunta a la bramata stanza,
m'inchinerò con le ginocchia in terra
al mio Apollo in scïenzia ed in sembianza;
  e da lui vinta in amorosa guerra,
seguiròl di timor con alma cassa   65
per la via del valor ond'ei non erra.
  Quest'è l'amante mio, ch'ogni altro passa
in sopportar gli affanni, e in fedeltate
ogni altro piú fedel dietro si lassa.

through tender pity for my suffering.

    Oh, how many times the trembling leaves   34
stood still and the breeze ceased to blow,
in order to listen to my bitter pain.

    And finally, never could I make my way   37
through any place where I did not see
even stones weep openly for my grief.

    I live, if a person can be said to live   40
who finds herself bereft of her own soul;
I live, but a life of misery and mourning,

    and I lament the hour and the day   43
that I was taken from my home and my beloved,
for whom my bones now melt into ash.

    Fortunate dwelling of mine, which still enfolds   46
the man to whom I always return in thought,
from whom I live at such distance and pain!

    I implore the little god, blindfolded archer,   49
who wounded my heart and stole away my life,
to show that man how I perish for love of him.

    Alas, how I curse my departure from you,   52
although, dear soul, in all my thoughts,
you are still tightly united with me,

    but joined to me by jealousy, too,   55
which, far from you, little by little, burns me,
with its freezing, dark, savage flame!

    The tears that I shed quench the fire, in part,   58
and I live only in the hope
of seeing you soon again, in that sweet place.

    The moment I reach the room I have longed for,   61
I will bow down, my knees on the ground,
before my Apollo in knowledge and beauty.

    Then, vanquished by him in loving war,   64
I'll follow after him, my soul freed from fear,
on valor's path, from which he never strays.

    This is the man I love, who surpasses   67
every other man in enduring pain,
and whose faithfulness leaves all others behind.

---

into the swallow and the nightingale after Philomela has been raped by her sister's husband
Tereus.

Ben vi ristorerò de le passate   70
noie, signor, per quanto è 'l poter mio,
giungendo a voi piacer, a me bontate,
    troncando a me 'l martír, a voi 'l desio.

I'll willingly make up to you for past suffering,   70
my lord, as far as my power allows,
bringing pleasure to you, good to myself,
   ending my suffering and your desire.   73

Capitolo 4

᠕

A voi la colpa, a me, donna, s'ascrive
il danno e 'l duol di quelle pene tante,
che 'l mio cor sente e 'l vostro stil descrive.

L'alto splendor di quelle luci sante
recando altrove, e 'l lor soave ardore,   5
ai colpi del mio amor foste un diamante.

Io vi pregai, dagli occhi il pianto fore
sparsi largo, e sospir gravi del petto:
non m'aiutò pietà, non valse amore.

Valse, via piú che 'l mio, l'altrui rispetto;   10
e benché umil mercé v'addimandai,
pur sol rimasi in solitario tetto.

D'ir altrove eleggeste, io sol restai,
com'a voi piacque ed a mia dura sorte:
sí che invidia ai piú miseri portai.   15

E s'or avvien che a voi pentita apporte
alcun dolore il mio grave tormento,
in ciò degno è ch'amando io mi conforte.

Dunque per me del tutto non è spento
quel foco di pietà, ch'ove dimora   20
fa d'animo gentil chiaro argomento.

Di voi, cui 'l ciel tanto ama e 'l mondo onora,
di bellezza e virtute unico vanto,
in cui le Grazie fan dolce dimora,

gran prezzo è ancor se nel corporeo manto,   25
dove star con Amor Venere suole,
virtú chiudete in ciel gradita tanto.

Se 'l vostro cor del mio dolor si duole,
s'egualmente risponde a' miei desiri,
oh vostre doti e mie venture sole!   30

Tra quanto Amor le penne aurate giri,
non ha chi, com'io, dolce arda e sospire,

Capitolo 4

A RESPONSE TO FRANCO FROM AN UNNAMED WRITER, WRITTEN IN THE SAME RHYMES AS HER POEM TO HIM

To you, lady, belongs the blame,
to me the pain of all the griefs
that my heart feels and your pen describes.

Taking away the bright shine and sweet fire   4
of those blessed eyes, you stood hard
as a diamond against my love's charge.

I implored you, I poured out my lament   7
from my eyes and deep sighs from my breast;
pity was no help and love of no avail.

Your concern for another was far stronger than for me, 10
and though I begged you humbly for mercy,
I still remained under a lonely roof.

You chose to go elsewhere, I stayed alone,   13
as your will and my cruel fate decreed,
so that I envied the most wretched creatures.

And if it's now the case that my heavy grief   16
makes you, repentant, suffer some pain,
it's right that I, loving you, take comfort from it.

So for me pity's fire is not entirely spent,   19
that pity which, wherever it dwells,
gives visible proof of a gentle soul.

From you, loved by heaven and praised by the world,   22
who alone can be proud of such beauty and virtue,
with whom the Graces make their sweet home,[14]

the honor's greater still if in the cloak of your body, 25
where Venus habitually tarries with Love,
you enclose virtue so valued by heaven.

If your heart grieves for my grief,   28
if your heart corresponds to my longing,
ah, your great gifts, and my unique good fortune!

Among all the men Love strikes with gold arrows,   31
and among all those the sun looks down on,

14. The three Graces were Aglaia (the youngest, goddess of beauty), Euphrosyne (serenity), and Thalia (prosperity).

né tra quanto del sol la vista miri.
    Dolc'è, quant'è piú grave, il mio languire,
se, qual nel vostro dir pietoso appare,   35
sentite del mio mal pena e martíre.
    Che poi non mi cediate nell'amare,
esser non può, ché la mia fiamma ardente
nel gran regno amoroso non ha pare.
    Troppo benigno a' miei desir consente   40
il ciel, se dal mio cor la fiamma mossa
vi scalda il ghiaccio della fredda mente.
    In voi non cerco affetto d'egual possa,
quel ch'a far di duo uno, un di duo, viene,
e duo traffigge di una sol percossa.   45
    Troppo del viver mio l'ore serene
fôrano, e tanto piú il mio ben intero,
quanto piú raro questo amando avviene:
    quanto Amor men sostien sotto 'l suo impero
che 'n duo cor sia una fiamma egual partita,   50
tanto piú andrei de la mia sorte altero.
    Sí come troppo è la mia speme ardita,
che sí audaci pensieri al cor m'invia,
per strada dal discorso non seguita:
    da l'un canto il pensar sí com'io sia,   55
verso 'l vostro valor, di merto poco,
dal soverchio sperar l'alma desvía;
    da l'altro Amor gentil ch'adegui invoco
la mia tanta con voi disagguaglianza,
e gridando mercé son fatto roco.   60
    D'Amor, ch'a nullo amato per usanza
perdona amar, dove un bel petto serra
pensier cortesi, invoco la possanza:
    quella, onde 'l ciel ei sol chiude e disserra,
e perch'a lui la terra è poco bassa,   65
gli spirti fuor de l'imo centro sferra,
    prego che l'alma travagliata e lassa
sostenga; e se non ciò, vaglia pietate

no other burns and sighs so sweetly as I.

    My suffering is sweet when it is most intense,   34
if, as it seems from your pitying speech,
you feel pain and grief for my woe.

    But that you love as much as I do you   37
is impossible, for my burning flame
has no equal in the kingdom of love.

    Heaven too kindly consents to my longing   40
if the flame that escaped from my heart
thaws the ice of your cold mind.

    In you I don't seek affection so strong   43
that it makes one of two and two of one,
and to transfix two with a single stroke.

    My life would be too full of happy hours   46
and my happiness too complete,
should love of such rarity happen to me.

    The less often Love decrees that two hearts   49
under his rule should equally share
one flame, the prouder I'll be of my fate.

    Because my hope is much too daring   52
to send such bold thoughts to my heart
on a path untraveled by everyday speech,

    on one hand, the thought of how slight is my merit,   55
compared to your worth, waylays my soul,
off the path of its high hope;

    on the other hand, I call on gentle Love   58
to lessen my great inferiority to you,
and I am hoarse from calling for mercy.

    Of Love, which by habit spares no one loved   61
from loving in return, wherever a fair breast
encloses courteous thoughts, I invoke the might—

    that might through which he alone   64
shuts and opens heaven, and unleashes the spirits
from the core of the earth, which is not deep to him,

    I pray him to sustain my troubled, weary soul;   67
and if not, then I pray that pity may reign

là dove 'l vostro orgoglio non s'abbassa.
   Di mercé sotto aspetto non mi date   70
lusingando martír, tanto piú ch'io
v'adoro; e quanto prima ritornate,
   ch'al lato starvi ognor bramo e desío.

there where your pride refuses to bend.
    Do not make me suffer under pretended pity,   70
all the more since I adore you;
and return as soon as you possibly can,
    for I long and desire to be always at your side.   73

Capitolo 5

ᴣ

    Signor, la virtú vostra e 'l gran valore
e l'eloquenzia fu di tal potere,
che d'altrui man m'ha liberato il core;
    il qual di breve spero ancor vedere
collocato entro 'l vostro gentil petto,   5
e regnar quivi, e far vostro volere.
    Quel ch'amai piú, piú mi torna in dispetto,
né stimo piú beltà caduca e frale,
e mi pento che già n'ebbi diletto.
    Misera me, ch'amai ombra mortale,   10
ch'anzi doveva odiar, e voi amare,
pien di virtú infinita ed immortale!
    Tanto numer non ha di rena il mare,
quante volte di ciò piango: ch'amando
fral beltà, virtú eterna ebbi a sprezzare.   15
    Il mio fallo confesso sospirando,
e vi prometto e giuro da dovero
mandar per la virtú la beltà in bando.
    Per la vostra virtú languisco e pèro,
disciolto 'l cor da quell'empia catena,   20
onde mi avolse il dio picciolo arciero:
    già seguí' 'l senso, or la ragion mi mena.

Capitolo 5

FRANCO TO AN UNNAMED MAN, PROBABLY DOMENICO VENIER

Sir, your virtue and your great valor
and your eloquence had such power
that they freed my heart from another's hand;
 and that heart I soon hope to see   4
placed within your noble breast,
and ruling there and doing your will.
 What I most loved I now despise,   7
and I no longer value weak and frail beauty
and repent of ever having delighted in it.
 Unhappy me, who loved a mortal shadow   10
that I should have hated and loved you instead,
endowed with infinite, undying virtue!
 The sea does not have as many grains of sand 13
as the number of times I weep over this:
loving frail beauty, I disdained endless virtue.
 Sighing, I confess my mistake,   16
and I promise and swear to you truly
that I'll banish beauty in favor of virtue.
 I languish and die, longing for your virtue, 19
my heart freed from that evil chain
with which the little archer god bound me;
 once I followed my senses, now reason is my guide. 22

Capitolo 6

જી

Contrari son tra lor ragion e amore,
e chi 'n amor aspetta antivedere,
di senso è privo e di ragion è fuore.
    Tanto piú in prezzo è da doversi avere
vostro discorso, in cui avete eletto   5
voler in stima la virtú tenere;
    e bench'io di lei sia privo in effetto,
con voi di possederla il desio vale,
sí che del buon voler premio n'aspetto:
    e se 'l timor de l'esser mio m'assale,   10
poi mi fa contra i merti miei sperare,
ché s'elegge per ben un minor male.
    Io non mi vanto per virtú d'andare
a segno che, l'amor vostro acquistando,
mi possa in tanto grado collocare;   15
    ma so ch'un'alma valorosa, quando
trova uom che 'l falso aborre e segue il vero,
a lui si va con diletto accostando:
    e tanto piú se dentro a un cor sincero
d'alta fé trova affezzïon ripiena,   20
come nel mio, ch'un dí mostrarvi spero,
    se 'l non poter le voglie non m'affrena.

Capitolo 6

AN ANSWER TO FRANCO'S PRECEDING POEM, WRITTEN
IN THE SAME RHYMES

Reason and love are contrary to each other,
and whoever expects to predict love's course
is bereft of wit and deprived of reason.
   So there is all the more cause to value   4
your declaration, in which you've resolved
to hold virtue in highest esteem,
   and though, in truth, I lack that quality,   7
my desire to possess it, with you, is strong enough
that I expect a reward for my good will:
   and, if fear of my true self assails me,   10
it makes me hope, too, in spite of my few merits,
that it may be a blessing to choose a lesser evil.
   I do not claim that I could attain,   13
by winning your love, sufficient virtue
to rise to such a lofty goal,
   but I do know that a gallant soul,   16
finding a man who hates lies and follows truth,
makes her way toward him with delight:
   and all the more if in a heart that's sincere   19
she finds affection, full of truest faith,
as in mine, which I hope to show you one day,
   if powerlessness does not rein in my desires.   22

Capitolo 7

ᴣ

Dunque l'alta beltà, ch'amica stella
con sí prodiga mano in voi dispensa,
d'amor tenete e di pietà rubella?
   Quell'alma, in cui posando ricompensa
di molt'anni l'error la virtú stanca,   5
dar la morte a chi v'ama iniqua pensa?
   Lasso, e che altro a far del tutto manca
orribile ed amara questa vita,
e rovinosa in strada oscura e manca,
   se non che sia col mal voler unita   10
d'una bellezza al mondo senza eguale
la forza insuperabile, infinita?
   Ma perché da l'inferno ancor non sale
Tesifone e Megera ai nostri danni,
se scende a noi dal ciel cotanto male?   15
   Ben sei fanciul piú d'ingegno che d'anni,
Amor, e d'occhi e d'intelletto privo,
se 'l tuo regno abbandoni in tanti affanni.
   Te, cui non ebbe di servir a schivo
Giove con tutta la celeste corte,   20
e ch'a Dite impiagar fêsti anco arrivo;
   te, del cui arco il suon vien che riporte
spoglie d'innumerabili trofei,
contra chi piú resiste ognor piú forte;
   te, cui soggetti son gli uomini e i dèi,   25
non so per qual destin, fugge e disprezza,
con la mia morte ne le man, costei.
   Ma se contrario a quel che 'n ciel s'avezza,
ella sen va da le tue forze sciolta,
per privilegio de la sua bellezza,   30
   a la tua stessa madre or ti rivolta,
ch'unico essempio di beltà fu tanto,

Capitolo 7

AN APPEAL TO FRANCO FROM AN UNREQUITED LOVER

So the great beauty that a kindly star
gave to you with such generous hands
you maintain as a rebel to love and to pity?
    Does that soul, which weary virtue rewards   4
by resting in it after many years of wandering,
wickedly plan to deal death to a man who loves you?
    Alas, and what else remains to make   7
this life of mine totally bitter and grim,
facing disaster on a dark and dire path,
    unless ill will be joined to the power   10
of a beauty unequaled anywhere in the world,
impossible to exceed and without any end?
    But why from hell do Tisiphone   13
and Megaera not rise to do us harm,[15]
since so much evil falls on us from heaven?
    Love, you are indeed a child,   16
more in mind than in years, without eyes or wit
if you leave your kingdom in such a dire state.
    You, whom even Jove does not refuse to serve,   19
with all the heavenly train, and who succeeded
in inflicting wounds even on Dis;[16]
    you from whose bow must spread the fame   22
of numberless trophies and prizes without number,
stronger against those who most resist;
    you to whom both men and gods are subject,   25
she flees and disdains, by a fate I know not,
with my death in her hands.
    But if, contrary to heaven's custom,   28
she eludes all those powers of yours
through the privilege of her beauty,
    have recourse now to your own mother,   31
who, though a perfect and unequaled beauty,

15. Tisiphone and Megaera were ancient Furies, goddesses of vengeance. Along with Allecto, they were represented as women with serpents for hair. They reappear in Dante's *Inferno* as the pilgrim awaits entry to Hell's city of Dis (*Inferno* 9.46–8).

16. Dis (or Pluto), the god of the underworld, fell in love with the young Proserpina and took her down to his realm.

pur piagata da te piú d'una volta:
  e s'a lei toglie la mia donna il vanto
d'ornamento e di grazie, a lei che giova   35
l'esserti madre poi da l'altro canto?
  Se vinta da costei Venere è in prova,
e se Minerva in scïenzia e in virtute
a costei molto inferïor si trova,
  tanto piú scegli le saette acute: 40
ché piú gloria ti fia di questa sola,
che di tutt'altre in tuo poter venute.
  Per l'universo l'ali stendi, e vola
di cerchio in cerchio, Amor, e sí vedrai
che questa il pregio a tutte l'altre invola;   45
  e s'al tuo imperio aggiunger la saprai,
quanto 'l tuo onor sovra i dèi tutti gío,
tanto maggior di te stesso verrai.
  Benché lo sventurato in ciò son io,
ché, benché stata sia costei sicura   50
da l'armi ognor del faretrato dio,
  non è stata però sempre sí dura,
che non abbia ad Amor dato ricetto
per pietà nel suo sen, non per paura.
  Com'ad ubidïente umil soggetto,   55
ad Amor ansïoso e di lei vago
l'adito aperse del suo gentil petto;
  quinci 'l suo desir proprio a render pago,
al suo arbitrio d'Amor l'armi rivolse
qual le piacque a fermar solingo e vago: 60
  sí che dovunque saettando colse
col doppio sol di quei celesti lumi,
a sé gran copia d'amadori accolse,
  e con leggiadri e candidi costumi
dilettò 'l mondo in guisa che la gente   65
d'amor per lei vien ch'arda e si consumi.
  Gran pregio, in sé tener unitamente
rara del corpo e singolar beltate
con la virtú perfetta de la mente:

you have wounded more than once,[17]
   and if my lady steals from her the prize   34
for beauty and grace, what use to her
is being your mother as well?
   If she outdoes Venus when put to the proof,   37
and if Minerva turns out to be
far less than she in wisdom and valor,
   all the more reason to choose your sharpest arrows,   41
for you'll win greater glory from this woman alone
than from all the others who've come under your sway.
   Stretch your wings throughout the universe and fly   43
from sphere to sphere, Love, and you will see indeed
that this woman steals the prize from all others;
   and if you are able to subdue her to your power,   46
however much your honor surpasses all the gods',
you will become greater still than you are now;
   yet in all this I am the unlucky one,   49
for though she has always been well defended
against the weapons of the quiver-bearing god,
   she has not always been so hardened   52
that she has not given love refuge
in her bosom, through pity, not through fear.
   Like an obedient and humble subject   55
to Love, anxious and yearning after her,
she has opened the entrance to her tender breast;
   to appease her desire, she has redirected   58
the weapons of love according to her will,
to keep any man she wished alone and off course;
   so wherever, aiming her arrows, she has struck   61
with the double sun of those heavenly eyes,
she has collected an abundance of lovers,
   and with her lovely and innocent manners   64
she has delighted the world in such a way
that for love of her, people burn and waste away.
   Most precious it is to unite in oneself   67
rare and unusual bodily beauty
with perfect capacity of mind;

---

17. Venus, the mother of Eros (the Roman Cupid), fell in love with the young Adonis and, in Roman literature, with Anchises, with whom she conceived the hero Aeneas.

di cosí doppio ardor l'alme infiammate   70
senton lor foco di tal gioia pieno,
che quanto egli è maggior, piú son beate.
    Anch'io lo 'ncendio, che mi strugge il seno,
sempre piú bramerei che 'n tale stato
s'augumentasse e non venisse meno,   75
    s'io non fossi, né so per qual mio fato,
in mille espresse ed angosciose guise
da lei, miser, fuggito e disprezzato:
    ché se 'l trovar l'altrui voglie divise
da le nostre in amor, è di tal doglia,   80
che restan le virtú del cor conquise,
    quanto convien ch'io lagrimi e mi doglia
di vedermi aborrir con quello sdegno,
che di speme e di vita in un mi spoglia?
    E s'io mi lagno, e se di pianto pregno   85
porto 'l cor, che 'l duol suo sfoga per gli occhi,
miser qual io d'Amor non ha 'l gran regno.
    Non basta che Fortuna empia in me scocchi
tanti colpi, ch'altrui mai non aviene
che 'n questa vita un sí gran numer tocchi;   90
    ché sospirar e pianger mi conviene
di ciò, che la mia donna, fuor d'ogni uso,
al mio strazio piú cruda ognor diviene;
    e s'io, del pianto il viso smorto infuso,
del cielo e de le stelle mi richiamo,   95
ed or Amor, or lei gridando accuso,
    che poss'io far se, in premio di quant'amo,
giunto da l'altrui orgoglio a tal mi veggo,
che la morte ancor sorda al mio mal chiamo?
    E col pensier, ond'io vaneggio, or chieggo   100
d'Amor aita, ed or per altra strada
sempre invano al mio scempio, oimè, proveggo.
    Ma poi che 'l ciel destina, e cosí vada,
che per sicura e dilettosa via,
dove 'l ben trovan gli altri, io pèra e cada,   105
    sàziati del mio mal, fortuna ria;

souls inflamed with such double love   70
feel their burning full of such joy
that the greater the fire, the more blessed they are.
    And I would also wish that the blaze   73
that consumes my breast in such a state
might always increase and never diminish,
    if I were not, I know not by what fate,   76
in a thousand deliberate and painful ways,
disdained and, miserable, fled from by her.
    For if finding others' desires in love   79
so divided from our own brings on such grief
that the powers of the heart are defeated,
    how much must I weep and lament   81
at seeing myself loathed and held in contempt,
and stripped in one moment of hope and of life?
    And though I lament with a heart full of tears,   84
which soothes its pain through my eyes,
love's realm holds no one as wretched as me.
    It's not enough that relentless Fortune   88
deals me so many blows that no one else living
will ever be struck with such a great number;
    for I must sigh and weep for this reason: 91
my lady, contrary to any known custom,
intent on my ruin, becomes ever more cruel;
    and if with a pale face, wet with tears,   94
I call upon heaven and the stars above,
and accuse now Love, now my lady, with cries,
    what can I do if in reward for so much love   97
I see myself so bound to her pride
that I call for death, always deaf to my pain?
    And in thought, as I rave, now I entreat   100
Love for help, and now alas in vain
by another path I try to save myself from ruin.
    But since heaven decrees it and so it must be,   103
that upon a safe and pleasant road
where others find good, I perish and fall,
    feast on my misery, merciless Fortune,   106

poi, di me quando sarai stanca e sazia,
qual tuo gran pregio e qual acquisto fia?
    E tu, Amor, dentro e fuor mi struggi e strazia,
ché tanto m'è 'l mio affanno di contento,   110
quant'ei l'orgoglio di madonna sazia.
    Ben ai successi de le cose intento,
di lei m'assale immoderata téma,
che 'n lei vendichi 'l cielo il mio tormento.
    Questo fa in parte la mia gioia scema,   115
anzi, s'io voglio raccontar il vero,
son sempre oppresso da una doglia estrema:
    che se meco madonna usasse impero,
gratissimo il servirla mi saría
con affetto di cor vivo e sincero;   120
    ma che invece di spender signoria,
a dilettar la circostante turba
mi strazie sotto acerba tirannia,
    questo m'afflige l'animo, e mi turba.
Né, per le mie querele e i miei lamenti,   125
l'opera incominciata ella disturba,
    ma, quasi mar nei procellosi venti,
nel mio chieder mercé via piú s'adira,
e cela di pietà gli occhi suoi spenti:
    da me torcendo altrove i lumi gira,   130
e gran materia è di sua crudeltate
quanto per me si lagrima e sospira.
    O donna, pregio de la nostra etate,
anzi di tutti i secoli, se 'n voi
non guastasse l'orgoglio la beltate,   135
    ond'avvien che 'l mio amor cosí v'annoi?
E s'a morir davanti non vi vengo,
ancora offesa vi chiamate poi:
    quanto faccio, e di quanto ch'io m'astengo,
di me le vostre voglie a render paghe,   140
vi spiace, e merto di vostr'odio ottengo.
    Ma perché 'l vostro sdegno ognor m'impiaghe,
dolci son di quèl volto le percosse,

but when you are weary and sated with me,
what prize and what profit will this be to you?
    And you, Love, waste and tear me inside and out,   109
for my agony brings me more contentment
the more that it satisfies my lady's pride.
    Carefully eyeing how things may turn out,   112
I am assailed by unreasoning fear
that heaven may avenge my misery on her;
    This in part makes my joy incomplete—   115
rather, if I am to tell the truth,
I am always weighed down by acute despair;
    for if my lady should use her power over me,   118
I would serve her most willingly,
with a heart full of true and earnest affection.
    But that instead of wielding her power   121
to delight the crowd that clusters around her,
she tears me apart under harsh tyranny—
    this afflicts and torments my soul.   124
Nor, for all my laments and complaints,
does she put a stop to the work she's begun,
    but like a sea in tempestuous winds   127
she grows angrier still when I ask for mercy
and shields her weary eyes against pity.
    Shifting her eyes from me, she looks elsewhere,   130
and however much I weep and sigh for myself,
I merely give further grounds to her cruelty.
    Oh, lady, treasure of our age,   133
indeed, of all centuries, if in you
pride did not destroy your beauty,
    why is it that my love vexes you so?   136
And if I don't come to die at your feet,
you will still say that you are offended;
    whatever I do or refrain from doing,   139
you refuse to fulfill your desire through me,
and the only reward I obtain is your hate.
    But though your disdain constantly wounds me,   142
blows are sweet coming from that face

e de le vostre man candide e vaghe.

   Qualunque affetto in voi giamai si mosse,   145
tutto fate con grazia: de' vostri atti
chïunque il dotto e buon maestro fosse.

   Quai tenesse con voi natura patti,
ancor de l'ire vostre e de l'offese
tutti gli uomini restan sodisfatti.   150

   Farvi perfetta a tutte prove intese
l'influsso donator d'ogni eccellenza,
e benigno la man verso voi stese:

   quinci del ciel l'altissima potenza
si vede in molti effetti discordanti,   155
c'han di virtute in voi tutti apparenza.

   Oh che dolci, oh che cari e bei sembianti,
ch'alte maniere quelle vostre sono,
da farvi i dèi venir qua giuso amanti!

   E se, com'io pur volentier ragiono   160
de le grazie che 'l ciel tante in voi pose
con singolar, non piú veduto dono,

   non mi teneste d'ogni parte ascose
quelle vostre divine e rare parti,
di che vostra persona si compose,   165

   non fôran sí angosciosi da me sparti
sospiri, né di lagrime vedresti
avampando, cor misero, innondarti.

   Ma dond'avien che 'n me, lasso, si desti
la speme, che per prova intendo come   170
faccia sempre i miei dí piú gravi e mesti?

   E pur chiamando di mia donna il nome,
vera, unica al mondo eccelsa dea,
convien ch'a lei mi volga, e ch'io la nome.

   Deh, non mi siate cosí iniqua e rea,   175
che 'l mio mal sia 'l ben vostro, e che m'ancida
quella vostra beltà che gli altri bea!

   Ma quell'Amor, che v'ha tolto in sua guida,
e che tien nel cor vostro il suo bel seggio,
la crudeltà per me da voi divida;   180

   ch'io piangendo umilmente ancor vel chieggio.

and from your pale and lovely hands.

Whatever feeling has ever stirred in you,   145
there is grace in everything you do,
whoever your wise, good master has been.

Whatever pacts nature has made with you,   148
even your rages and your misdeeds
leave all men full of contentment.

Her influence made you fit for every challenge,   151
giving you every excellent attribute,
reaching her beneficent hand out to you;

here on earth the highest powers of heaven   154
are discerned in many different forms,
which in you all seem to be virtues.

Oh, what sweet, what dear and fair looks,   157
what lofty manners are these of yours,
enough to draw gods as your lovers from heaven!

And since I speak so willingly   160
of the many graces granted you by heaven,
in an extraordinary gift never seen since,

if you did not hide from me on all sides   163
those divine and matchless limbs
of which your body is composed,

I would not have heaved such anguished sighs,   166
nor, unhappy heart, would you have seen
yourself, flaming, engulfed by tears.

But how does it happen that hope rises up   169
in me, alas, so that I feel through experience
how it makes all my days woeful and dreary?

And even as I invoke my lady's name,   172
true and unique goddess, supreme on earth,[18]
I must turn to her and say her name.

Pray, be not so wicked and cruel to me   175
that my sorrow is your boon, and your beauty,
which blesses others, murders me!

But let Love, who has taken you for his guide,   178
and whose lovely throne resides in your heart,
remove, for my sake, cruelty from you;

which, humbly weeping, I also beg of you.   181

---

18. "True and only," *vera, unica* in the Italian, is another pun on "Veronica." Compare *capitoli* 1, 11, 16.

Capitolo 8

Ben vorrei fosse, come dite voi,
ch'io vivessi d'Amor libera e franca,
non còlta al laccio o punta ai dardi suoi;
    e se la forza in ciò d'assai mi manca
da resister a l'armi di quel dio,   5
che 'l cielo e 'l mondo e fin gli abissi stanca,
    ch'ei s'annidasse fôra 'l desir mio
dentro 'l mio cor, in modo ch'io 'l facessi
non repugnante a quel che piú desío.
    Non che sovra lui regno aver volessi,   10
ché folle a imaginarlo sol sarei,
non che ch'un sí gran dio regger credessi;
    ma da lui conseguir in don vorrei
che, innamorar convenendomi pure,
fosse 'l farlo secondo i pensier miei.   15
    Ché se libere in ciò fosser mie cure,
tal odierei, ch'adoro; e tal, ch'io sdegno,
con voglie seguirei salde e mature.
    E poi ch'Amor anch'io biasmar convegno,
imaginando non si trovería   20
cosa piú ingiusta del suo iniquo regno.
    Egli dal proprio ben l'alme desvía;
e mentre indietro pur da ciò ti tira,
nel precipizio del tuo mal t'invia.
    E se 'l cor vostro in tanto affanno ei gira,   25
credete che per me certo non meno
sua colpa, si languisce e si sospira;
    e se voi del mio amor venite meno
(nol so, ma 'l credo), anch'io d'un crudel angue
soffro al cor gli aspri morsi e 'l rio veneno.   30
    Cosí, quanto per me da voi si langue
vedete ristorato con vendetta

Capitolo 8

FRANCO DESCRIBES A SET OF MISMATCHED LOVERS, INCLUDING HERSELF

I wish it were the case, as you say it is,
that I led my life free from Love, and frank,
not caught in his snare or pierced by his arrows;
    and if in this affair I lack by far   4
the strength to resist the weapons of that god
who wearies heaven and earth and even hell,
    my desire would still be that he nestled in my heart,   7
so that I could make him become
less resistant to what I most desire.
    Not that I want to rule over him,   10
for I would be mad even to imagine it,
nor would I presume to rule such a great god;
    but I would like him to grant me as a gift   13
that even if I must fall in love,
I may do so according to my own design.
    For if my feelings were free in this affair,   16
I would despise the man I adore;
and with steady, mature desire, I'd pursue the one I scorn.
    And since I, too, must complain of Love,   19
anything more unfair than his wicked reign
would be impossible to imagine or find.
    He leads souls astray from their own good,   22
and even as he pulls you back,
he sets you on the brink of your own ruin.
    And if he turns your heart toward such distress,   25
believe me, through his doing I myself
certainly languish and sigh no less;
    and if you swoon with love for me   28
(I know not, but believe it), I, too, suffer at heart
from a cruel snake's sharp bite and killing venom.
    So however much you suffer on my account,   31
you see fully paid back, in return,

de le mie carni e del mio infetto sangue.

E se 'l mio mal vi spiace e non diletta,
anch'io 'l vostro non bramo, e quel ch'io faccio   35
contra voi 'l fo da l'altrui amor costretta;

benché, s'oppressa inferma a morte giaccio,
com'è ch'a voi recar io possa aita
nel martír ch'entro grido e di fuor taccio?

Voi, s'a lagnarvi il vostro duol v'invita   40
meco, nel mio languir soverchio impietra
e rende un sasso di stupor mia vita:

via piú nel cor quella doglia penètra,
che raggela le lagrime nel petto,
e l'uom, qual Niobe, trasfigura in pietra.   45

Il vostro duol si può chiamar diletto,
poiché parlando meco il disfogate,
del mio, ch'al centro il cor chiude, in rispetto.

Io vi rispondo ancor, se mi parlate;
ma le preghiere mie supplici il vento   50
senza risposta ognor se l'ha portate,

se pur ebbi mai tanto d'ardimento,
che in voce o con inchiostro addimandassi
qualche mercede al grave mio tormento.

E cosí portar gli occhi umidi e bassi   55
convengo, e converrò per lungo spazio,
se morte al mio dolor non chiude i passi.

Del mio amante non dico: ché 'l mio strazio
è 'l dolce cibo, ond'ei mentre si pasce
divien nel suo digiun manco ognor sazio.   60

E dal suo orgoglio pur sempre in me nasce
novo desio d'appagar le sue voglie,
ch'unqua non vien che riposar mi lasce;

ma dal mio nodo Amor l'arretra e scioglie:
forse con lui fa un'altra donna quello   65
ch'egli fa meco; e qual dà, tal ritoglie.

Cosí di quanto è 'l mio desir rubello
ai desir vostri, a la medesma guisa
ne riporto supplizio acerbo e fello.

by my flesh and my afflicted blood.

    And if my pain hurts and does not delight you,   34
nor do I want yours, and what I do against you
I do driven by love for another;

    and if I lie abject and sick unto death,   37
how can I help you in your pain
when I shriek within and am outwardly silent?

    If your grief leads you to lament to me,   40
in my travail, greater yet, my life
turns to stone and hardens into unfeeling rock:

    such grief penetrates the heart far more deeply,   43
so that it freezes the tears within the breast,
and changes man, like Niobe, into stone.[19]

    Your suffering could be called delight   47
since you ease it by speaking of it to me,
unlike mine, which my heart shuts up in its core.

    I still answer you if you speak to me;   50
but the wind has carried my imploring prayers
off with it every moment, without an answer,

    whenever I have had sufficient daring   53
to appeal, through my voice or in ink,
for mercy in return for my dire pain.

    And so I must lower my tearful eyes   56
and keep them low for a long time to come,
unless death cuts short the path of my woe.

    Of my lover, I say nothing; for my agony   59
is sweet nourishment to him, so that as he feeds on it,
it is ever less satisfied by its own starvation.

    And even from his pride a strange desire   61
is born in me to satisfy all his wishes,
and it never allows me to rest;

    but Love loosens and frees him from my embrace,   64
and perhaps another woman does to him
what he does to me, and as he gives, he receives.

    So as much as my desire resists yours,   67
in the same way, in return for my desire,
I receive agony, piercing and sharp.

---

19. Niobe, the daughter of Tantalus, bragged so much about her seven children's beauty that Apollo and Artemis slew them in revenge. Niobe was turned to stone, with a spring, like tears, flowing down her face (*Metamorphoses*, 6.146–312).

Fors'ancor voi del vostro amor conquisa   70
altra donna sprezzate, e con la mente
dal piacerle v'andate ognor divisa;
   e s'a lei sète ingrato e sconoscente,
in suo giusto giudizio Amor decide
ch'un'altra sí vi scempia e vi tormente.   75
   Fors'anco Amor del comun pianto ride,
e per far lagrimar piú sempre il mondo,
l'altrui desir discompagna e divide;
   e mentre che di ciò si fa giocondo,
de le lagrime nostre il largo mare   80
sempre piú si fa cupo e piú profondo:
   ché s'uom potesse a suo diletto amare,
senza trovar contrarie voglie opposte,
l'amoroso piacer non avría pare.
   E se tai leggi fûr dal destin poste,   85
perché ne la soverchia dilettanza
al ben del cielo il mondan non s'accoste,
   tant'è piú 'l mio dolor, quant'ho in usanza
d'innamorarmi e di provar amando
quest'amata in amor disagguaglianza.   90
   Ben quanto a l'esser mio vo ripensando:
veggo che la fortuna mi conduce
ove la vita ognor meni affannando;
   e se potessi in ciò prender per duce
quella ragion ch'or, da l'affetto vinta,   95
d'Amor sotto l'imperio si riduce,
   sarebbe nel mio cor la fiamma estinta
de l'altrui foco, e di quel fôra in vece
del vostro l'alma ad infiammarsi accinta.
   E se l'ordine a me mutar non lece,   100
s'a disfar o corregger quel non viene,
ch'o ben o mal una volta il ciel fece,
   posso bramar che chi cinta mi tiene
d'indegno laccio in libertà mi renda,
sí ch'io mi doni a voi, come conviene;   105
   ma ch'altro in ciò fuor del desir io spenda,

Perhaps you, too, disdain another woman   70
conquered by love for you, and your mind
roams far from ever wanting to please her;
    and if you are heedless and ungrateful to her,   73
Love, in his fair judgment, decrees
that another woman should ravage and torment you.
    Perhaps Love even laughs at these shared tears   76
and, to make the world weep even more,
divides and sunders yet another's desire;
    and, while he makes merry over this,   79
the wide sea of all our tears
darkens and deepens further still:
    for if man could love to his heart's content,   82
without confronting contrary desires,
the pleasure of love would have no equal.
    And if destiny has laid down the law   85
that in supreme delight, earthly good
may not attain the bliss of heaven,
    my woe is all the greater as my habit is   88
to fall in love, and to feel, through loving,
this beloved mismatch in love.
    However much I reflect on myself,   91
I see that fortune leads me wherever
life follows an always troubled path;
    and if I were able to take reason as my guide,   94
which now, defeated by emotion,
is subjected to the reign of Love,
    the flame for the other man would burn out   97
in my heart, and my soul would be prompt
to flare up with fire for you instead.
    And if I lack the right to change this scheme   100
of things, if he whom heaven once made,
for good or ill, does not undo or improve it,
    I may hope that he who holds me tied   103
in an unworthy bond gives my freedom back,
so I may give myself to you, as is more fit;
    but, dear sir, you must no longer expect   106

e questo ancor con non picciola noia,
non è che piú da voi, signor, s'attenda.

    Ben sarebbe compita la mia gioia,
s'io potessi cangiar nel vostro amore   110
quel ch'in altrui con diletto m'annoia.

    A voi darei di buona voglia il core,
e dandol, crederei riguadagnarlo
nel merito del vostro alto valore:

    cosí verrei d'altrui mani empie a trarlo,   115
e in luogo di conforto e di salute
aventurosamente a ben locarlo.

    Anch'io so quanto val vostra virtute,
e de le rare eccellenti vostr'opre
molte sono da me state vedute.   120

    Chiaro il vostro valor mi si discopre,
e s'io non vengo a dargli ricompensa,
Amor non vuol che tanto ben adopre.

    Com'io 'l potessi far, da me si pensa;
e se, dov'al desio manca il potere,   125
il buon animo i merti ricompensa,

    che v'acquietate meco è ben dovere:
forse ch'a tempo di miglior ventura
ve ne farò buon effetto vedere.

    Tra tanto l'esser certo di mia cura   130
conforto sia ch'al vostro dolor giovi,
e mi faccia stimar da voi non dura,

    fin che libera un giorno io mi ritrovi.

that I should devote more than a wish
to this, and that with no small annoyance.
    Certainly my joy would be complete   109
if I could change into love for you
what in that man teases me with delight.
    I would gladly give my heart to you,   112
and by giving it, believe I earned it back
in the merit of your high distinction:
    so I should take my heart from his cruel hands,   115
and safely set it, by fortune's favor,
in a place of comfort and good health.
    I know very well how to value your virtue,   118
and of your rare and excellent works
many examples have come to my notice.
    Your valor is clearly evident to me,   121
and if I cannot reward it rightly,
Love keeps me from availing myself of so much good.
    I consider how I might be able to do so,   124
and if where desire falls short of power,
good will still deserves a return,
    certainly your duty is to make peace with me: 127
at a more propitious time, perhaps,
I will show you an outcome that turns all this to good.
    Meanwhile, let the certainty of my care   130
be a comfort to you and assuage your grief
and make you judge me not unkind,
    'til one day I find myself free again.   133

Capitolo 9

ॐ

Donna, la vostra lontananza è stata
a me, vostro fedel servo ed amante,
morte tanto crudel quanto insperata.
   Nel gentil vostro angelico sembiante
abitar l'alma e 'l mio cor vago suole,   5
e ne le luci sí leggiadre e sante:
   queste fûr risplendente unico sole
sovra i miei dí, senza lor tristi e negri,
e di quel pieni, ond'uom via piú si duole,
   come sono a me adesso orbati ed egri,   10
in questa sepoltura de la vita,
che non fia, senza voi, che si reintègri.
   Con voi l'anima mia s'è dipartita,
anzi 'l mio spirto e l'anima voi sète,
e tutta la virtú vitale unita: 15
   e s'uom morto parlar vien che si viete,
non io, ma di me parla in cambio quella
che ne le vostre man mia vita avete.
   Questa non pur vi scrive e vi favella,
per miracol d'amor, in cotal guisa,   20
che, ne l'esser io morto, in voi vive ella;
   ma stando dal cor vostro non divisa,
vi susurra a l'orecchie di segreto,
e 'l mio misero stato vi divisa.
   Né perciò del mio male altro ben mieto,   25
se non ch'agli occhi vostri ei si figura
con spettacolo a voi gioioso e lieto;
   e mentre meco ognor v'innaspra e indura,
superate ne l'essermi crudele
le fiere mostrüose a la natura.   30
   Lasso, ch'io spargo ai venti le querele,
anzi è un percuoter d'onde a duro scoglio,

Capitolo 9

**BY AN UNKNOWN AUTHOR, LAMENTING
FRANCO'S ABSENCE**

Lady, your absence has been to me,
your faithful servant and devoted lover,
a death as cruel as it was foreseen.
    My soul and my enamored heart   4
once lived in your gentle, angelic face
and in your eyes, so beautiful and blessed:
    these were the bright and only sun   7
on my days, without them sad and dark,
and full of what grieves man by far the most,
    as bereaved and weak as are my eyes   10
in this sepulcher of life, which, without you,
will not be restored to health.
    With you my soul took leave of me,   13
or, rather, you are my spirit and soul
and all my vital strength conjoined in one;
    and if a dead man is barred from speaking,   16
not I but my life, which you hold in your hands,
speaks here in exchange for me.
    My life not only writes and speaks to you,   19
by a miracle of love, in such a way
that in my death, it lives in you;
    not being divided from your heart,   22
it whispers secretly in your ear,
and describes my wretched state to you.
    Nor do I win any ease for my pain,   25
except that it appears before your eyes
in a spectacle joyful and pleasant to you;
    and as you sharpen and harden toward me,   28
in your cruelty to me you surpass
the monstrous wild beasts of nature.
    Alas, that I cast my laments to the winds—   31
rather, it's the beating of waves on a stone,

quanto mai di voi pianga e mi querele.
   Mosso s'insuperbisce il vostro orgoglio,
sí come 'l mar a l'impeto de' venti,   35
mentre a ragion con voi di voi mi doglio;
   ed or, per far piú gravi i miei tormenti,
per levarmi 'l ristoro ch'io sentía
nel formarvi propinquo i miei lamenti,
   n'andaste a volo per diversa via,   40
quando men sospettava, a dimostrarvi
in tutti i modi a me contraria e ria.
   Qual neve sotto 'l sol, piangendo sparvi
con quest'orma di vita, e con quest'ombra
vana e insufficïente a seguitarvi;   45
   anzi, da' miei sospir cacciata e sgombra,
col vento, ch'a voi venne, si risolse,
che spirando al bel sen fors'or v'ingombra.
   Empio destin, ch'altrove vi rivolse
dal mirar lo mio strazio e quella pena,   50
che infinita al mio cor per voi s'accolse!
   Troppo era la mia vita alta, serena,
darvi in presenzia de la mia gran fede
col vicin pianger mio certezza piena,
   e riceverne asprissima mercede   55
di presenti minacce e di ripulse,
contrario a quel ch'a la pietà si chiede.
   Ben certo allor benigno il ciel m'indulse;
e troppo chiara ancor nel sommo sdegno
la luce de' vostr'occhi a me rifulse.   60
   Di gustar quel piacer non era degno,
ch'io sentía, nel vedervi, aspro e mortale
far piú sempre 'l mio duol, con ogni ingegno:
   or lasso piango il mio passato male,
quando a le mie d'amor gravi percosse   65
non fu in dolcezza alcun diletto eguale.
   Amor d'acerbo colpo mi percosse,
di quel che di piacer è in tutto privo,
quando da me, madonna, vi rimosse.

no matter how much I weep and complain.
    Shaken, your pride grows haughtier still,   34
much like the blast of winds on the sea,
while I rightly complain of you to yourself.
    And now, to make my torments more grievous still,   37
to deny me the comfort I used to feel,
close to you declaring my woe,
    you flew away on a different path   40
when least expected, in order to appear
in all ways contrary and cruel to me.
    Like snow in the sun, you vanished in tears,   43
with this mere trace of life and this vain shadow,
powerless to follow after you,
    or rather, pursued and weighed down by my sighs,   46
it dissolved in the oncoming wind, which now,
blowing on your breast, perhaps holds you back.
    Cruel fate, which has taken you away,   49
far from the sight of my ruin and pain,
which, endless, has settled in my heart through you!
    My life was too lofty and too serene   52
to show you in person my great loyalty
and how close I was to weeping,
    receiving in exchange the harshest reward   55
of these threats and rejections, contrary
to anything that pity demands.
    Certainly, then, kind heaven indulged me,   58
and shone down upon me the light of your eyes,
now far too bright at the height of your scorn.
    It was not right to enjoy this pleasure,   61
for seeing you, I felt, with all my wit,
my grief become ever more mortal and dire;
    alas, now I lament my past misery,   64
when no delight was equal in sweetness
to the hard blows that I suffered for love.
    Love struck me down with a violent blow,   67
of the kind that is totally deprived of pleasure,
when, my lady, he took you from me.

Dianzi fu 'l viver mio lieto e giulivo,   70
ed or, a prova del mio mal cotanto,
sento 'l mio ben, mentre di lui mi privo.
  Deh tornate a veder il mio gran pianto,
venite a rinovar l'aspre mie piaghe,
senza lasciarmi respirar alquanto: 75
  di ciò contente fían mie voglie e paghe,
che 'l mio duol, da voi fatto ancor maggiore,
mirin da presso l'alme luci vaghe.
  A me fia d'alta gioia ogni dolore;
e in gran pietà riceverà lo strazio,   80
e in dolce aita ogni aspra offesa il core,
  pur ch'a noi ritorniate in breve spazio.

Before, my life was joyous and cheerful,   70
and now, as a test of my immense pain,
I feel my good as I am deprived of it.
    Pray, return to see my flood of tears,   73
come to reopen my bitter wounds,
not letting me take a single breath;
    by this all my wishes would be met and fulfilled: 76
that your kind, noble eyes, close by, should see
the pain that you constantly increase in me.
    To me every pain will be a great joy,   79
and my heart will interpret torment as compassion
and every harsh injury as sweet relief,
    provided that you come back to us soon.   82

Capitolo 10

ॐ

In disparte da te sommene andata,
per frastornarti da l'amarmi, avante
ch'unqua mostrarmi a tanto amore ingrata:
    né mia colpa fia mai ch'alcun si vante
giovato avermi in opre od in parole,   5
senza mercede assai piú che bastante;
    ma s'uom, seguendo ciò che 'l suo cor vuole,
di quel m'attristi, ond'ei via piú s'allegri,
meco non merta, e mi sprezza, e non cole.
    Quei sí, che son d'amor meriti intègri,   10
quando, per far a me cosa gradita,
per me ti sono, i tuoi dí tristi, allegri!
    E nondimeno tu con infinita
doglia sentisti che mai cose liete
non m'incontrâr dal tuo amor disunita.   15
    Che mi prendesti a l'amorosa rete,
presa da un altro pria, vietò mia stella,
non so se per mio affanno, o per quïete:
    basta che, fatta d'altro amante ancella,
l'anima, ad altro oggetto intenta e fisa,   20
rendersi ai tuoi desir convien rubella.
    Con tutto questo, e ch'al mio ben precisa
la strada fosse, e fattomi divieto,
dal tuo seguirmi poco men che uccisa,
    con giudicio amorevole e discreto   25
tanto stimai 'l tuo amor senza misura,
quanto piú al mio voler fosti indiscreto:
    e di te preso alcuna dolce cura,
bench'a me tu temprasti amaro fele
col tuo servirmi, in ciò non ti fui dura;   30
    e per te non avendo in bocca il mèle
di quell'affetto ch'entro 'l sen raccoglio,

FRANCO'S REPLY, WRITTEN IN THE SAME RHYMES

I went away, departing from you,
in order to force you out of loving me,
not at all to seem thankless for so much love;
   nor is it my fault if anyone boasts   4
of giving me favors in word or deed
without having received more than ample reward.
   But if a man, following his heart's desire,   7
makes me regret it, which delights him even more,
he deserves nothing, and scorns and dishonors me.
   But those are certainly love's just rewards   10
when, to please me, your sad days
turn to happy ones, on my account.
   And yet you've heard with infinite sorrow   13
that any joy has ever come to me
since I was parted from your love.
   My star forbade you to trap me in love's net,   16
for I was caught already by another man,
for woe or peace I do not know;
   it's enough that my soul, to another enslaved,   19
intent and fixed on this other man,
rightly rebels against sharing your desire.
   In spite of all this, and that my path to joy   22
was straight and direct, yet I was pushed off it
and all but slain by your persistence,
   with a loving and tempered judgment,   25
I believed your love was as boundless
as, in fact, you failed to respect my will;
   having taken loving care of you,   28
though you mixed bitter bile with your duty to me,
I was not harsh to you as a result;
   and since toward you my mouth lacks the honey   31
of the affection I feel in my breast,

che in altrui pro convien che si rivele,
   liberamente, come teco soglio,
ti raccontai ch'altrove erano intenti   35
i miei spirti, e mostraiti il mio cordoglio.
   Or, perché teco ad un non mi tormenti,
tentando invan ch'a mio gran danno io sia
pietosa a te, con tuoi dogliosi accenti,
   da te partimmi; e non potendo pia   40
esserti, almen veridica t'apparvi:
non rea, qual da te titol mi si dia.
   Quanto è 'l peggio talvolta il palesarvi
effetti d'alma di pietate ingombra,
dov'altri soglia male interpretarvi!   45
   Benché, se vaneggiando erra ed adombra
il tuo pensier, che da ragion si tolse,
seguendo Amor per via di lei disgombra,
   non però quel ch'ad util tuo si vòlse
da me, da cui 'l desir tuo si raffrena,   50
che d'ir al precipizio i piè ti sciolse,
   a meritar alcun biasmo mi mena;
anzi di quel ch'aiuto in ciò ti diede,
la mia chiara pietà si rasserena:
   ché s'io mossi da te fuggendo 'l piede,   55
fu perché le presenti mie repulse
m'eran de la tua morte espressa fede.
   E quante volte fu che ti repulse
da sé 'l mio sguardo, o ti mirò con sdegno,
so che 'l gran duol del petto il cor t'evulse.   60
   Ch'io ti vedessi d'alta doglia pregno
morirmi un dí davante, eccesso tale
era a me sconvenevole ed indegno.
   Da l'altra parte, assai potev'io male
risponder al tuo amor: non men che fosse   65
il tentar di volar non avendo ale.
   E che far potev'io contra le posse
di quell'arcier che, del tuo bene schivo,
d'oro in te, in me di piombo il suo stral mosse?

which I must reveal only to another,
    freely, as is my custom with you,   34
I told you that my thoughts were turned
elsewhere, and I showed you my regret.
    Then, not to torture myself and you both,   37
since you tried in vain with your sorrowful words
to make me feel pity, at great cost to myself,
    I left you; and though I was unable   40
to give you mercy, at least I was truthful,
not, as you want to label me, cruel.
    Sometimes the worst one can do is be open,   43
though this is the act of a soul full of pity,
which others are likely to misunderstand!
    Although your thought, straying from reason, 46
wanders aimless and disturbed,
following Love unimpeded by judgment,
    even so, I am not to be held to blame   49
for anything that I did to help you,
on my side, as I curb your desire,
    and I kept you from a precipitous fall.   52
On the contrary, the help I gave you
clearly shows my exceptional good will;
    so if I fled from you, the reason was   55
that the refusals I am making now
were a firm guarantee to me then of your death.
    And whenever my glance drove you away   58
or I looked at you with scorn, I know
that great pain tore your heart from your breast.
    That I should see you, overwhelmed   61
with grief, die before me one day—
such an extreme seemed wrong and unfit.
    On the other hand, I could hardly return   64
your love, especially because
it was an attempt to fly without wings.
    And how could I resist the power of that archer, 67
who, opposed to your desire, shot you
with a golden arrow, me with one of lead?[20]

20. Cupid's golden arrow made the person receiving it fall in love, while the leaden arrow
made its victim resist love (*Metamorphoses*, 1.468–71).

Ma d'òr prima anco al mio cor fece arrivo   70
la sua saetta, stand'io ferma intanto,
mirando incauta l'altrui volto divo.
    Quinci un lume, ch'al sol toglieva il vanto,
m'abbagliò sí, che non fia che s'appaghe
d'alcun ben altro mai l'anima tanto.   75
    E perch'errando 'l mio stil piú non vaghe,
io partí' per disciôrti dal mio amore,
con le mie piante a fuggir pronte e vaghe.
    So che la lontananza il suo furore
mitiga; e quando tu, del viver sazio,   80
pur vogli amando uscir di vita fuore,
    te, con quest'occhi, e me insieme non strazio.

But earlier still, his gold shaft reached my heart,   70
as I stood firm, incautiously gazing
at the other man's celestial face.
 There a light that robbed the sun of its pride   73
so dazzled me that never will my soul
be as contented by any other love.
 And so my wavering style would no longer stray,   76
I left, to free you from love for me,
with feet eager and longing for flight.
 I know that absence lessens love's fury;   79
and when you, having lived to the full,
still loving, decide to leave life behind,
 with these eyes I'll not torture both you and myself.   82

Capitolo 11

ᴈ

Invero una tu sei, Verona bella,
poi che la mia Veronica gentile
con l'unica bellezza sua t'abbella.
    Quella, a cui non fu mai pari o simíle
d'Adria ninfa leggiadra, or col bel viso   5
t'apporta a mezzo 'l verno un lieto aprile;
    anzi ti fa nel mondo un paradiso
il sol del volto, e degli occhi le stelle,
e 'l tranquillo seren del vago riso;
    ma l'intelletto, che sí chiaro dièlle   10
il celeste Motor a sua sembianza,
unito in lei con l'altre cose belle,
    quegli altri pregi in modo sopravanza,
che l'uman veder nostro non perviene
a mirar tal virtute in tal distanza.   15
    A pena l'occhio corporal sostiene
lo splendor de la fronte, in cui mirando
abbagliato e confuso ne diviene:
    questa la donna mia dolce girando,
l'aria fa tutta sfavillar d'intorno,   20
e pon le nubi e le tempeste in bando.
    Di rose e di vïole il mondo adorno
rende 'l lume del ciglio, con cui lieta
primavera perpetua fa soggiorno.
    Oimè! qual empio influsso di pianeta,   25
unica di quest'occhi e vera luce,
subito mi t'asconde e mi ti vieta?
    Chi 'l nostro paradiso altrove adduce,
Adria, meco perciò dogliosa e trista,
ché 'n tenebre il dí nostro si riduce?   30
    Ogni altro oggetto, lasso me, m'attrista,
or che del vago mio splendor celeste

Capitolo 11

BY AN UNKNOWN AUTHOR, IN PRAISE OF VERONA, WHERE FRANCO IS STAYING

Truly, fair Verona, you are one of a kind, [21]
now that my gentle Veronica
beautifies you with her unique beauty.
    She, who's never had an equal or peer,   4
Adria's nymph, now with her fair face
brings you in midwinter an April full of joy;
    the sun of her face and the stars of her eyes   7
and the calm serenity of her sweet laugh
turn you, indeed, to a heaven on earth;
    but the brilliant intellect that the heavenly Mover   10
gave her, in his image, united
with her other beautiful qualities,
    so far surpasses all those other gifts   13
that our human vision cannot reach far enough
to perceive such great virtue at such a distance.
    The bodily eye can scarcely bear   16
the splendor of her brow; beholding it,
human sight becomes dazzled and dazed:
    this lady of mine, gently turning around,   19
sets the air all about her to sparkling
and banishes tempests and clouds far away.
    The gleam of her eye bedecks the world   22
with roses and violets, and with her,
gay, everlasting spring comes to stay.
    Alas! what cruel planet's influence,   25
unique and truthful light of her eyes,
suddenly hides you and keeps me away?
    Adria, who takes our paradise elsewhere?—   28
so that, like me, you are saddened and grieving,
since our bright day has been turned into darkness?
    Alas, every other object repels me   31
now that I'm denied the sight that I long for,

21. This first line (*Invero una,* "truly unique") sets up a pun similar to those on the name "Veronica" in *capitoli* 1, 7, and 16.

mi si contende la bramata vista.

Ben del pensier con l'egre luci e meste
scorgo Verona invidïosamente,   35
che de' miei danni lieta si riveste.

Veggo, lasso, e rivolgo con la mente
ne l'altrui gioia e ne l'altrui diletto
via piú grave 'l mio danno espressamente.

Adria, per costei fosti almo ricetto   40
di tutto 'l ben ch'a noi dal ciel deriva,
quant'ei ne suol piú dar sommo e perfetto:

or di lei tosto indegnamente priva,
per questa del tuo lido antica sponda
torbido 'l mar risuona in ogni riva.   45

Ben tanto piú si fa lieta e gioconda
Verona, e di fiorito e dolce maggio,
nel maggior nostro verno e ghiaccio, abonda.

Quivi del mio bel sol l'amato raggio
spiega le tante sue bellezze eterne,   50
che d'ir al cielo insegnano il vïaggio.

Per virtú di tal lume in lei si scerne
vestir le piante di novel colore,
e giunger forza a le radici interne.

L'aura soave e 'l prezïoso odore,   55
che da le rose de la bocca spira
questa figlia di Pallade e d'Amore,

nutrimento vital per tutto inspira,
sí ch'a quel refrigerio in un momento
tutto risorge e rinasce e respira;   60

e de la voce angelica il concento
i fiumi affrena, e i monti ad udir move,
e 'l ciel si ferma ad ascoltarla intento:

il ciel, che in Adria piange e ride altrove,
là 've la dolce mia terrena dea   65
grazia e dolcezza dal bel ciglio piove,

e quel ricetto estremamente bea,
dov'ella alberga, per destin felice
d'un altro amante e per mia stella rea.

of my beautiful radiance, bright as the sky.
    Clearly, in my feeble, woeful mind's eye,   34
I enviously see the town of Verona
happily preening herself to my cost;
    amid other people's joy and contentment,   37
I see, alas, and deliberately in my mind,
turn over and over my increasing loss.
    Adria, for her you were the kindly shelter   40
of all the most perfect and highest blessings
that heaven habitually bestows upon us:
    now of her lately and unfairly deprived,   43
along the ancient line of your coast
the troubled sea roars on all of your shores.
    All the more does Verona grow gay and merry,   46
and she abounds in a sweet, flowering May
while we must endure deep winter and hard frost.
    There the dear ray of my beautiful sun   49
displays her multiple, undying graces,
which point out the pathway to heaven.
    Through the force of her bright-shining light   52
plants can be seen taking on new hues
and gaining strength for their hidden roots.
    The mild air and precious scent   55
exhaled from the rosy lips
of this daughter of Pallas and Love[22]
    infuse vital nourishment in every place,   58
so that all at once, from this freshening force,
all rises, is reborn, and inhales anew:
    the harmoniousness of her angelic voice   61
stops rivers in their course and convinces the hills
to pause and listen, and heaven stops, intent on hearing:
    weeping in Adria, the sky, laughing elsewhere,   64
wherever my sweet goddess on earth
rains down sweetness and grace from her eyes,
    pours down every blessing on the place where she dwells,   67
through the fortunate fate of that other lover
and the hard-heartedness of my star to me.

---

22. Pallas (Greek Athena, Roman Minerva) was the goddess of wisdom and the arts.

Altri del mio penar buon frutto elice,   70
del mio bel sol la luce altri si gode,
ed io qui piango nudo ed infelice.
   Ma s'ella 'l mio dolor intende ed ode,
perch'a levarmi l'affamato verme
non vien dal cor, che sí 'l consuma e rode?   75
   E se non m'ode, o mie speranze inferme!
poi che 'l ciel chiude a' miei sospir la strada,
contra cui vano è quanto uom mai si scherme.
   Ma tu sí aventurosa alma contrada,
ch'a pena un tanto ben capi e ricevi,   80
qual chi confuso in gran dolcezza cada,
   d'Adria i diletti, a fuggir pronti e lievi,
mira, e dal nostro danno accorta stima
il volar de' tuoi dí fugaci e brevi.
   Or ti vedi riposta ad alta cima,   85
né pensi forse come d'alto grado
le cose eccelse la fortuna adima:
   stabil non è di qua giú 'l bene, e rado
piú d'un momento dura, e 'l pianto e 'l duolo
trova per mezzo l'allegrezza il guado.   90
   Ma pur felice aventuroso suolo,
che quel momento al goder nostro dato
possiedi un ben cosí perfetto e solo.
   Pian, poggio, fonte e bosco fortunato,
ch'a un guardo, a un sol toccar del vago piede,   95
forma prendete di celeste stato,
   l'alto e novo miracol, che 'n voi siede,
a farvi basti, in tanto spazio, eterno
tutto quel ben ch'al suo venir vi diede:
   sí che mai non v'offenda o ghiaccio o verno,   100
ned altro influsso rio, ma sempre in voi
sia la stagion de' fior lieta in eterno;
   pur che tosto colei ritorni a noi,
al nido ov'ella nacque, che senz'essa
mena tristi ed oscuri i giorni suoi.   105
   Deh torna, luce mia, del raggio impressa

Another man makes good gain from my loss,   70
another enjoys the light of my fair sun,
and I, stripped bare, weep in misery here.

But if she hears and understands my grief,   73
why doesn't she come to remove from my heart
the famished worm that devours and gnaws it?

And if she hears me not, woe to my frail hopes!   76
for the sky cuts off any path for my sighs,
and against the sky man struggles in vain.

But you, countryside so blessed and fertile,   79
who've just taken in and welcomed such a boon,
like a man overwhelmed by falling into bliss,

look on those delights, so quick and so swift   82
to leave Adria behind; and wiser for our loss,
judge how brief and fleeting is the passing of your days.

Now you see yourself up at the top   85
and perhaps don't consider how from any peak
fortune can bring down the highest things;

Here on earth there is no good that's stable,   88
rarely does it last more than a moment,
and even in joy, tears and grief find their way.

But happy and fortunate country indeed,   91
that at that moment given for our pleasure,
you possess a good so perfect and unique.

Plain, hill, fountain, and wood blessed by fate,   94
for at a glance, at one touch of her fair foot,
you take on the form of a heavenly place.

May the high, unheard of miracle   97
dwelling within you preserve forever
all the good brought you by her arrival:

may neither ice nor winter nor any other harm   100
ever wound you, but may the flowery season
remain with you forever,

provided that she returns to us soon,   103
to the place she was born, which, now without her,
lives out its days in sadness and shadow.

Pray, my dear light, do come back,   106

de la divinità, qui dove mai
pianger la tua partita non si cessa.
    Tempo è di ritornar, madonna, omai
a consolar de la vostr'alma vista   110
di questa patria i desïosi rai,
    a dar a la mia mente inferma e trista,
col dolce oggetto del bel vostro lume,
rimedio contra 'l duol che sí l'attrista:
    e se troppo 'l mio cor di voi presume,   115
datemi in pena che del vago volto
da vicin lo splendor m'arda e consume;
    né de' begli occhi altrove sia rivolto
il doppio sol, fin che 'n polve minuta
non mi vediate dal mio incendio vòlto;   120
    e per farlo, affrettate la venuta.

marked by the ray of divinity, to the place
which never ceases to mourn for your going.

    It is time, my lady, at last to return,   109
to bring comfort, with your blessed sight,
to the longing eyes of this, your native land,

    and to grant my ailing and sorrowful mind   112
by the sweet visibility of your fair light
a remedy for the woe that so aggrieves it:

    and if my heart demands too much of you,   115
let my penance be that your fair face's splendor
may consume and burn me at close hand;

    and let the double sun of those lovely eyes   118
be turned nowhere else, until you see me
reduced to fine dust by this fire of mine.

    And in order to do this, speed your return.   121

Capitolo 12

～

Oh quanto per voi meglio si faría,
se quel che 'l cielo ingegno alto vi diede
riconosceste con piú cortesia,
    sí ch'a impiegarlo in quel che piú si chiede
veniste, disdegnando il mondo frale,   5
che quei piú inganna, che gli tien piú fede;
    e se lodaste pur cosa mortale,
lasciando quel ch'è sol del senso oggetto,
lodar quel ch'al giudicio ancor poi vale,
    lodar d'Adria il felice almo ricetto,   10
che, benché sia terreno, ha forma vera
di cielo in terra a Dio caro e diletto:
    questa materia del vostro ingegno era,
e non gir poetando vanamente,
oblïando la via del ver primiera.   15
    Senza discorrer poeticamente,
senza usar l'iperbolica figura,
ch'è pur troppo bugiarda apertamente,
    si poteva impiegar la vostra cura
in lodando Vinegia, singolare   20
meraviglia e stupor de la natura.
    Questa dominatrice alta del mare,
regal vergine pura, invïolata,
nel mondo senza essempio e senza pare,
    questa da voi deveva esser lodata,   25
vostra patria gentile, in cui nasceste,
e dov'anch'io, la Dio mercé, son nata;
    ma voi le meraviglie raccoglieste
d'altro paese; e de la mia persona,
quel ch'Amor cieco vi dettò, diceste.   30
    Una invero è, qual dite voi, Verona,
per le qualità proprie di se stessa,

Capitolo 12

FRANCO'S RESPONSE, IN WHICH SHE ADVISES THE POET
TO WRITE IN PRAISE OF VENICE

Oh, how much better you would do
if you acknowledged with greater courtesy
the lofty intellect heaven gave you
    by using it in a more fitting way,   4
disdaining the frail world, which more
disappoints a man the more he has faith in it:
    and, if you had to praise a mortal thing,   7
leaving behind what pleases only the senses,
you were to praise what good judgment values more:
    you praised Adria, the blessed, noble retreat,   10
which, earthly though it is, has the true form
of heaven on earth, precious and dear to God.
    This was a subject fit for your intellect,   13
not wandering off in vain versifying,
forgetful of the pathway of primal truth.
    Without running on in poetical fashion,   16
without using hyperbolic figures of speech,
which are all too clearly obvious lies,
    you might have turned your attention instead   19
to praising Venice, the one and only
miracle and wonder of nature.
    This high ruler of the sea,   22
lofty virgin, inviolate and pure,
without equivalent or peer in the world,
    this is what you should have praised,   25
this gentle land, in which you were born,
and where I, too, thank God, was born;
    but you gathered together the marvels   28
of another city, and you said of me
what blind Love dictated to you.
    Verona is indeed unique, as you say,   31
but for her own qualities,

e non per quel che da voi si ragiona;
   ma tanto piú Vinegia è bella d'essa,
quanto è piú bel del mondo il paradiso,   35
la cui beltà fu a Vinegia concessa.
   In modo dal mondan tutto diviso,
fabricata è Vinegia sopra l'acque,
per sopranatural celeste aviso:
   in questa il Re del cielo si compiacque   40
di fondar il sicuro, eterno nido
de la sua fé, ch'altrove oppressa giacque;
   e pose a suo diletto in questo lido
tutto quel bel, tutta quella dolcezza,
che sia di maggior vanto e maggior grido.   45
   Gioia non darsi altrove al mondo avezza
in tal copia in Vinegia il ciel ripose,
che chi non la conosce, non l'apprezza.
   Questo al vostro giudicio non s'ascose,
che de le cose piú eccellenti ha gusto;   50
ma poi la benda agli occhi Amor vi pose:
   dal costui foco il vostro cor combusto,
vi mandò agli occhi de la mente il fumo,
che vi fece veder falso e non giusto.
   Ned io di me tai menzogne presumo,   55
quai voi spiegaste, ben con tai maniere,
che dal modo del dir diletto assumo;
   ma non perciò conosco per non vere
le trascendenti lodi che mi date,
sí che mi son con noia di piacere.   60
   Ma se pur tal di me concetto fate,
perch'al nido, ov'io nacqui, non si pensa
da voi, e 'n ciò perch'ognor nol lodate?
   Perch'ad altr'opra il pensier si dispensa,
se per voi deve un loco esser lodato,   65
che dia al mio spirto posa e ricompensa?
   Ricercando del ciel per ogni lato,
se ben discorre in molte parti il sole,
però vien l'orïente piú stimato:

not for those you attribute to her;
    but the beauty of Venice exceeds hers   34
as far as the earth is surpassed by paradise,
with whose beauty Venice was endowed.

    In a way set apart from what is seen on earth,   37
Venice was built upon the waters
according to supernatural, heavenly intent:

    In her the King of heaven took pleasure   40
in founding the secure, eternal nest
of his faith, which elsewhere lay oppressed,

    and for his own delight he placed on this shore   43
all the beauty and all the sweetness
that is most acclaimed and praised on earth.

    Nowhere else in the world is used to the joy   46
that heaven bestowed so abundantly on Venice,
so that whoever does not know her cannot appreciate her.

    This was not concealed from your judgment,   49
which has a taste for the most excellent things;
but Love at the time blindfolded your eyes,

    and your heart, burned by his flame,   52
sent smoke up into your mind's eye,
which made you see falsely, not according to truth.

    Nor do I believe such lies about myself   55
as those you invented in so mannered a way
that I do take some pleasure in the style;

    but on that account I do not take as true   58
the high-flown praises that you give to me,
which leave me both flattered and annoyed.

    But if you make such a conceit even of me,   61
why do you not consider the place I was born,
and why do you not constantly sing its praise?

    Why do you devote your thought to other tasks,   64
if you must praise some place or another
that can give repose and reward to my spirit?

    Looking at the sky from one side or the other,   67
we see that the sun moves all the way through it,
yet we still esteem most highly the east:

perché quasi dal fonte Febo suole   70
quindi spiegar il suo divino raggio,
quando aprir ai mortali il giorno vuole;
    cosí anch'io 'n questo e in ogni altro vïaggio,
senza col sol però paragonarmi,
per mio orïente, alma Venezia, t'aggio.   75
    Questa, se in piacer v'era dilettarmi,
dovevate lodar, e con tal modo
al mio usato soggiorno richiamarmi.
    Lunge da lei, di nullo altro ben godo,
se non ch'io spero che la lontananza   80
dal mio vi scioglia o leghi a l'altrui nodo.
    Continuando in cotal mia speranza,
prolungherò piú ch'io potrò 'l ritorno:
tal che m'amiate ha lo sdegno possanza!
    Cosí vuol chi nel cor mi fa soggiorno: 85
amor di tal, che per vostra vendetta
forse non meno il mio riceve a scorno;
    ma, come sia, non ritornerò in fretta.

for here Phoebus, as if from his source,   70
looses his divine ray when he desires
to open up the day for mortal beings:

so I, too, in this and any other voyage,   73
though without equaling myself to the sun,
think of you, dear Venice, as my east.

You should have praised her, if your will   76
was to please me, and in that way, to call me
back to the place where I usually live.

Away from her, I enjoy nothing else,   79
except to hope that our separation may free you
from your bond to me or tie you to another.

Persisting in this hope of mine,   82
I will delay my return as long as I can:
so much do I disdain your love for me!

This is what the man who dwells in my heart wants: 85
whose love, perhaps to right your wrong,
responds to mine with no less scorn; but

be that as it may, I will not come back soon.   88

Capitolo 13

⌁

Non piú parole: ai fatti, in campo, a l'armi,
ch'io voglio, risoluta di morire,
da sí grave molestia liberarmi.
　　Non so se 'l mio « cartel » si debba dire,
in quanto do risposta provocata: 5
ma perché in rissa de' nomi venire?
　　Se vuoi, da te mi chiamo disfidata;
e se non, ti disfido; o in ogni via
la prendo, ed ogni occasïon m'è grata.
　　Il campo o l'armi elegger a te stia,   10
ch'io prenderò quel che tu lascerai;
anzi pur ambo nel tuo arbitrio sia.
　　Tosto son certa che t'accorgerai
quanto ingrato e di fede mancatore
fosti, e quanto tradito a torto m'hai.   15
　　E se non cede l'ira al troppo amore,
con queste proprie mani, arditamente
ti trarrò fuor del petto il vivo core.
　　La falsa lingua, ch'in mio danno mente,
sterperò da radice, pria ben morsa   20
dentro 'l palato dal suo proprio dente;
　　e se mia vita in ciò non fia soccorsa,
pur disperata prenderò in diletto
d'esser al sangue in vendetta ricorsa;
　　poi col coltel medesmo il proprio petto,   25
de la tua occisïon sazia e contenta,
forse aprirò, pentita de l'effetto.
　　Or, mentre sono al vendicarmi intenta,
entra in steccato, amante empio e rubello,
e qualunque armi vuoi tosto appresenta.   30
　　Vuoi per campo il segreto albergo, quello
che de l'amare mie dolcezze tante

Capitolo 13

A CHALLENGE TO A LOVER WHO HAS OFFENDED HER

No more words! To deeds, to the battlefield, to arms!
For, resolved to die, I want to free myself
from such merciless mistreatment.
    Should I call this a challenge? I do not know,   4
since I am responding to a provocation;
but why should we duel over words?
    If you like, I will say that you've challenged me;   7
if not, I challenge you; I'll take any route,
and any opportunity suits me equally well.
    Yours be the choice of place or of arms,   10
and I will make whatever choice remains;
rather, let both be your decision.
    At once, I am sure, you will realize   13
how ungrateful and faithless you have been
and how wrongfully you have betrayed me.
    And unless my rage yields to overwhelming love,   16
with these very hands I will, in all boldness,
tear your living heart from your very breast.
    The deceiving tongue that lies to do me harm   19
I will tear out by its root, after it's been bitten
against the palate with repentant teeth;
    and if this brings no relief to my life,   22
abandoning all hope, I will rejoice
at having turned to bloodshed for my revenge.
    Then, with the same knife, my own breast,   25
satisfied and appeased by slaying you,
I may cut open, regretting my deed.
    Now, while I'm intent on pursuing revenge,   28
enter the arena, cruel, rebellious lover,
and present at once whatever arms you wish.
    Do you wish, for the field, the secret inn   31
that, hardhearted and deceptive, once watched

mi fu ministro insidïoso e fello?

Or mi si para il mio letto davante,
ov'in grembo t'accolsi, e ch'ancor l'orme   35
serba dei corpi in sen l'un l'altro stante.

Per me in lui non si gode e non si dorme,
ma 'l lagrimar de la notte e del giorno
vien che in fiume di pianto mi trasforme.

Ma pur questo medesimo soggiorno,   40
che fu de le mie gioie amato nido,
dov'or sola in tormento e 'n duol soggiorno,

per campo eleggi, accioch'altrove il grido
non giunga, ma qui teco resti spento,
del tuo inganno ver' me, crudele infido: 45

qui vieni, e pien di pessimo talento,
accomodato al tristo officio porta
ferro acuto e da man ch'abbia ardimento.

Quell'arme, che da te mi sarà pòrta,
prenderò volontier, ma piú, se molto   50
tagli, e da offender sia ben salda e corta.

Dal petto ignudo ogni arnese sia tolto,
al fin ch'ei, disarmato a le ferite,
possa 'l valor mostrar dentro a sé accolto.

Altri non s'impedisca in questa lite,   55
ma da noi soli due, ad uscio chiuso,
rimosso ogni padrin, sia diffinita.

Quest'è d'arditi cavalier buon uso,
ch'attendon senza strepito a purgarsi,
se si senton l'onor di macchie infuso: 60

cosí o vengon soli ad accordarsi,
o se strada non trovano di pace,
pòn del sangue a vicenda sazïarsi.

Di tal modo combatter a me piace,
e d'acerba vendetta al desir mio   65
questa maniera serve e sodisface.

Benché far del tuo sangue un largo rio
spero senz'alcun dubbio, anzi son certa,
senza una stilla spargerne sol io;

over so many of my now bitter delights?

    Here before me now stands the bed   34
where I took you in my arms, and which still
preserves the imprint of our bodies, breast to breast.

    In it I find now neither joy nor sleep,   37
but only weeping, by night and by day,
which transforms me into a river of tears.

    But this very place, which once was   40
the cherished shelter of my joys,
where I now live alone, in torment and grief,

    choose this as a battleground, so that the news   43
of your betrayal will reach no other place
but die here with you, cruel, faithless man.

    Come here, and, full of most wicked desire,   46
braced stiff for your sinister task,
bring with daring hand a piercing blade.

    Whatever weapon you hand over to me,   49
I will gladly take, especially if it is sharp
and sturdy and also quick to wound.

    Let all armor be stripped from your naked breast,   52
so that, unshielded and exposed to blows,
it may reveal the valor it harbors within.

    Let no one else intervene in this match,   55
let it be limited to the two of us alone,
behind closed doors, with all seconds sent away.

    This is the custom of noble knights,   58
who, without clamor, strive to clear their names
when they consider their honor to be stained:

    either they reach an agreement on their own,   61
or, if they can find no road to peace,
they may sate their thirst for each other's blood.

    This is the style in which I like to fight,   64
and this manner fulfills and satisfies
my desire for bitter revenge.

    Although I hope, without any doubt, to spill   67
a river of your blood—indeed, I am certain
I can, without shedding a drop of my own—

ma se da te mi sia la pace offerta?   70
se la via prendi, l'armi poste in terra,
a le risse d'amor del letto aperta?

   Debbo continuar teco anco in guerra,
poi che chi non perdona altrui richiesto,
con nota di viltà trascorre ed erra?   75

   Quando tu meco pur venissi a questo,
per aventura io non mi partirei
da quel ch'è convenevole ed onesto.

   Forse nel letto ancor ti seguirei,
e quivi, teco guerreggiando stesa,   80
in alcun modo non ti cederei:

   per soverchiar la tua sí indegna offesa
ti verrei sopra, e nel contrasto ardita,
scaldandoti ancor tu ne la difesa,

   teco morrei d'egual colpo ferita.   85
O mie vane speranze, onde la sorte
crudel a pianger piú sempre m'invita!

   Ma pur sostienti, cor sicuro e forte,
e con l'ultimo strazio di quell'empio
vendica mille tue con la sua morte;   90
   poi con quel ferro ancor tronca il tuo scempio.

what if you were to offer me peace? 70
What if, all weapons laid aside, you took
the path opened to a love match in bed?

Must I continue to battle against you, 73
since whoever refuses pardon when asked
wends his erring way reputed a coward?

When you finally came to this point 76
with me, I'd not, perhaps, depart
from what is decent and proper to do.

Perhaps I would even follow you to bed, 79
and, stretched out there in skirmishes with you,
I would yield to you in no way at all.

To take revenge for your unfair attack, 82
I'd fall upon you, and in daring combat,
as you too caught fire defending yourself,

I would die with you, felled by the same blow. 85
Oh, empty hopes, over which cruel fate
forces me to weep forever!

But hold firm, my strong, undaunted heart, 88
and with that felon's final destruction,
avenge your thousand deaths with his one.

Then end your agony with the same blade. 91

Capitolo 14

ᘐ

Non piú guerra, ma pace: e gli odi, l'ire,
e quanto fu di disparer tra noi,
si venga in amor doppio a convertire.
    La mia causa io rimetto in tutto a voi,
con patto che, per fin de le contese,   5
amici piú che mai restiamo poi:
    non mi basta che l'armi sian sospese,
ma, per stabilimento de la pace,
d'ogni parte si lievino l'offese.
    Che nascesse tra noi rissa, mi spiace;   10
ma se lo sdegno in amor s'augumenta,
che tra noi si sdegnassimo, mi piace:
    e se pur ragion vuol ch'io mi risenta
e vendicata sia l'ingiuria mia,
de la qual foste ognor ministra intenta,   15
    voglio con l'armi de la cortesia
invincibil durar tanto a la pugna,
che conosciuto alfin vincitor sia.
    Né questo da l'amor grande repugna,
anzi con queste e non mai con altre armi   20
ogni spirto magnanimo s'oppugna.
    O se voleste incontra armata starmi,
se voleste tentar, con forza tale,
se possibil vi sia di superarmi,
    fôra 'l mio stato a quel di Giove eguale;   25
forse troppo è la speranza ardita,
che studia di volar non avendo ale.
    Somma felicità de la mia vita
sarebbe, in questo stato, che teneste
da nuocermi la mente disunita;   30
    ma s'a l'opere mie ben attendeste,
cosí precipitosa ne lo sdegno

Capitolo 14

FROM THE MAN WHOM FRANCO CHALLENGED IN 13, INVITING HER TO MAKE PEACE WITH HIM

No more war, but peace! and may the hate and rage,
and whatever disagreement has arisen between us
be transformed into twice as much love.

    I entrust my case completely to you,   4
on the condition that, to end our quarrel,
we remain better friends than we ever were.

    To me it's not enough that we hang up our weapons,   7
but to ensure peace, let attacks
be put an end to on both sides.

    I am sorry that strife rose up between us;   10
but if disdain grows into love,
I am glad that we felt disdain for each other;

    and even though reason requires of me   13
that I resent and avenge the injury
that you were always intent on dispensing to me,

    I intend, through the use of the weapons of courtesy,   16
to stand up so well to this battle, unvanquished,
that in the end I am acclaimed the victor.

    True love has no objection to this;   19
with these and never with any other weapons
every great-hearted spirit undertakes battle.

    Oh, if you were willing to face me, armed yourself,   22
if you wanted to test, with such strength,
whether you are able to overcome me,

    my state would be equal to that of Jove;   25
but perhaps my hope is too daring,
for it seeks to fly without wings.

    The greatest happiness of my life   28
would be, in this state, that you changed
your mind from doing me harm;

    but if you had really considered my deeds,   31
you would not have been so sudden

a ciascun passo meco non sareste.
    L'ira è bensí de l'affezzïon segno,
ma che attende a introdur nel nostro petto,   35
quanto può, l'odio con acuto ingegno;
    cosí 'l languir, giacendo infermo in letto,
segno è di vita, perché l'uom ch'è morto
cosa alcuna patir non può in effetto:
    ben per l'infermità vien altri scorto   40
a morir, e quant'è piú 'l mal possente,
al fin s'affretta in termine piú corto.
    Del vostro sdegno súbito ed ardente,
s'è in voi punto ver' me d'amore, attendo
che siano tutte le reliquie spente.   45
    E per questo talvolta anch'io m'accendo,
e non per ira, ma per dolor molto,
batto le man, vocifero e contendo:
    vedermi del mio amor il premio tolto,
né questo pur, ma in altretanta pena   50
vederlomi in su gli occhi (oimè!) rivolto,
    per disperazïon questo mi mena
a quel che piú mi spiace; e pur l'eleggo,
poi che 'l preciso danno assai s'affrena.
    Con la necessità mi volgo e reggo,   55
da poi che la rüina manifesta
de le speranze mie tutte preveggo;
    ma non perciò nel cor sempre mi resta
di piacervi talento e di servirvi,
anzi in me piú tal brama ognor si desta.   60
    La mia ragion verrei talvolta a dirvi,
ma perché so che romor ne sarebbe,
col silenzio m'ingegno d'obedirvi.
    Non so, ma forse ch'a taluno increbbe
del viver nostro insieme; che 'l suo tòsco,   65
nel nostro dolce a spargerlo, pronto ebbe.
    Insomma, dal mio canto non conosco
d'avervi offeso, se 'l mio amor estremo
meritar pena non m'ha fatto vosco;

at every moment to feel disdain for me.
    Anger is indeed a sign of affection,   34
but it attempts to put into our breasts,
as much as it can, hatred and sharp wit.
    In the same way, languishing weakly in bed   37
is a sign of life, for a man who is dead
cannot endure anything, in fact;
    by illness another is led on to death,   40
and the more powerful his disease,
the faster he hastens to his end.
    If there is even a little love in you   43
for me, may it be that all the remains
of your sudden and burning disdain are extinguished.
    On this account I myself sometimes burn,   46
and not from anger but from great pain
I clap my hands, cry out, and fight myself;
    to see my love's reward snatched away from me,   49
and not only this, but to see it transformed
into equal pain, alas, before my very eyes—
    this leads me, through desperation,   52
to what I most dislike; and even so, I choose it,
for in this way the hurt is somewhat subdued.
    I behave and obey as necessity demands,   55
given that I see ahead of me now
the obvious destruction of all my hopes;
    but even so, in my heart stays forever   58
the desire to please and to serve you;
indeed, this longing arises every moment.
    I would sometimes come to defend myself to you,   61
but since I know there would be gossip about it,
in silence I devise ways to obey you.
    I am not sure, but perhaps someone was offended   64
by our living together, so that he was quick
to scatter his poison over our sweetness.
    In short, I do not see how on my side   67
I have offended you, unless my extreme love
has made me deserve pain from you.

ma seguite, crudel: questo mai scemo   70
non diverrà, ma nel mio cor profondo
vivo si serberà fino a l'estremo.
 Vivrà di questo il mio pensier giocondo,
benché per tal cagion di pianto amaro,
di lamenti e sospiri e doglia abondo.   75
 Ecco che nel düello mi preparo,
con l'armi del mio mal, de le mie pene,
de l'innocenzia mia sotto 'l riparo.
 Non so se 'l vostro orgoglio ne diviene
maggior, o se s'appiana, mentre mira   80
ch'io verso 'l pianto da le luci piene:
  ben talor l'umiltà estingue l'ira,
ma poi talor l'accende, onde quest'alma
tra speranza e timor dubbia si gira.
 Ma d'armi tali pur sotto aspra salma,   85
mi rendo in campo a voi, madonna, vinto,
e nuda porgo a voi la destra palma.
 Se non s'è l'odio nel cor vostro estinto,
mi sia da voi col preparato ferro
un mortal colpo in mezzo 'l petto spinto: 90
  pur troppo armata, e so ben ch'io non erro,
contra me sète; ed io del seno ignudo
l'adito ai vostri colpi ancor non serro.
 Quel dolce sguardo umanamente crudo
son l'armi ond'ancidete il tristo core,   95
in cui viva, bench'empia, ognor vi chiudo;
  gli strali e 'l foco e 'l laccio son d'Amore
l'alte vostre bellezze, a me negate,
onde cresce 'l desio, la speme more.
 Queste in mio danno, aspra guerriera, usate,   100
e quanto piú di lor sète gagliarda,
tanto piú pronta a le ferite siate.
 Qual cosa dal ferirmi vi ritarda?
Forse vi giova che d'acerba fiamma,
senza morir, per voi languisca ed arda.   105
 Lasso, ch'io mi distruggo a dramma a dramma,

But, cruel one, go on as you are;   70
this love of mine will never decrease,
but deep in my heart, it will live till the end;
   my joyful thought will live on this,   73
even though I abound for this reason
in bitter tears and sighs and laments.
   So now I ready myself for our duel,   76
armed with my suffering and with my sorrows,
underneath the shield of my innocence.
   I do not know whether your pride   79
will increase or be milder as a result
when you see me weep with eyes full of tears;
   often humility extinguishes anger,   82
yet sometimes it fuels it; so my doubtful soul
hesitates between hope and fear.
   But with such weapons, heavily burdened,   85
I enter the field, defeated already,
and offer you, lady, my bare right hand.
   If the hatred has not died down in your heart,   88
may a mortal blow from your ready sword
be struck into the center of my breast;
   you are—and I know I'm not wrong—   91
armed against me all too well, and I do not even shield
my naked breast against your penetrating blows.
   That sweet glance, kindly cruel,   94
is the weapon with which you slay my sad heart,
in which, living, I enclose you, fierce as you are;
   Love's arrows, his fire and his bow   97
are your high beauties, denied to me,
so that my desire grows, my hope expires.
   Use these to harm me, fierce warrior,   100
and to the extent that you're braver than they,
by so much be quicker to deal me wounds.
   What delays you from striking me?   103
It does you good, perhaps, that in biting flame,
without dying, I languish and burn for you.
   Alas, I'm destroyed, little by little,   106

né de la mia nemica il mio gran foco
punto il gelido petto accende o infiamma:
    ella si prende i miei martíri in gioco,
misero me, ché pur a nòve piaghe   110
dentro 'l mio petto non si trova loco.
    Di quella fronte e de le luci vaghe,
e del dolce parlar fûr gli aspri colpi,
che 'n parte fêr quell'empie voglie paghe.
    Volete ch'io non pianga e non v'incolpi,   115
e di quanto in mio scempio avete fatto
di voi mi lodi, e non sol vi discolpi?
    L'armi prendete ad impiagarmi ratto,
e 'l mio duol disgombrando con la morte,
fate degno di voi magnanimo atto.   120
    A riconcilïar l'irata sorte,
onde 'l ciel mi minaccia oltraggio e scorno,
pigliate in man la spada, ardita e forte.
    Ecco che disarmato a voi ritorno,
e per finir il pianto a qualche strada,   125
ai vostri piedi umil mi volgo intorno:
    del vostro sdegno la tagliente spada,
s'altro non giova, omai prendete in mano,
e sopra me ferendo altèra cada.
    Ripetete pur via di mano in mano,   130
mentre dal segno alcun colpo non erra,
e che l'oggetto avete non lontano:
    breve fatica queste membra atterra,
lacere e tronche d'amorosa doglia,
non punto accinte a contrastar in guerra;   135
    e s'ancor ben potessi, non n'ho voglia,
ma di morirvi inanzi eleggo, pria
ch'alcun riparo in mia difesa toglia.
    Potete, se vi piace, essermi ria;
e quando usar l'asprezza non vi piaccia,   140
potete, se vi piace, essermi pia.
    Quanto a me, pur ch'a voi si sodisfaccia,
vi dono sopra me podestà franca,

but my great fire does not inflame
my enemy's icy breast at all.

    Instead, she makes light of my torments.   109
Oh, woe is me, for in my breast
no room at all remains for new wounds.

    From that forehead and those lovely eyes   112
and that sweet speech came the hard blows
that partly satisfied those cruel desires.

    Do you want me not to weep or blame you,   115
and to praise you for how much harm
you've done me, not only to excuse you?

    Take up your weapons to wound me at once,   118
and, relieving my suffering with my death,
perform a great feat worthy of your honor.

    To make peace at last with my angry fate,   121
through which heaven assails me with outrage and scorn,
daring and strong, take your sword in hand.

    Here I am, returning to you unarmed,   124
and to end my lament by some route or another,
I bow down, humble, at your feet;

    if nothing else pleases you, take up in your hand 127
the cutting sword of your disdain
and let it fall, indignant, on me.

    Strike your blows, with one hand and the other, 130
while not one blow misses the mark
and you have your target not far from you;

    one quick effort will fell these limbs to the ground, 133
torn and cut off through the pain of love,
not girded at all to do battle in warfare.

    And even if I could, I do not wish to,   136
but I choose to die in front of you instead,
before I seek shelter in self-defense.

    You can, if you wish, be heartless to me;   139
and when you no longer enjoy using cruelty,
you can, if you like, be compassionate to me.

    As for myself, as long as you are satisfied,   142
I grant you complete dominion over me,

legato piedi e mani e gambe e braccia;
e vi mando per fede carta bianca,   145
ch'abbiate del mio cor dominio vero,
sí che veruna parte non vi manca.
Del resto assai desío piú, che non spero,
né so se in via di strazïar m'abbiate
fatto l'invito, o se pur da dovero.   150
Aspetterò che voi me n'accertiate.

bound hand and foot, and legs and arms;
    and I send you, in faith, carte blanche   145
to have total sovereignty over my heart,
so that no part of it does not belong to you.
    Altogether, I wish for far more than I hope,   148
nor do I know if you made your invitation
to torture me or because you truly meant it.
    I shall wait for you to tell me which is the case.   151

Capitolo 15

⤳

Signor, ha molti giorni ch'io non fui
(come doveva) a farvi riverenza:
di che biasmata son forse d'altrui;
    ma se da far se n'ha giusta sentenza,
le mie ragioni ascoltar pria si dènno   5
da me scritte, o formate a la presenza:
    che, quanto dritte ed accettabili ènno,
non voglio ch'altri s'impedisca, e solo
giudicar lascerò dal vostro senno.
    Con questo in tanti mali mi consolo,   10
che non sète men savio che cortese,
e che pietà sentite del mio duolo:
    sí che s'alcun di questo mi riprese,
ch'a voi d'alquanto tempo io non sia stata,
prodotte avrete voi le mie difese.   15
    Io so pur troppo che da la brigata
far mal giudizio de le cose s'usa,
senza aver la ragion prima ascoltata.
    Signor, non solo io son degna di scusa,
ma che ciascun, c'ha gentil cor, m'ascolti   20
di tristo pianto con la faccia infusa.
    Non posso non tener sempre rivolti
i sentimenti e l'animo e l'ingegno
ai gravosi martír dentro a me accolti,
    sí ch'ora ch'a scusarmi con voi vegno,   25
entra la lingua a dir del mio dolore,
e di lui ragionar sempre convegno;
    benché quest'è mia scusa, che l'amore
ch'io porto ad uom gentile a maraviglia
mi confonde la vita e toglie il core;   30
    anzi pur dal girar de le sue ciglia
la mia vita depende e la mia morte,

Capitolo 15

TO DOMENICO VENIER, WHOM SHE HAS NOT BEEN
ABLE TO VISIT

Sir, for many days I did not come
(as I should have) to pay you my respects,
for which perhaps I may be blamed by some;

but if just sentence is to be decreed,   4
first my reasons must be heard,
in written form or in your presence;

I do not want another party to intrude   7
into whether my reasons are sufficient and true,
and only your wisdom shall be the judge.

Amid so much trouble, it comforts me   10
that you are no less wise than courteous,
and that you feel pity for my sorrow;

so much so that if someone reproached me   13
for not having come to see you in some time,
you would have come to my defense.

I know only too well that our circle   16
is bound to judge matters for the worse,
without hearing first what the reason might be.

Sir, I deserve not only to be pardoned   19
but to be heard as well by all those
of gentle heart, while sad tears drench my face.

I cannot help constantly turning   22
my feelings, my soul, and my intellect
to the heavy woes gathered within me;

so that now, as I come to excuse myself to you,   25
my tongue enters in to speak of my distress,
and I always come around to speaking of him.

But this is my excuse: the love I bear   28
a man, noble to a wondrous degree,
confounds my life and robs me of my heart;

indeed, my life depends, as does my death,   31
on the slightest movement of his brow,

e quindi gioia e duol l'anima piglia.
    Permesso alfine ha la mia iniqua sorte
che 'n preda del suo amor m'abbandonassi,   35
di che fíen l'ore del mio viver corte;
    ed ei, crudel, da me volgendo i passi,
quando piú bramo la sua compagnia,
fuor de la nostra comun patria vassi:
    senza curar de la miseria mia,   40
a far l'instanti ferie altrove è gito,
ma d'avantaggio andò sei giorni pria;
    di ch'è rimaso in me duolo infinito,
e 'l core e l'alma e 'l meglio di me tutto,
col mio amante, da me s'è dipartito.   45
    Corpo dal pianto e dal dolor distrutto,
ne l'allegrezza senza sentimento,
rimasta son del languir preda in tutto:
    quinci 'l passo impedito, e non pur lento,
ebbi a venir in quella vostra stanza,   50
secondo 'l mio devere e 'l mio talento,
    peroché i membri avea senza possanza,
priva d'alma; e se in me di lei punto era,
dietro 'l mio ben n'andava per usanza.
    Cosí passava il dí fino a la sera,   55
e le notti piú lunghe eran di quelle
ch'ad Alcmena Giunone fêr provar fiera:
    sovra le piume al mio posar rubelle,
non ritrovando requie nel martíre,
d'Amor, di lui doleami, e de le stelle.   60
    Standomi senza lui volea morire:
spesso levai, e ricorsi agli inchiostri,
né confusa sapea che poi mi dire.
    Ben prego sempre Amor che gli dimostri
le mie miserie e 'l suo gran fallo espresso,   65
oltre a tanti da me segni fuor mostri.
    Certo da un canto e lungamente e spesso
egli m'ha scritto in questa sua partita,
ed ancor piú di quel che m'ha promesso:

and so my soul receives both joy and woe.

    At last my cruel fate has allowed me   34
to abandon myself, prey to love for him,
so cutting short the hours of my life;

    and he, cruel man, walking away from me   37
when I most long for his company,
has left the country that is home to us both.

    With no concern for my wretched state,   40
he has traveled elsewhere to spend these holidays,
and, worse, he left six days early;

    so that endless grief has stayed with me,   43
and my heart and soul and all that's best in me
have departed from me along with my lover.

    With my body wracked by weeping and pain,   46
in the midst of joy without any feeling,
I remain entirely prey to languor.

    So with halting step, not only slow,   49
I had to make my way into your room,
following my duty and my desire,

    and yet I felt my limbs deprived of strength   52
and myself bereft of soul; and if in it anything
of myself was left, it had gone, as usual, after him.

    And so the day led on to evening   55
and the nights were longer still
than those fierce Juno made Alcmena endure;[23]

    upon the pillows, unfriendly to my rest,   58
finding no respite in my misery,
I upbraided Love, and him, and my stars.

    Being without him, I wanted to die,   61
often I rose and took up my inks,
but in my daze, I knew not what to say.

    At all hours I pray Love to make him see   64
my miseries and his own deliberate wrong,
and the many signs of love I've shown.

    On one hand, in his absence, certainly   67
he has written often and at length
and even more than he promised he would;

23. Juno was jealous of Alcmena, the wife of Amphitrion, because Jove, disguised as her hus-
band, transformed the single night he spent with her into three nights. In revenge, Juno made
Alcmena suffer seven days in labor before she gave birth to Hercules (Ovid, *Metamorphoses*,
9.281–312).

col suo cortese scrivermi la vita   70
senza dubbio m'ha reso, ed io 'l ringrazio
con un pensier ch'a sperar ben m'invita.
    Da l'altra parte intento a lo mio strazio,
poiché senza di sé mi lascia, io 'l veggo,
e ch'ei sta senza me sí lungo spazio.   75
    Le sue lettere mandatemi ognor leggo,
e tenendole innanzi a lor rispondo,
e parte a la mia doglia in ciò proveggo.
    Alti sospir dal cor m'escon profondo
nel legger le sue carte e in far risposte,   80
piene di quel languir che in petto ascondo.
    In ciò fûr tutte dispensate e poste
l'ore; e del mio signor basciava in loco
le sue grate e dolcissime proposte.
    Peggio che morta, in suon tremante e fioco   85
sempre chiamarlo lagrimando assente,
il mio sol rifugio era e 'l mio gioco:
    e desïandol meco aver presente,
altrui noiosa, a me stessa molesta,
lassa languía del corpo e de la mente.   90
    Come deveva over potea, con questa
oppressa dal martír gravosa spoglia,
venir da voi, meschina, inferma e mesta,
    a crescer con la mia la vostra doglia,
e in cambio di parlar con buon discorso,   95
aver di pianger, piú che d'altro, voglia?
    In quel vostro sí celebre concorso
d'uomini dotti e di giudicio eletto,
da cui vien ragionato e ben discorso,
    come, senza poter formar un detto,   100
dovev'io ne la scola circostante
uom tal visitar egro infermo in letto?
    Furono appresso le giornate sante,
ch'a questo officio m'impedîr la via;
benché la cagion prima fu 'l mio amante,   105
    a cui sempre pensar mi convenía,

without doubt through his courteous writing   70
he has restored my life, and I give him thanks
with a thought that bids me to hope for the best.
   On the other hand, I see him intent on my ruin   73
because he leaves me without him
and remains without me so long.
   The letters he sends me I constantly read,   76
and I hold them before me as I write my reply,
and this way, in part, I relieve my pain.
   Deep sighs arise from the depth of my heart   79
as I read his letters and write answers back,
full of the languor I hide in my breast.
   My hours have all been devoted to this,   82
and in the place of my lord,
I kissed his cherished and tenderest words.
   Worse than dead in his absence, constantly weeping,   85
calling him in trembling and uneven voice
was my only relief and amusement.
   And longing to have him present before me,   88
I languish, alas, in body and mind,
annoying to others and a trial to myself.
   How should, or could, I come to see you,   91
with this dreary body tormented by pain,
wretched, unhealthy, and in such sad state,
   to increase your grief by adding my own,   94
and instead of making good conversation,
wanting to cry more than anything else?
   In that assembly of yours, so famous,   97
of learned men of distinguished judgment,
who know how to argue and discourse so well,
   how was I, unable to say one word,   100
amid an academy such as yours,
to visit an invalid, confined to bed?[24]
   And then the holy days were upon us,   103
which kept me again from doing this duty,
although the main reason was really my lover,
   about whom I have been constantly forced   106

---

24. This line identifies the recipient of this letter as Domenico Venier, confined to bed because of his gout of the foot (Bianchi, 206 n. 102).

e legger, e risponder, in ciò tutta
spendendo la già morta vita mia.
   Ed ora a stato tal io son ridutta,
che s'ei doman non torna, com'io spero,   110
fia la mia carne in cenere distrutta.
   Di rivederlo ognor bramosa pèro,
bench'ei tosto verrà, com'io son certa,
per quel ch'ei sempre m'ha narrato il vero:
   de la promessa fé di lui s'accerta   115
con altre esperïenzie la mia spene,
né qual dianzi ha da me doglia è sofferta.
   Egli verrà, l'abbraccerò 'l mio bene:
stella benigna, ch'a me 'l guida, e ria
quella ond'ei senza me star sol sostiene.   120
   Mi resta un poco di malinconia,
ch'egro è 'l mio colonello, ed io non posso
mancargli per amor e cortesia:
   sí che, gran parte d'altro affar rimosso,
attendo a governarlo in stato tale,   125
ch'ei fôra senza me di vita scosso.
   Per troppo amarmi ei giura di star male,
convenendo da me dipartir tosto,
e verso Creta andar quasi con l'ale.
   Di ciò nel cor grand'affanno ei s'ha posto,   130
ed io non cesso ad ogni mio potere
di consolarlo a ciascun buon proposto.
   Vorreil dal suo mal libero vedere,
perché tanto da lui mi sento amata,
e perch'ei langue fuor d'ogni dovere;   135
   e come donna in questa patria nata,
vorrei ch'ov'ha di lui bisogno andasse,
e ch'opra a lei prestasse utile e grata:
   le virtú del suo corpo afflitte e lasse,
per ch'ei ne gisse ov'altri in Creta il chiama,   140
grato mi fôra ch'ei ricuperasse.
   Del suo nobil valor la chiara fama
fa che quivi ciascun l'ama e 'l desía,

to think and to read and to write in return,
wasting my life, already dead.
    And now I'm reduced to such a condition 109
that unless, as I hope, he comes back tomorrow,
my flesh will melt away into ashes.
    I perish, always longing to see him again, 112
though soon he will come, of that I am certain,
because he has always told me the truth;
    my hope in his sworn faith is affirmed 115
by my diverse experience of him,
nor have I suffered such grief before.
    My dear one will come, I will embrace him, 118
benign is the star that leads him to me,
and cruel the one that keeps him away.
    Yet I still feel a lingering sadness, 121
for my colonel is ill, and love and courtesy
demand of me that I should not fail him;
    and so, having set other business aside, 124
I expect to minister to him in a way
that makes him, without me, bereft of life.
    He swears he is ill because he loves me too much, 127
and he has agreed to leave me at once
and to head down to Crete as though he had wings.
    About this he's set great concern in his heart 130
and I never cease, the best that I'm able,
to console him whenever the chance comes my way.
    I would like to see him freed from his ailment 133
because I feel that he loves me so deeply,
and because he suffers far more than he should;
    and, as a woman born in this city, 136
I want him to go where he is needed
and to aid Venice with useful, bold deeds.
    I would be pleased if he recovered 139
the strength of his body, now ailing and weary,
to travel to Crete, where others call him.
    The widespread fame of his noble valor 142
makes everyone there love and desire him,

e come esperto in guerreggiar il brama.
    Dategli, venti, facile la via,   145
e perché fuor d'ogni molestia ei vada,
la dea d'amor propizia in mar gli sia:
    sí che con l'onorata invitta spada
a la sua illustre immortal gloria ei faccia
con l'inimico sangue aperta strada.   150
    Ciò fia ch'al mio voler ben sodisfaccia,
poi che, rimosso questo impedimento,
il mio amor sempre avrò ne le mie braccia.
    E se costui perciò parte scontento,
ch'ad altro ho 'l core e l'anima donato,   155
rimedïar non posso al suo tormento.
    E che poss'io? Che s'egli è innamorato,
io similmente il mio signor dolce amo,
e 'l mio arbitrio di lui tutt'ho in man dato.
    A lui servir e compiacer sol bramo,   160
valoroso, gentil, modesto e buono;
e fortunata del suo amor mi chiamo.
    Lassa! che mentre di lui sol ragiono,
né presente l'amato aspetto veggio,
da novo aspro martír oppressa sono;   165
    e pietra morta in viva pietra seggio
sopra del mio balcone, afflitta e smorta,
poi che 'l mio ben lontano esser m'aveggio.
    A questa che da me scusa v'è pòrta
di non esser venuta a visitarvi,   170
priva di vita senza la mia scorta,
    piacciavi, s'ella è buona, d'appigliarvi,
considerando ben voi questa parte,
senz'a quel ch'altri dice riportarvi.
    E se le mie ragion confuse e sparte   175
senz'argomenti e senza stil v'ho addutto,
a dir la verità non richiede arte.
    Bench'io non son senza un salvocondutto,
e senza da voi esserne invitata,
per tornar cosí presto a quel ridutto,   180

and long for him as an expert in warfare.
 Grant him, winds, an easy passage   145
and so that he travels without any danger,
may the goddess of love guard him on the sea,
 so that with his honored, invincible sword   148
through the blood of our enemies he may carve out
a straightforward path to undying fame.
 Let this be done to my satisfaction,   151
so that, with this obstacle out of my way,
I will always have my love in my arms.
 And if the other man leaves, discontented   154
that I have given my heart and soul to another,
I will not be able to assuage his torment.
 And what can I do? For if he is in love,   157
I love my sweet lord in the same way,
and I have put all my will in his hands.
 I long to serve and please him alone,   160
courageous, gentle, modest, and good;
and I call myself lucky on account of his love.
 Alas! I'm brought down by a new misery: 163
that at the moment I am speaking of him,
I do not see, present, his beloved face,
 and, dead stone, I sit in living stone,   166
upon my balcony, troubled and pale,
because I realize my love is far away.
 This excuse, carried from me to you,   169
for not having come to you for a visit,
deprived of life without my escort,
 please, if it's acceptable, accept it firmly,   172
considering well this side of the story,
without depending on what others tell you.
 And if I have recited my reasons to you,   175
in confusing disorder, without logic or style,
telling the truth does not require art.
 Although I am not without a safe-conduct   178
to return so quickly to that salon
without having been invited by you,

    basta che quando vi sarò chiamata,
lascerò ogni altra cosa per venirvi;
né questo è poco a donna innamorata.
    E stimerò che sia vero obedirvi
star pronta a quel che mi comanderete,   185
non venendo non chiesta ad impedirvi.
    Se con vostro cugin ne parlerete,
son certa ch'egli mi darà ragione,
e voi medesmo ve n'accorgerete.
    Gli altri amici son poi buone persone,   190
e senza costo voglion de l'altrui,
s'altri con loro a traficar si pone.
    Forse che quanto tarda a scriver fui,
tanto son lunga in questa mia scrittura,
senza pensar chi la manda ed a cui.   195
    Ma io son cosí larga di natura,
tal che tutta ricevo entro a me stessa
la virtú vostra e la viva figura:
    questa mi siede in mezzo l'alma impressa,
come di mio signor effigie degna,   200
ch'onorar il cor mio giamai non cessa.
    Cosí vostra mercé per sua mi tegna,
e per me inchini quella compagnia,
sin ch'a far questo a la presenzia io vegna;
    benc'ho mutato in parte fantasia,   205
e in ciò ch'io mi ritoglio, o ch'io mi dono,
non sarà quel che tal crede che sia.
    Questo dico, perché dar in man buono,
venendo, non vorrei di chi perduta
mi tenne del suo amor, che non ne sono: 210
    cosí la sorte ora offende, ora aiuta.

it suffices, if I am summoned there,   181
that I'll leave everything else to come,
no small thing for a woman in love.
    And I will assume that truly to serve you   184
is to be ready for whatever you command,
not coming to bother you without being asked.
    If you will speak to your cousin of this,   187
I am certain that he will say I am right,
and that you will see it yourself.
    And, then, our other friends are good people,   190
and if someone enters into relations with them,
they always want someone else, free of cost.
    Perhaps in this script I am as longwinded   193
as I was slow to write you at first,
not considering who sends it and to whom.
    But I am so receptive by nature   196
that I take in, in their entirety,
all your virtues and your lively being;
    and this remains at the center of my soul   199
as an image worthy of my lord,
whom my heart never ceases to honor.
    So may your grace think me entirely his,   202
and persuade the group to forgive me,
until I come to do it in person,
    although I have partly changed my wish,   205
and whether in this I hold back or yield,
the outcome will not be what someone may think.
    I say this because I don't want, by coming,   208
to encourage the man who thinks me madly in love
with him to believe it, for I am not.
    In this way fate now attacks and then saves us.   211

Capitolo 16

ॐ

D'ardito cavalier non è prodezza
(concedami che 'l vero a questa volta
io possa dir, la vostra gentilezza),
   da cavalier non è, ch'abbia raccolta
ne l'animo suo invitto alta virtute,   5
e che a l'onor la mente abbia rivolta,
   con armi insidïose e non vedute,
a chi piú disarmato men sospetta
dar gravi colpi di mortal ferute.
   Men ch'agli altri ciò far poi se gli aspetta   10
contra le donne, da natura fatte
per l'uso che piú d'altro a l'uom diletta:
   imbecilli di corpo, ed in nulla atte
non pur a offender gli altri, ma se stesse
dal difender col cor timido astratte.   15
   Questo doveva far che s'astenesse
la vostra man da quell'aspre percosse,
ch'al mio feminil petto ignudo impresse.
   Io non saprei già dir onde ciò fosse,
se non che fuor del lato mi traeste   20
l'armi vostre del sangue asperse e rosse.
   Spogliata e sola e incauta mi cogliesti,
debil d'animo, e in armi non esperta,
e robusto ed armato m'offendeste:
   tanto ch'io stei per lungo spazio incerta   25
di mia salute; e fu per me tra tanto
passïon infinita al cor sofferta.
   Pur finalmente s'è stagnato il pianto,
e quella piaga acerba s'è saldata,
che da l'un mi passava a l'altro canto.   30
   Quasi da pigro sonno or poi svegliata,
dal cansato periglio animo presi,

Capitolo 16

A CHALLENGE TO A POET WHO HAS DEFAMED HER

It is not a brave knight's gallant deed
(if, gentle sir, you permit me
this time to declare the truth),
   it is not the deed of a knight who's gathered   4
lofty virtue in his undefeated heart
and set his mind entirely on honor,
   with insidious and hidden weapons   7
to strike without warning an unarmed woman
and to deal her blows that mean her death.
   Even less than to any other should a man   10
do this to women, whom nature created
for the use that brings most delight to men:
   weak in body, and not only quite unfit   13
to injure others, but also far distant,
through their timid hearts, from self-defense.
   This should have restrained your hand   16
from striking those relentless blows
now marked on my naked female breast.
   How this came about I can't really say,   19
except that from my side you pulled out
your weapons, dripping and red with blood.
   You found me defenseless, alone, off my guard,   22
fainthearted and never practiced in combat,
and strong, fully armed, you wounded me sorely;
   so that long after, I was uncertain   25
whether I would survive, and through all this
I suffered endless pain in my heart.
   Yet my tears are stanched at last and dried,   28
and the bitter wound has finally healed
that pierced me through from one side to the other.
   As if jolted awake from sweet sleep all at once,   31
I drew courage from the risk I'd avoided,

benché femina a molli opere nata;
  e in man col ferro a essercitarmi appresi,
tanto ch'aver le donne agil natura,   35
non men che l'uomo, in armeggiando intesi:
  perché 'n ciò posto ogni mia industria e cura,
mercé del ciel, mi veggo giunta a tale,
che piú d'offese altrui non ho paura.
  E se voi dianzi mi trattaste male,   40
fu gran vostro diffetto, ed io dal danno
grave n'ho tratto un ben che molto vale.
  Cosí nei casi avversi i savi fanno,
che 'l lor utile espresso alfin cavare
da quel che nuoce da principio sanno;   45
  e cosí ancor le medicine amare
rendon salute; e 'l ferro e 'l foco s'usa
le putrefatte piaghe a ben curare:
  benché non serve a voi questa per scusa,
che m'offendeste non già per giovarmi,   50
e 'l fatto stesso parla e sí v'accusa.
  Ed io, poi che 'l ciel vòlse liberarmi
da sí mortal periglio, ho sempre atteso
a l'essercizio nobile de l'armi,
  sí ch'or, animo e forze avendo preso,   55
di provocarvi a rissa in campo ardisco,
con cor non poco a la vendetta acceso.
  Non so se voi stimiate lieve risco
entrar con una donna in campo armato;
ma io, benché ingannata, v'avvertisco   60
  che 'l mettersi con donne è da l'un lato
biasmo ad uom forte, ma da l'altro è poi
caso d'alta importanza riputato.
  Quando armate ed esperte ancor siam noi,
render buon conto a ciascun uom potemo,   65
ché mani e piedi e core avem qual voi;
  e se ben molli e delicate semo,
ancor tal uom, ch'è delicato, è forte;
e tal, ruvido ed aspro, è d'ardir scemo.

though a woman, born to milder tasks;
    and, blade in hand, I learned warrior's skills,   34
so that, by handling weapons, I learned
that women by nature are no less agile than men.

    So, devoting all my effort to arms,   37
I see myself now, thanks to heaven, at the point
where I no longer fear harm from anyone.

    And if you once treated me unfairly,   40
it was a serious error you made;
but from great harm I've acquired great good.

    Thus in adversity wise people behave,   43
knowing just how to put to advantage
what seems at first certain to harm them.

    And bitter medicines likewise bring health,   46
and we make use of steel and fire
to clean and cauterize infected wounds,

    although you can't use this as an excuse,   49
for you didn't wound me to do me good;
the fact speaks for itself and puts you in the wrong.

    And I, since heaven condescended to free me   52
from such mortal danger, day and night
fix my attention on the noble art of arms,

    so that now, having summoned up courage and strength,   55
I dare to defy you to combat in the field,
with a heart entirely aflame for revenge.

    I do not know if you think it a trifling risk   58
to enter the field to joust with a woman,
but though you once fooled me, I warn you now

    that if on one hand it might be unseemly   61
for a strong man to contend with a woman,
on the other, it's thought a weighty event.

    When we women, too, have weapons and training,   64
we will be able to prove to all men
that we have hands and feet and hearts like yours;

    and though we may be tender and delicate,   67
some men who are delicate also are strong,
and some, though coarse and rough, are cowards.

Di ciò non se ne son le donne accorte;
che se si risolvessero di farlo,
con voi pugnar porían fino a la morte.
E per farvi veder che 'l vero parlo,
tra tante donne incominciar voglio io,
porgendo essempio a lor di seguitarlo.   75
A voi, che contra tutte sète rio,
con qual'armi volete in man mi volgo,
con speme d'atterrarvi e con desio;
e le donne a difender tutte tolgo
contra di voi, che di lor sète schivo,   80
sí ch'a ragion io sola non mi dolgo.
Certo d'un gran piacer voi sète privo,
a non gustar di noi la gran dolcezza;
ed al mal uso in ciò la colpa ascrivo.
Data è dal ciel la feminil bellezza,   85
perch'ella sia felicitate in terra
di qualunque uom conosce gentilezza.
Ma dove 'l mio pensier trascorre ed erra
a ragionar de le cose d'amore,
or ch'io sono in procinto di far guerra?   90
Torno al mio intento, ond'era uscita fuore,
e vi disfido a singolar battaglia.
Cingetevi pur d'armi e di valore:
vi mostrerò quanto al vostro prevaglia
il sesso feminil; pigliate quali   95
volete armi, e di voi stesso vi caglia,
ch'io vi risponderò di colpi tali,
il campo a voi lasciando elegger anco,
ch'a questi forse non sentiste eguali.
Mal difender da me potrete il fianco,   100
e stran vi parrà forse, a offenderne uso,
da me vedervi oppresso in terra stanco:
cosí talor quell'uom resta deluso,
ch'ingiuria gli altri fuor d'ogni ragione,
non so se per natura, o per mal uso.   105
Vostra di questa rissa è la cagione,

Women so far haven't seen this is true;   70
for if they'd ever resolved to do it,
they'd have been able to fight you to the death.
 And to prove to you that I speak the truth,   73
among so many women I will act first,
setting an example for them all to follow.
 On you, who are so savage to us all,   76
I turn, with whatever weapon you choose,
with the hope and will to throw you to the ground.
 And I undertake to defend all women   79
against you, who despise them so
that rightly I'm not alone to protest.
 It is certain that you miss great pleasure   82
by being unable to savor our sweetness,
and I blame your bad habits for being the cause.[25]
 Feminine beauty is a gift from heaven,   85
intended to be a source of joy
to every man with a gentle heart.
 But where is my thought wandering and roaming   88
by speaking of matters related to love
now that I'm about to make war?
 I return to the purpose from which I have strayed,   91
and I now challenge you to single combat:
gird yourself with weapons and valor.
 I'll show you how far the female sex   94
excels your own. Arm yourself however you please
and take good heed for your survival,
 for I will answer you with blows   97
(though leaving the choice of field to you)
unlike any you've ever felt before.
 You'll defend yourself poorly against my flank attack,   100
and it may seem strange to you, used to wounding others,
exhausted, to see yourself thrown to the ground.
 Thus disappointed sometimes is the man   103
who insults others without provocation,
by nature or bad habit I do not know.
 You are the cause of this quarrel between us,   106

---

25. Franco may be alluding to Maffio's homosexuality here (Bianchi, 208 n. 84).

ed a me per difesa e per vendetta
carico d'oppugnarvi ora s'impone.
    Prendete pur de l'armi omai l'eletta,
ch'io non posso soffrir lunga dimora,   110
da lo sdegno de l'animo costretta.
    La spada, che 'n man vostra rade e fóra,
de la lingua volgar venezïana,
s'a voi piace d'usar, piace a me ancora;
    e se volete entrar ne la toscana,   115
scegliete voi la seria o la burlesca,
ché l'una e l'altra è a me facile e piana.
    Io ho veduto in lingua selvaghesca
certa fattura vostra molto bella,
simile a la maniera pedantesca: 120
    se voi volete usar o questa o quella,
ed aventar, come ne l'altre fate,
di queste in biasmo nostro le quadrella,
    qual di lor piú vi piace, e voi pigliate,
ché di tutte ad un modo io mi contento,   125
avendole perciò tutte imparate.
    Per contrastar con voi con ardimento,
in tutte queste ho molta industria speso:
se bene o male, io stessa mi contento;
    e ciò sarà dagli altri ancora inteso,   130
e 'l saperete voi, che forse vinto
cadrete, e non vorreste avermi offeso.
    Ma prima che si venga in tal procinto,
quasi per far al gioco una levata,
non col ferro tagliente ancora accinto,   135
    de la vostra canzone, a me mandata,
il principio vorrei mi dichiaraste,
poi che l'opera a me vien indrizzata.
    « Ver unica » e 'l restante mi chiamaste,
alludendo a Veronica mio nome,   140
ed al vostro discorso mi biasmaste;
    ma al mio dizzïonario io non so come
« unica » alcuna cosa propriamente

and I am bound by honor to battle
in the name of vengeance and self-defense.
    So take up at last the weapon you've chosen,   109
for I cannot bear any further delay,
compelled as I am by the scorn in my soul.
    The sword that strikes and stabs in your hand—   112
the common language spoken in Venice—
if that's what you want to use, then so do I;
    and if you want to enter into Tuscan,   115
I leave you the choice of high or comic strain,
for one's as easy and clear for me as the other.
    I've seen, in mock-heroic verse,   118
a very fine work of yours that resembles
the style that mixes Italian and Latin.[26]
    Whichever of these you wish to use,   121
as you do elsewhere, to speed on your arrows
in a contest of insults exchanged between us,
    choose the language that you prefer,   124
for I am equally happy with them all,
since I have learned them for exactly this purpose.
    To compete with you as boldly as I may,   127
I have studied all these styles in depth;
whether well or ill, I myself am content;
    and others as well will understand this.   130
And so will you, for you may fall, beaten,
wishing you had not insulted me.
    But before the two of us reach that stage,   133
as an entering salute to the joust we begin,
not yet opened with your cutting blade,
    I would like to ask you to recite   136
the beginning of the *canzone* you sent my way,[27]
since this written work is addressed to me.
    "Verily unique," among other things, you called me,   139
alluding to Veronica, my name,
and in your discourse you blamed me severely.
    But, according to my dictionary, I fail to see   142
how one can properly call something "unique"

---

26. In the 1570s, *burlesca* (line 118) meant mock-heroic, that is, a low style parodying elevated subjects; *pedantesca* referred to a comic mixture of Latin and Italian words.

27. Maffio's attack was not a *canzone* (a long poem with a final *envoi*) but, rather, a *sonetto caudato*, a sonnet ending with an extra couplet.

in mala parte ed in biasmar si nome.

 Forse che si direbbe impropriamente,   145
ma l'anfibologia non quadra in cosa
qual mostrar voi volete espressamente.

 Quella di cui la fama è glorïosa,
e che 'n bellezza od in valor eccelle,
senza par di gran lunga virtüosa,   150

 « unica » a gran ragion vien che s'appelle;
e l'arte, a l'ironia non sottoposto,
scelto tra gli altri, un tal vocabol dïelle.

 L'« unico » in lode e in pregio vien esposto
da chi s'intende; e chi parla altrimenti   155
dal senso del parlar sen va discosto.

 Questo non è, signor, fallo d'accenti,
quello, in che s'inveisce, nominare
col titol de le cose piú eccellenti.

 O voi non mi voleste biasimare,   160
o in questo dir menzogna non sapeste.
Non parlo del dir bene e del lodare,

 ché questo so che far non intendeste;
ma senz'esser offeso da me stato,
quel che vi corse a l'animo scriveste,   165

 altrui volendo in ciò forse esser grato;
benché me non ingiuria, ma se stesso,
s'altri mi dice mal, non provocato.

 E 'l voler oscurar il vero espresso
con le torbide macchie degli inchiostri   170
in buona civiltà non è permesso;

 e spesso avien che 'l mal talento uom mostri,
giovando in quello onde piú nuocer crede:
essempi in me piú d'una volta mostri,

 sí come in questo caso ancor si vede,   175
ché voi, non v'accorgendo, mi lodate
di quel ch'al bene ed a la virtú chiede.

 E se ben « meretrice » mi chiamate,
o volete inferir ch'io non vi sono,
o che ve n'èn tra tali di lodate.   180

in a critical sense, by way of condemnation.
    Perhaps you're speaking in an ironic way,   145
but amphibology fails to communicate[28]
the point you evidently want to make.
    A woman whose fame makes her right to be proud,   148
who stands out for beauty or for courage,
and far exceeds all others in virtue—
    such a woman is rightly called "unique";   151
and art, without irony, chooses to bestow
this word, selected from others, upon her.
    "Unique" is used in praise and esteem   154
by those who know; and whoever speaks otherwise
digresses from the true meaning of words.
    It is not, sir, merely mistaken emphasis,   157
when one hurls abuse and insult at someone,
to use a term meant for most excellent things.
    Either your purpose was not to defame me,   160
or you were, unaware, lying when you said it.
I am not speaking of good words or praise,
    for I know that you intended neither one;   163
but without receiving any offense from me,
you simply wrote what came into your head,
    wishing perhaps to please somebody else—   166
though a man in fact insults himself,
not me, by slandering me without cause.
    The desire to cover over manifest truth   169
with turbid splatterings of black ink
is not acceptable in civil company;
    and often a man shows his evil nature   172
by delighting in what he thinks can do most harm.
In my case, you've proved this true more than once,
    as can be seen again in this instance,   175
for, without realizing it, you give me praise
for qualities based upon goodness and virtue.
    And though you call me "prostitute,"[29]   178
either you imply that I'm not one of them,
or that among them some merit praise.

---

28. *Amphibology,* or speech contrary to the intended meaning, was a figure of speech listed under "irony" in rhetorical handbooks.

29. In *meretrice,* the word Franco uses here, she may want her readers to hear the sound of *merito* (merit).

Quanto le meretrici hanno di buono,
quanto di grazïoso e di gentile,
esprime in me del parlar vostro il suono.
  Se questo intese il vostro arguto stile,
di non farne romor io son contenta,   185
e d'inchinarmi a voi devota, umíle;
  ma perch'al fin de la scrittura, intenta
stando, che voi mi biasimate trovo,
e ciò si tocca e non pur s'argomenta,
  da questa intenzïon io mi rimovo,   190
e in ogni modo questïon far voglio,
e partorir lo sdegno ch'entro covo.
  Apparecchiate pur l 'inchiostro e 'l foglio,
e fatemi saper senz'altro indugio
quali armi per combatter in man toglio.   195
  Voi non avrete incontro a me rifugio,
ch'a tutte prove sono apparecchiata,
e impazïentemente a l'opra indugio:
  o la favella giornalmente usata,
o qual vi piace idïoma prendete,   200
ché 'n tutti quanti sono essercitata;
  e se voi poi non mi risponderete,
di me dirò che gran paura abbiate,
se ben cosí valente vi tenete.
  Ma perché alquanto manco dubitiate,   205
son contenta di far con voi la pace,
pur ch'una volta meco vi proviate:
  fate voi quel che piú vi giova e piace.

Whatever goodness prostitutes may have,   181
whatever grace and nobility of soul,
the sound of your word assigns to me.

If this was the purpose of your witty style,   184
I'm happy not to raise objections,
and I bow down, your humble and devoted servant.

But since, reading carefully what you write,   187
I find that in fact you are reproaching me—
and this is clear, not a matter for debate—

I distance myself from that purpose of yours;   190
I insist on disputing it at any cost,
and I long to give birth to the anger I breed.

So make ready now your paper and ink   193
and tell me, this time, without further delay
which weapons I must wield in combat with you.

You will have nowhere to run from me   196
for I am prepared for any test of skill
and I wait impatiently to start the fight.

You may choose the language of every day,   199
or whatever other idiom you please,
for I have had practice in them all;

and if you do not write me a response,   202
I will say that you feel great fear of me,
even though you think yourself so brave.

But since I'm unwilling to leave you in doubt,   205
I happily offer to make peace with you,
on the condition that you joust with me just once.

Do whatever suits and pleases you best.   208

Capitolo 17

ॐ

Questa la tua Veronica ti scrive,
signor ingrato e disleale amante,
di cui sempre in sospetto ella ne vive.
   A te, perfido, noto è bene in quante
maniere del mio amor ti feci certo,   5
da me non mai espresse altrui davante.
   Non niego già che 'n te non sia gran merto
di senno, di valor, di gentilezza,
e d'arti ingenue onde sei tanto esperto;
   ma la mia grazia ancor, la mia bellezza,   10
quello che 'n se medesma ella si sia,
da molti spirti nobili s'apprezza.
   Forse ch'è buona in ciò la sorte mia;
e forse ch'io non son priva di quello
ch'ad arder l'alme volontarie invia: 15
   almen non ho d'ogni pietà rubello
il rigido pensier, né, qual tu, il core
in ogni parte insidïoso e fello.
   E pur contra ragion ti porto amore:
quel che tu meco far devresti al dritto,   20
teco 'l fo a torto, e so ch'è a farlo errore.
   Tu non m'avresti in tanti giorni scritto,
che star t'avvenne di parlarmi privo,
mostrando esser di ciò mesto ed afflitto,
   com'io cortesemente ora ti scrivo;   25
e se ben certo m'offendesti troppo,
teco legata in dolce nodo vivo,
   il qual mentre sciôr tento, e piú l'ingroppo,
e sí come d'Amor disposto fue,
non trovo in via d'amarti alcun intoppo.   30
   Ma pur furono ingrate l'opre tue,
poi che pensar ad altra donna osasti,

FRANCO'S ANGRY REPROACH TO A MAN AND POET WHOSE INFIDELITY SHE HAS DISCOVERED

This letter your Veronica writes to you,
ungrateful lord and disloyal lover,
she who lives in constant mistrust of you.
    Faithless man, you know full well   4
how many ways I've assured you of my love,
ways I never revealed to anyone else.
    I deny in no way the merit you possess   7
in wisdom, in courage, and in gentility,
and in the liberal arts, in which you're so skilled;
    but my charm and my beauty,   10
whatever it may really be worth,
is still prized and valued by many noble souls.
    Perhaps it is just good luck that this is so;   13
or perhaps I don't lack what is required
to lead willing spirits to catch on fire.
    At least I don't have an unbending mind,   16
a foe to all pity; nor, like you, a heart
treacherous and cruel through and through.
    Yet against all reason I feel love for you: 19
what you should rightly do for me
I do for you wrongly, knowing I do wrong.
    You'd not have written me, however many days   22
you were prevented from speaking to me,
showing you were on this account gloomy and sad,
    so courteously as I write to you now.   25
Yet though you've certainly offended me too much,
I still live tied to you in a sweet knot,
    which entangles me more the more I try to loose it;   28
and since you've been so inclined to love,
I find, myself, no hindrance to loving you.
    But your writings were unkind indeed,   31
for you dared to think of another woman,

e limar versi de le lodi sue:
  farlo celatamente ti pensasti,
ma io ti sopragiunsi a l'improviso,   35
quando manco di me tu dubitasti.
  Ben ti vidi perciò turbar nel viso,
e per la forza de la conscïenza
ne rimanesti timido e conquiso,
  sí che gli occhi d'alzar in mia presenza   40
non ti bastò l'errante animo allora.
Ahi teco estrema fu mia pazïenza!
  Chiudesti 'l libro tu senza dimora,
ed io gli occhi devea con mie man trarti:
misera chi di tale s'innamora!   45
  Io non ho perdonato per amarti
ad alcuna fatica, ad alcun danno,
sperando intieramente d'acquistarti:
  e tu, falso, adoprando occulto inganno
per cogliermi al tuo laccio, or che mi tieni,   50
mi dai, d'amor in ricompensa, affanno.
  Ben son di vezzi e di lusinghe pieni
i tuoi detti eloquenti, e con pia vista
sempre a strazio maggior, empio, mi meni.
  D'odio e d'amor gran passïon or mista   55
m'ingombra l'alma, e 'l torbido pensiero
agitando contamina e contrista:
  e 'n te dal ciel quella vendetta spero,
ch'io non vorrei; ed infelicemente
d'alto sdegno e d'amor languisco e pèro.   60
  Contra gli error si deve esser clemente,
che dimostrati a quel che gli commise,
sí com'è ragionevole, si pente.
  Quel libro d'altrui lodi in sen si mise
questo importuno, acciò ch'io nol vedessi: 65
ahi contrarie in amor voglie divise!
  D'ira tutta infiammata allor non cessi,
fin che di sen per forza non gliel tolsi,
e quel che v'era scritto entro non lessi.

and to polish verses written in her praise.
    You hoped to carry all this out on the sly,   34
but suddenly I took you by surprise
when you least suspected that I might.
    At this, I clearly saw worry in your face,   37
and under the power of your conscience
you remained timid and contrite,
    so that in my presence your wandering mind   40
didn't permit you to raise your eyes.
Ah, my patience with you was extraordinary!
    The book you had written in, you hastily closed,   43
and I should have torn out your eyes with my hands.
Unhappy the woman who loves a man like you!
    I have spared no effort to love you entirely,   46
avoided no pain, for I had high hopes
that I might be able to win you entirely;
    and you, false man, using devious tricks   49
to entrap me, now that you hold me fast,
in return for love, give me only anguish.
    Your eloquent discourse is full through and through   52
of endearments and fine turns, and with loyal mien
you lead me to ever worse ruin, faithless man!
    A great passion, confused between hatred and love,   55
now weighs down my soul, and jarring,
disturbs and bereaves my clouded thought.
    And I wish for vengeance from heaven against you,   58
which I don't really want; and, miserably,
between scorn and love I languish and die.
    Toward others' errors one should be forgiving,   61
for when they are shown to the man who commits them,
as long as he's reasonable, he repents of them.
    He hid in his breast that book praising another,   64
this stubborn man, so that I wouldn't see it;
mismatched desires opposed, alas, in love!
    Then, all aflame with rage, I didn't give up   67
until I had grabbed the book from his breast,
and had read what was written there.

Quanto 'l caso chiedea, teco mi dolsi,   70
amante ingrato; e 'l libro stretto in mano,
altrove il piè da te fuggendo volsi,
    bench'ir non ti potei tanto lontano,
ch'al lato non mi fosti, e non facesti
tue scuse, e 'l libro mi chiedesti invano.   75
    Dimandereiti or ben quel che vedesti,
da farti pur alzar gli occhi a colei;
ma tu senz'esser chiesto mel dicesti:
    piena dentro e di fuor di vizii rei,
forse perch'io di tal non sospettassi,   80
la ponesti davanti agli occhi miei:
    agli occhi miei, che 'n tutto schivi e cassi
d'ogni altro lume, tengon te per sole,
benché spesso in gran tenebre gli lassi.
    Dubito se fûr vere le parole   85
che dicesti; né so di che, ma temo,
e dentro sospettando il cor si dole.
    Di gelosia non ho 'l pensier mai scemo,
tal ch'avampando in freddo verno al ghiaccio,
nel mezzo de le fiamme aggelo e tremo;   90
    e quanto piú di liberar procaccio
l'alma dal duolo, in maggior duol la invoglio,
e 'l mio mal dentro 'l grido e teco 'l taccio.
    Pur romper il silenzio or teco voglio;
e perché t'amo e perch'altri il comanda,   95
teco fo quel che con altrui non soglio.
    La buonasera in nome suo ti manda
per me 'l buono e cortese Lomellini,
e ti saluta e ti si raccomanda.
    Tu hai, non so perché, buoni vicini,   100
che ti lodano e impètranoti il bene,
se ben per torta strada tu camini.
    A questi d'obedir a me conviene,
e in quel ch'imposto m'han significarti,
questi versi di scriverti m'avviene.   105
    Di costor gran cagion hai di lodarti,

As the case called for, I told you my pain,   70
ungrateful lover; book tight in my hand,
I turned my steps elsewhere, fleeing from you,
    though I failed to put you far enough behind   73
to avoid you at my side, still making excuses,
and begging me, in vain, to give the book back.
    I could ask you what you had seen   76
that could make you raise your eyes to her,
but you told me yourself, without being asked.
    Perhaps because I suspected no such thing,   79
you set her, full inside and out
with wicked vice, right before my eyes—
    before my eyes, which, void and deprived   82
of any other light, took you for the sun,
even though you've often left them in darkness.
    I doubt now that any of the words you said were true,   85
but I am afraid, though I know not of what,
and my heart grieves, suspicious to its core.
    From jealousy my thoughts are never free,   88
so, as if blazing up from ice in cold winter,
in the midst of flames I freeze and shake;
    and the more I try to free my soul   91
from sorrow, the more sorrow I inflict upon it;
I cry out my pain within, with you I am silent.
    But now I want to break my silence with you;   94
both because I love you and because another wills it,
I do with you what I do with no other;
    on his behalf, good and courteous Lomellini   97
wishes you through me a good evening
and he greets you and awaits your command.
    You have, I don't know why, loyal neighbors,   100
who sing your praises and wish you the best,
even though you walk a crooked path.
    These people I am obliged to obey;   103
and to tell you of the duty that they've assigned me,
it happens that I write you these verses now.
    You are quite right to praise yourself for them,   106

bench'io convengo ancor per viva forza,
crudel, protervo e sempre ingrato, amarti.
   Contra mia voglia scriverti mi sforza
Amor, che tutto il conceputo sdegno   110
cangia in dolce desio, non pur l'ammorza:
   spinta da lui, mandarti ora convegno
queste mie carte, accioché tu le legga;
anzi sempre con l'alma a te ne vegno.
   Ma perché in corpo ancor ti parli e vegga,   115
ch'a bocca la risposta tu mi porte
forz'è che con instanzia ti richiegga,
   e che tu venghi in spazio d'ore corte.

though I, by sheer force, am compelled to love you,
cruel, haughty, and ungrateful man.

    Against my will, Love decrees that I write you,   109
for love turns whatever anger is born
to sweet desire, and abates it not at all.

    Driven by Love, I must send you now   112
these papers of mine for you to read;
or, rather, in them I come to you in spirit.

    But so that I may see and speak to you in person,   115
I am forced insistently to ask
that you answer me with your own mouth

    and that you come while time is short.   118

Capitolo 18

॰

Molto illustre signor, quel che iersera
ne recai mio capitolo a mostrarvi,
scritto di mia invenzïon non era;
    ma non per tanto di ringrazïarvi
non cesso, ch'avvertita voi m'abbiate   5
che ch'io nol mandi a quell'amico parvi;
    e vi so grado che mi consigliate
di quello c'ho da far, quando a voi vengo
perché i miei versi voi mi correggiate.
    Grand'obligazïone al cielo tengo   10
ch'un vostro pari in protezzïon m'abbia,
e piú da voi di quel ch'io merto ottengo.
    La gelosia, che dentro 'l cor m'arrabbia,
mi fece scriver quello ch'io non dissi;
ma fu del mio signor martello e rabbia.   15
    Egli pria mi narrò quello ch'io scrissi,
e molte cose mi soggiunse appresso,
perché di lui 'n sospetto non venissi.
    Non so quel che sia in fatto, ma confesso
ch'io mi sento morir da passïone   20
di non averlo a ciascun'ora presso:
    e questi versi scritti a tal cagione,
con scusa di mandargli quei saluti
di iersera, invïarli il cor dispone.
    Prego la mercé vostra che m'aiuti   25
in racconciarli, e in far ch'a me ne venga
il mio amante e lo sdegno in pietà muti:
    gli altri versi di ieri ella si tenga,
ch'io farò poi di lor quel ch'a lei piace;
e pur ch'umil l'amante mio divenga,   30
    d'ogni altra avversità mi darò pace.

Capitolo 18

TO A FRIEND, ASKING FOR HELP WITH REVISIONS

Most illustrious sir, the *capitolo*
that I came yesterday to show you
was not, in fact, my own invention;
   but nonetheless I can't thank you enough   4
for warning me that in your opinion
I should not send it to that friend;
   and I am grateful to you for advising me   7
about what I ought to do
when I call on you to correct my verses.
   I am greatly indebted to heaven   10
for the protection of someone like you,
and from you I receive more than I deserve.
   Jealousy, which enrages my heart,   13
made me write what I did not say,
but the pain and anger came from my lord.
   He first told me what to write,   16
and later he added many things
so that I should not suspect him.
   I don't know what the truth in this matter is,   19
but I confess that I feel myself dying of pain
at not having him nearby at all hours:
   and my heart persuades me to send him the verses   22
I composed for this reason, with the excuse
of sending him greetings written last night.
   I ask your kindness to help me revise them   25
and so lead my lover to come back to me
and to transform his scorn into pity;
   please keep yesterday's other verses,   28
and later I'll do with them what you wish;
and as long as my lover shows that he's become humble,
   I will resign myself to all other harm.   31

Capitolo 19

ᴖ

Quel che ascoso nel cor tenni gran tempo
con doglia tal, ch'a la lingua contese
narrar le mie ragioni a miglior tempo;
   quelle dolci d'amor amare offese,
che di scovrirle tanto altri val meno,   5
quanto ha piú di far ciò le voglie accese;
   or che la piaga s'è saldata al seno
col rivoltar degli anni, onde le cose
mutan di qua giú stato e vengon meno,
   vengo a narrar, poi che se ben noiose   10
a sentir fûro, ne la rimembranza
or mi si volgon liete e dilettose.
   Cosí spesso di far altri ha in usanza
dopo 'l corso periglio, e maggiormente
se d'uscirne fu scarsa la speranza.   15
   Or sicura ho 'l pericolo a la mente,
quando da' be' vostr'occhi e dal bel volto
contra me spinse Amor la face ardente:
   ed a piagarmi in mille guise vòlto,
dal fiume ancor de la vostra eloquenza   20
il foco del mio incendio avea raccolto.
   L'abito vago e la gentil presenza,
la grazia e le maniere al mondo sole,
e de le virtú chiare l'eccellenza,
   fûr ne la vista mia lucido sole,   25
che m'abbagliâr e m'arser di lontano,
sí ch'a tal segno andar Febo non suole.
   Ben mi fec'io solecchio de la mano,
ma contra sí possente e fermo oggetto
ogni riparo mio fu frale e vano;   30
   pur rimasi ferita in mezzo 'l petto,
sí che, perduto poscia ogni altro schermo,

Capitolo 19

A POEM OF RECOLLECTION, IN WHICH FRANCO RECOUNTS HER EARLY AND LATER LOVE FOR A MAN OF THE CHURCH

The feeling I kept long concealed in my heart
with such pain that my tongue was prevented
from explaining my reasons at a better time,
    those bittersweet offenses of love   4
(which least deserve revealing to others
the more one has the desire to reveal them),
    now that the wound in my heart has mended   7
with the passing of years, through whose effect
earthly things change and fade away,
    I am going to tell of now,   10
for though they were certainly painful to feel,
in memory now they seem joyful and sweet.
    This sort of recall often happens to people   13
who have lived through a danger, especially to those
whose hope of escaping it was only slight.
    Safely now I recollect   16
the danger when Love reached forth to me
the flaming torch of your fair eyes and face,
    and, set on wounding me in a thousand ways,   19
he had intensified the fire of my passion
even further with the flow of your eloquence.
    Your becoming attire and noble presence,   22
your grace and manners, unique in the world,
the excellence of your luminous virtues
    were a brilliant sun to my sight,   25
which dazzled and burned me from far away,
to a degree that Phoebus himself does not reach.
    I tried to shield my eyes with my hand,   28
but against such a powerful and steady object,
all my defenses were weak and vain:
    indeed, I was pierced in the center of my breast,   31
so that, with all protection lost,

arder del vostro amor fu 'l cor costretto:
e con l'animo in ciò costante e fermo
vi seguitai; ma mover non potea   35
il piede stretto d'assai nodi e infermo.

Tanta a me intorno guardia si facea,
che d'assai men dal cielo a Danae Giove
in pioggia d'oro in grembo non cadea.

Ma l'ali, che 'l pensier dispiega e move,   40
chi troncar mi potéo, se mi fu chiuso
al mio arbitrio l'andar co' piedi altrove?

Pronto lo spirto a voi venía per uso,
né tardava il suo volo, per trovarsi
del grave pianto mio bagnato e infuso.   45

E bench'al mio bisogno aiuti scarsi
fosser questi, vivendo mi mantenni,
come in necessità spesso suol farsi;

e cosí sobria in mia fame divenni,
ch'assai men che d'odor nel mio digiuno   50
sol di memoria il cor pascer convenni.

Cosí, senza trovar conforto alcuno,
la soverchia d'amor pena soffersi,
in stato miserabile importuno:

nel qual ciò che i tormenti miei diversi   55
far non potêr, col tempo i miei pensieri
vari da quel ch'esser solean poi fêrsi.

Voi ve n'andaste a popoli stranieri,
ed io rimasi in preda di quel foco,
che senza voi miei dí fea tristi e neri;   60

ma procedendo l'ore, a poco a poco
del bisogno convenni far virtute,
e dar ad altre cure entro a me loco.

Questa fu del mio mal vera salute:
cosí divenne alfin la mente sana   65
da le profonde mie gravi ferute:

il vostro andar in regïon lontana
saldò 'l colpo, benché la cicatrice
render non si potesse in tutto vana.

my heart was forced to burn with love for you:
    and I followed you with a constant and unswerving soul;   34
but I was unable to take one step,
bound and weakened by many ties.

    I was kept everywhere under such close guard   37
that Jove fell much more easily from heaven
in a golden shower into Danae's lap.[30]

    But who could deprive me of the wings   40
that thought frees and moves, even if taking steps
in another direction was forbidden to my will?

    My spirit turned eagerly toward you by habit,   43
and its flight was not delayed
by being laden and drenched with my sorrowful tears.

    And though these brought me only slight help   46
in my need, I managed to continue to live,
as of necessity one often must do,

    and so in my hunger I became frugal,   49
so much that I had to nourish my heart
less on scent than on memory alone.

    So, without finding any consolation,   52
I endured the extremity of love's pain,
in a miserable and wretched condition;

    in this state, with the passing of time   55
as my many torments could not do,
my thinking changed from what it had been.

    You went away to foreign peoples,   58
and I stayed behind, the prey of that fire
which, without you, made my days black and sad;

    but as the hours progressed, little by little,   61
I resolved to make a virtue of my need,
and to make room in myself for other concerns.

    This was the true solution to my pain: 64
in this way my mind discovered at last
a cure for its deep and serious wounds;

    your departure for foreign lands   67
mended the blow, although the scar
could not be completely erased.

---

30. Danae, locked in a tower by her father, was nonetheless visited by Jove in the form of a golden shower (Ovid, *Metamorphoses*, 4.611).

Forse stata sarei lieta e felice   70
nel potervi goder a mio talento,
e forse in ciò sarei stata infelice.

La gran sovrabondanza del contento
potría la somma gioia aver cangiato
in noioso e gravissimo tormento;   75

e se da me 'n disparte foste andato,
in tempo di mio tanto e di tal bene,
infinito il mio duol sarebbe stato.

Cosí non vòlse 'l ciel liete e serene
far l'ore mie, per non ridurmi tosto   80
in prova di piú acerbe e dure pene.

Ond'io di quanto fu da lui disposto
restar debbo contenta; e pur non posso
non desïar ch'avenisse l'opposto.

Da quel che sia 'l mio desiderio mosso   85
in questo stato, non so farne stima,
ché s'è da me quel primo amor rimosso.

Quanto cangiato in voi da quel di prima
veggo 'l bel volto! Oh in quanto breve corso
tutto rode qua giuso il tempo, e lima!   90

Di molta gente nel comun concorso
quante volte vi vidi e v'ascoltai,
e dal bel vostro sguardo ebbi soccorso!

E se ben il mio amor non vi mostrai,
o che 'l faceste a caso, o per qual sia   95
altra cagion, benigno vi trovai:

per ch'ora in una ed ora in altra via
di devoto parlar, con atto umano,
volgeste a me la fronte umile e pia;

e nel contar il ben del ciel sovrano,   100
v'affisaste a guardarmi, e mi stendeste,
or larghe or giunte, l'una e l'altra mano;

ed altre cose simili faceste,
ond'io tolsi a sperar che del mio amore
cautamente pietoso v'accorgeste.   105

Quinci s'accrebbe forte il mio dolore

Perhaps I would have been happy and glad   70
if I could have enjoyed you to my heart's content,
and perhaps I'd have been unhappy instead.
    The great excess of happiness   73
might have transformed the highest joy
into cruel, burdensome pain;
    and if you'd gone, leaving me behind   76
at a time so full of such delight,
my distress would have had no end.
    So heaven refused to make my hours   79
joyful and serene, to avoid reducing me
soon after to the worst, most bitter pain.
    And I, freed by heaven to such a degree,   82
must remain content; and yet I'm not able
to hope that the opposite had not occurred.
    I cannot judge what it was   85
that caused my desire in that state,
for the love I first felt has left me since.
    How changed from what it was before   88
your handsome face now seems to me!
How quickly time eats away all earthly things!
    How often I saw you at services in church,   91
shared by others, as well, and listened to you,
and took consolation from your beautiful gaze!
    And though I never showed you my love,   94
whether it was by chance or for another reason,
I always found that you were kind;
    for now in one way, now in another,   97
in holy speech, in benevolent ways,
you turned your humble and pious brow toward me;
    and as you spoke of heaven's supreme good,   100
you sent me your glance, and now open, now closed,
you held out both your hands to me:
    and you did other similar things,   103
so I started to hope that with careful pity
you might have taken notice of my love.
    And so my grief increased acutely   106

di non poter al gusto d'ambo noi
goder la vita in gioia ed in dolzore.
    Mesi ed anni trascorsero da poi,
ond'a me varïar convenne stile,   110
com'ancor forse far convenne a voi.
    Or vi miro non poco dissimíle
da quel che solevate esser davante,
de l'età vostra in sul fiorito aprile.
    Oh che divino angelico sembiante,   115
quel vostro, atto a scaldar ogni cor era
d'agghiacciato e durissimo diamante!
    Or, dopo cosí lieta primavera,
forma d'autunno, assai piú che d'estate,
varia vestite assai da la primiera.   120
    E se ben in viril robusta etate,
l'oro de la lanugine in argento
rivolto, quasi vecchio vi mostrate;
    benché punto nel viso non s'è spento
quel lume di beltà chiara e serena,   125
ch'abbaglia chi mirarvi ardisce intento.
    Questa con la memoria mi rimena
del vostro aspetto a la prima figura,
ond'ebbi già per voi sí crudel pena;
    e mentre 'l pensier mio stima e misura,   130
e pareggia l'effigie di quegli anni
con questa de l'età d'or piú matura,
    di fuor sento scaldarmi il petto e i panni,
senza che però 'l cor dentro si mova,
per la memoria de' passati affanni.   135
    In questo l'alma un certo affetto prova,
ch'io non so qual ei sia; se non che vosco
l'esser e 'l ragionar mi piace e giova;
    e se 'l giudicio non ho sordo e losco,
quest'è de l'amicizia la presenza,   140
ch'al volto ed a la voce io la conosco.
    Del mio passato amor da la potenza
queste faville in me sono rimaste,

that we could not enjoy life together,
as we both wished, in joy and sweet rest.
  Then the months and years passed by   109
so that I had to change my style,
as perhaps you also did.
  Now I see you very changed   112
from what you used to be before,
in the flowering April of your life.
  Oh, what a heavenly, angelic countenance   115
yours was then, able to warm anyone's heart,
even one frozen or as solid as diamonds!
  Now, after such a joyful spring,   118
far more than summer's, you wear autumn's guise,
very different from the first.
  And though of a vigorous and manly age,   121
with the gold of your hair turned to silver,
you appear to be almost old,
  although, in your face, the former light   124
of noble, calm beauty is not at all spent,
and it dazzles whoever dares watch you closely.
  This light returns me in recollection   127
to the first impression of your appearance,
which made me feel such agony for you:
  and while my thought assesses and compares   130
the image of those early years
to that of your now maturer age,
  I feel outer warmth in my breast and my clothing,   133
yet within me my heart is not stirred
by the memory of my past pain.
  My soul feels some emotion at this,   136
but what it is, I don't know, unless
speaking and being with you thrills and delights me.
  And if I don't judge deafly or aslant,   139
it is, in fact, the presence of friendship
that I perceive in your face and your voice.
  These sparks of the power of my past love remain   142
in me from then, though milder now

piú temperate e di minor fervenza:
    da queste accesa, le mie voglie caste   145
in quella guisa propria di voi formo,
che 'l santo amor a circonscriver baste.
    In amicizia il folle amor trasformo,
e pensando a le vostre immense doti,
per imitarvi l'animo riformo;   150
    e se 'n ciò i miei pensier vi fosser noti,
i moderati onesti miei desiri
non lascereste andar d'effetto vuoti.
    Per cui convien ch'ognor brami e desiri
de le vostre virtú gustar il frutto,   155
e quando far nol posso, ne sospiri.
    Ma se convien a voi cangiar ridutto,
e peregrin da noi gir in disparte,
non mi negate il favor vostro in tutto.
    Basta che se ne porti una gran parte   160
seco la mia fortuna: in quel che resta
supplite con gli inchiostri e con le carte.
    Non vi sia la fatica in ciò molesta,
poi che l'alma affannata, piú ch'altronde,
quinci gloriosa si può far di mesta.   165
    Quando siate di là da le salse onde,
vi prego con scritture visitarmi
piene d'amor che grato corrisponde:
    e volendo piú a pieno sodisfarmi,
questo potrete agevolmente farlo   170
con alcuna vostr'opera mandarmi.
    E quand'io non sia degna d'impetrarlo,
per alcun vanto espresso che 'n me sia,
da la vostra bontà voglio sperarlo;
    da la vostra infinita cortesia,   175
benché convien a l'amor ch'io vi porto
che da voi ricompensa mi si dia.
    E facendo altrimenti, avreste il torto:
ond'io, per non far debil mia ragione,
del dever v'ammonisco, e non v'essorto.   180

and burning less fiercely:
    afire with them, I form chaste desires   145
in a manner worthy of you,
which holy love is enough to control.

    I turn my passionate love to friendship,   148
and considering your immense gifts,
I reshape my soul in imitation of you;

    and if my thoughts on this were known to you, 151
you wouldn't permit my present desire,
honest and moderate, to go unfulfilled.

    So I must always long and yearn   154
to taste the fruit of your virtues,
and when I cannot, sigh for them.

    But if you must change your dwelling,   157
and travel far away from us,
don't deny me your favor completely.

    Let it suffice that you take away with you   160
a great part of my good fortune;
fill what remains of it with paper and ink.

    May the effort to do this not weigh you down, 163
for from this writing more than anything else
my suffering soul can leave sadness for joy.

    When you are far beyond these salty waves, 166
I beg you to visit me by means of letters,
full of glad love that corresponds to mine;

    and should you wish to please me   169
more fully, you can easily do so
by sending some of your works to me.

    And should I be unworthy to obtain this   172
for any particular fame of my own,
I wish to place my hope in your generosity;

    give me this recompense from the abundance 175
of your courtesy, even though doing so
is only fitting to the love I bear you.

    And you would be wrong to do otherwise: 178
accordingly, so as not to weaken my appeal,
I remind you of your duty but do not insist.

Si voglion certo amar quelle persone,
da le quai noi amati si sentimo:
cosí la buona civiltà dispone;
   e tanto importa ad amar esser primo,
che se l'amato a ridamar non vola,   185
macchia ogni sua virtú d'oscuro limo.
   Questo è che mi confida e mi consola:
che cader non vorrete in cotal fallo,
ch'ogni ornamento a la virtute invola.
   Come bel fiore in lucido cristallo,   190
traspar ne le vestigie vostre esterne
lo spirto ch'altrui rado il ciel tal dàllo:
   l'alma in voi nel sembiante si discerne,
che di vaghezza esterïor contende
con le virtuti de la mente interne.   195
   Ben chi è tal, se lo specchio inanzi prende,
dilettato dal ben che 'n lui fuor vede,
a far simile al volto il senno attende;
   e mentre move per tai scale il piede,
nel proporzïonar tal di se stesso,   200
ogni condizïon mortale eccede.
   Beato voi, cui far questo è concesso,
e cotanto alto già sète salito,
che nullo avete sopra, e pochi presso!
   Ben quindi fate ognor cortese invito,   205
la man porgendo altrui, perché su monti,
di zelo pien di carità infinito;
   ma tutti non han piè veloci e pronti,
sí come voi, in cosí ardua strada,
e voi 'l sapete, senza ch'io 'l racconti.   210
   Ma però nulla in suo valor digrada
la vostra dignità, se in ciò s'abbassa
per sostener chi v'ama, che non cada.
   Io, sol nel primo entrar già vinta e lassa,
il vostro aiuto di lontan sospiro   215
con occhi lagrimosi e fronte bassa:
   volgete il guardo a me con dolce giro,

We certainly want to love those people   181
by whom we feel that we are loved:
proper civility inclines us this way;
 and it is so important to be the first to love   184
that if the loved one does not love in return,
he stains his every virtue with dark-colored mud.
 This gives me confidence and consolation: 187
that you will not want to fall into such error,
the kind that steals away every sign of virtue.
 Like a beautiful flower in brilliant crystal,   190
your spirit, rarely given by heaven to others,
shines out through your external features:
 your soul can be seen in your appearance,   193
which competes in outward beauty
with the virtues of your inner mind.
 He is a good man who, when he sets a mirror   196
before him, pleased by his outer countenance,
attempts to make his wisdom correspond to his face;
 and as he moves his feet upon such stairs,   199
assessing himself in such a way,
he rises above any human condition.
 Blessed are you, to whom this is permitted,   202
and you have already ascended so high
that you have no one above you and few even close!
 Indeed, you always offer a kind invitation,   205
holding out your hands so that others may climb,
full of eagerness and infinite charity;
 but not everyone has feet as fast and ready   208
as yours to attempt such an arduous path,
and you know it without my telling you.
 But your dignity loses none of its value   211
if it lowers itself to offer support
to the woman who loves you, so that she does not fall.
 Tired and spent at even the first step,   214
I sigh for your help, far down below,
with eyes full of tears and a downcast brow.
 Turn your eyes kindly in my direction,   217

ed a la mia devozïone atteso,
degnatemi d'alcun vostro sospiro.
    Ciò ne la vostra assenza a me conteso   220
prego non sia, e del vostro ozio ancora
alcuno spazio a scrivermi sia speso:
    alcuna rara e minima dimora
in quest'uso per me da voi si spenda,
poi ch'a servirvi io son pronta ad ogni ora.   225
    Dal mio canto, non fia mai che sospenda
il suo corso la penna, e che con l'alma
a compiacervi tutta non intenda.
    E se non vi sarà gravosa salma
il legger le mie lettere, vedrete   230
che di scrivervi spesso avrò la palma:
    questa con vostra man voi mi darete,
e de l'amor in amicizia vòlto,
dagli andamenti miei v'accorgerete.
    Non tengo ad altro il mio pensier rivolto,   235
se non a farvi di mia fede certo,
e mostrarvi 'l mio cor simile al volto,
    senza richieder da voi altro in merto,
se non che 'n grado il mio affetto accettiate,
a voi da me pien d'osservanzia offerto;   240
    e che innanzi al partir mi concediate
ch'io vi parli e v'inchini; e quando poi
siate altrove, di me vi ricordiate,
    perch'io 'l farò con usura con voi.
Del visitarne scrivendo, non parlo,   245
scambievolemente intra di noi,
    ché ben son certa che verrete a farlo,
questo officio gentil meco pigliando,
che 'n alcun modo io non son per lasciarlo.
    Né altro: di buon cor mi raccomando.   250

and, attentive to my devotion to you,
consider me worthy of a sigh of your own.

    Do not allow your absence to leave   220
this prayer unanswered, and use some moments
of your leisure to write to me:

    employ some rare and brief part of your time   223
in this way for my sake, for I am prepared
at every moment to be of service to you.

    For my part, it never will happen   226
that my pen's motion ceases or that my soul
no longer intends to please you in all ways.

    And if reading my letters does not become   229
a burden too great for you, you will see
that by writing you often, I win the palm:[31]

    this you will give me with your own hand,   232
and you will recognize in my behavior
love that has turned into friendship.

    I direct my thought to no other matter   235
than to assure you of my loyalty
and to show you that my heart and face are the same,

    without asking from you any other reward   238
than that you should graciously accept my affection,
offered to you with profound respect:

    and that before your departure you grant   241
that I may speak to you and bow down
and when you're away, that you remember me,

    for I'll do the same, and more, for you.   244
Of mutual visits in even exchange
through writing, I say not a word,

    for I am quite sure that you will do this,   247
taking this kind of trouble on my behalf,
for I certainly have no plan of letting go.

    No more: wholeheartedly, I remind you of this.   250

---

31. Among the Romans, the palm branch was a sign of victory.

Capitolo 20

ᴣᴐ

Questa quella Veronica vi scrive,
che per voi, non qual già libera e franca,
or d'infelice amor soggetta vive;
    per voi rivolta da via dritta a manca,
uom ingrato, crudel, misera corre   5
dove 'l duol cresce e la speranza manca.
    Con tutto questo non si sa disciôrre
dal vostro amor, né puote, né desía,
e del suo mal la medicina aborre;
    disposta o di trovar mente in voi pia,   10
o, del servirvi nell'acerba impresa,
giunger a morte intempestiva e ria.
    Senza temer pericolo od offesa,
a la pioggia, al sereno, a l'aria oscura
vengo, da l'alma Citerea difesa,   15
    per veder e toccar almen le mura
del travïato lontan vostro albergo,
per disperazïon fatta sicura.
    Per strada errando, gli occhi ai balconi ergo
de la camera vostra; e fuor del petto   20
sospiri e pianto d'ambo i lumi aspergo.
    Di buio ciel sotto povero tetto,
de la sorte mi lagno empia e rubella,
e del mio mal ch'a voi porge diletto.
    Senza veder con cui dolermi stella,   25
ne le tenebre fisi i lumi tengo,
che fûr duci d'Amor ne la via fella;
    e poi ch'al terren vostro uscio pervengo,
porgo i miei preghi a l'ostinate porte,
né di basciar il limitar m'astengo.   30
    — Deh siatemi in amor benigne scorte;
apritemi 'l sentier del mio ben chiuso,

Capitolo 20

FRANCO'S ROMAN ELEGY, TO A MAN WHO LOVES
ANOTHER WOMAN

This letter is written to you by that Veronica
who now lives neither free nor frank
but as a slave of unrequited love.
 Turned for your sake from the right path to the wrong,   4
thankless, cruel man, in misery she runs
where sorrow grows and hope decreases.
 In the midst of all this she cannot free herself   7
from loving you; she could not nor does she want to;
and she loathes the medicine that might cure her ill,
 willing either to discover a pitiful mind in you   10
or through serving you in this bitter endeavor,
to reach the point of an early, cruel death.
 With no fear of danger or insult,   13
in rain, in clear weather, and in the dark,
I come, protected by kind Cytherea,[32]
 to see and touch at least the walls   16
of your house, isolated and remote,
drawing confidence from my desperation.
 Wandering in the street, I lift my eyes   19
to your bedroom's balconies; and from my breast
I pour forth sighs, and tears from both my eyes.
 Under the poor shelter of the dark sky,   22
I lament my cruel and relentless fate
and my pain, which gives you pleasure.
 Seeing no star to which I might complain,   25
I stare ahead into the shadows,
which were Love's guides onto his fatal path;
 and as soon as I reach the entrance to your house,   28
I make my appeals to the stubborn doors,
and do not refrain from kissing the threshold.
 —Ah, be my kindly guides to love;   31
open to me the way to my beloved within,

32. Cytherea is another name for Venus, based on the name of the island on which she landed
after her birth from the waves: Cythera, in the Ionian Sea.

del notturno mio error per uso accorte.
     Di letal sonno e tu, custode, infuso,
desto al latrar de' tuoi vigili cani,   35
non far il prego mio vano e deluso:
     deh, pietoso ad aprirmi usa le mani,
cosí i ceppi servili aspri dal piede
del continuo ti stian sciolti e lontani! —
     Ma ch'è quel che da me, lassa, si chiede?   40
— Vattene in pace — il portinaio dice, —
ché le notti il signor qui non risiede;
     ma del suo amor a far lieta e felice
un'altra donna, con lei dorme e giace,
e tu invan qui ti consumi, infelice.   45
     Vattene, sconsolata; e s'aver pace
non puoi, pur con saldo animo sopporta
quel ch'al destino irrevocabil piace. —
     Talor, per gran pietà di me, la porta
geme in suon roco, come quando è mossa,   50
nei cardini, a serrarsi o aprir, distorta;
     ed io, quindi col piè debil rimossa,
ne le braccia di tal che m'accompagna
del viver cado poco men che scossa.
     Il suo pianto dal mio non discompagna   55
quel mio fedel ch'è meco, e d'un tenore
meco del mio martír grida e si lagna.
     Dure disagguaglianze in aspro amore,
poi ch'a chi m'odia corro dietro, e fuggo
da chi de l'amor mio languisce e more!   60
     E cosí ad un me stessa ed altrui struggo,
e 'l sangue de le mie e l'altrui vene
col mio grave dolor consumo e suggo:
     benché da l'altro canto le mie pene
forse consolan altra donna, e 'l pianto   65
con piacer del mio amante al cor perviene.
     Ma chi puote esser mai spietato tanto,
che s'allegri, se pur non può dolersi,
lacero il sen vedermi in ogni canto?

accustomed as you are to my nocturnal roaming.
And you, doorkeeper, full of death-like sleep,   34
awakened by the barking of your watchful dogs,
do not reject and disappoint my pleas—
ah, lift your hand and, in pity, open the door;   37
so may the heavy, enslaving chains
fall from your feet and be taken off forever.
But what am I asking, unhappy woman?   40
"Be gone in peace," the watchman says,
"my master no longer resides here at night.
Making another happy and blessed   43
with his love, he lies and sleeps by her side,
while you, unhappy, waste away here in vain.
So go away, poor wretch, and if you find no peace,   46
you must then endure with steadfast soul
what unchangeable destiny is pleased to give you."
Now and then through heartfelt pity, the door   49
lets out a grating moan, as a door often does
when it opens or closes on twisted hinges;
and I, now wavering on unsteady feet,   52
step away and fall back into my companion's arms,
not simply weak but shaken unto death.
My faithful follower does not cease   55
to accompany my wailing with his own,
and in harmony with me he wails and laments my woe.
Wretched mismatches in cruel love—   58
for I pursue a man who hates me
and shun one, who, languishing, dies for my love!
I destroy at the same time myself and another,   61
and in my grief I drink up and drain the blood
from my own veins and from his, as well,
while, on the other hand, my heartfelt pain   64
perhaps consoles another woman,
and my lament comes with pleasure to my lover's heart.
But who could ever be so ruthless   67
as not to pity me, but rather to enjoy
seeing my breast ripped open from every side?

Lassa, la notte e 'l dí far prose e versi   70
non cesso in varia forma, in vario stile,
sempre a un oggetto coi pensier conversi;
    e s'ha quest'opre il mio signor a vile,
men mal è assai che se 'n mia onta e in strazio
leggerle con colei ha preso stile.   75
    Per me lieto non è di tempo spazio,
e di quel dond'a me si niega il gusto
altra si stanca, e fa 'l suo desir sazio.
    Quant'è per me difficultoso, angusto,
quel ch'ad altri è camin facile e piano!   80
Colpa d'Amor iniquitoso, ingiusto.
    Ma da la crudeltà se 'l gir lontano
ad uom nobil s'aspetta veramente,
e l'aver facil alma in petto umano;
    se quanto altri è piú chiaro e piú splendente   85
per natura, per sangue e per fortuna,
chi l'ama ridamar deve egualmente;
    voi 'n cui 'l ciel tutte le sue grazie aduna,
dovete aver pietà di me, che v'amo
sí che 'n questo non trovo eguale alcuna.   90
    E quanto piú ne' miei sospir vi chiamo,
d'esser udita (a dir il vero) io 'merto,
e quanto piú con voi conversar bramo.
    Non è d'ingegno indizio oscuro e incerto,
c'ha gusto de le cose piú eccellenti,   95
conoscer e stimar il vostro merto.
    Deh sentite pietà de' miei tormenti,
se de le tigri non sète del sangue,
e se non vi nudrîr l'idre e i serpenti.
    Ne la mia faccia pallida ed essangue   100
fede acquistate de la pena cruda,
onde 'l mio cor innamorato langue.
    Né anch'io d'orsa, che 'n cieco antro si chiuda,
nacqui; né l'erbe stesa mi nudrîro,
come vil bestia, in su la terra ignuda;   105
    ma tai del mio buon seme effetti uscîro,

Alas, night and day I never cease   70
writing verse and prose in diverse forms and styles,
all focused, like my thoughts, upon a single theme.

And if my lord holds these writings in contempt,   73
I care less than if, to my shame and pain,
he has made it his habit to read them with her.

For me there is no happy time in sight,   76
while of him, though I may never enjoy him,
another grows weary and has had her fill.

How difficult of approach and narrow for me   79
is the path that's easy and smooth for others!—
this is the doing of relentless, unjust Love.

But if a noble man can be truly expected   82
to travel far from cruelty and always maintain
a yielding spirit in a humane breast,

if, however more famous and splendid he may be   85
by nature, in blood and in good fortune,
he should love in return the woman who loves him,

you, in whom all heaven's graces unite,   88
should pity me, for I love you so much
that I find no other woman to match me.

And the more I call out for you in sighs,   91
and the more I long to speak to you,
the more (in truth) I deserve to be heard.

It is no unclear or doubtful sign   94
of a mind with a taste for most excellent things
that it recognizes and values your merit.

Alas, feel some pity for the pain I endure   97
if you are not born of the race of tigers
and were not fed by hydras and snakes.

In my face, pale and bloodless,   100
you may be certain of the cruel distress
in which my fond heart pines away.

I wasn't born of a bear, concealed in a dark cave,   103
nor was I fed with forked out hay,
like a low animal, on the bare ground;

the results of my good breeding ensure   106

ch'alcun non ha da recarsi ad oltraggio,
se del suo amor io lagrimo e sospiro.
　　Ciò dir basti parlando con uom saggio,
ché far con voi per questa strada acquisto　　　　110
nel mio pensiero intenzïon non aggio;
　　ma del mio stato ingiurïoso e tristo
cerco indurvi a pietà con le preghiere,
e di sospir col largo pianto misto.
　　Ch'al segno de le doti vostre altiere　　　　115
alcun raro in me pregio non arrive,
questo ogni ragion porta, ogni dovere;
　　ma quel che dentro 'l petto Amor mi scrive
con lettre d'oro di sua man, leggete,
se 'l mio merto ha con voi radici vive.　　　　120
　　L'obligo de l'amante vederete
d'esser grato a l'amor simile al mio,
se con occhio sottil v'attenderete.
　　Ma né con questo voglio acquistarvi io:
solo a l'alta pietà del mio martíre　　　　125
farvi per cortesia benigno e pio.
　　Il mio continuo e misero languire,
l'amorose querele ond'io vi prego,
vi faccian del mio duol pietà sentire:
　　gran forza suol aver di donna prego　　　　130
negli animi gentil ch'ancor non ame;
ed io, d'amor accesa, a voi mi piego.
　　Prima che 'l duol di me si sazii e sbrame,
e mi riduca in cenere quest'ossa,
date ristoro a le mie ardenti brame;　　　　135
　　porgete alcun rimedio a la percossa,
che d'aspra angoscia versa un largo fonte,
e mi spolpa, e mi snerva, e mi disossa;
　　scemate il grave innaccessibil monte
di quei ch'amando voi sostengo affanni,　　　　140
con voglie in tutti i casi a soffrir pronte;
　　movetevi a pietà de' miei verdi anni,
onde, da la virtú vostra sospinta,

that no one need think he's insulted by me,
even though I weep and sigh for his love.
 Let me say no more to a man who's wise,   109
for to retrace with you a path already taken
does not lie in my thought or my plan;
 but I am trying to make you feel some pity   112
for my scorned and wretched state,
through pleas and laments mingled with tears.
 For my isolated good qualities   115
cannot match the evidence of your noble talents—
this follows by reason and by necessity;
 but read what Love writes in my heart[33]   118
in his own hand, with letters of gold,
if my merit lives in you at all.
 You would see that the duty of a lover   121
is to welcome love like mine,
if you were to attend with a discerning eye.
 But I do not want to win you this way: 124
I only wish, through deep pity for my woe,
to make you through courtesy kind and tenderhearted.
 May my unceasing misery and grief,   127
the loving complaints by which I appeal,
make you feel compassion for my pain.
 A lady's prayer often has great power   130
in gentle souls, even if she is not in love;
and I, inflamed with love, bow down to you.
 Before grief has had enough and disdains me   133
and reduces these bones of mine to ash,
give new life to my burning desire.
 Give me some remedy against this blow,   136
which looses a fountain of bitter anguish
and strips away my flesh, nerves, and bones.
 Lessen the huge and endless mountain   139
of agonies I suffer for love of you,
and my longing in every case to suffer more;
 have pity on my tender, youthful years,   142
which, responding to your virtue, are the cause

33. Here Franco alludes, with some variation, to the scene in Dante's *Purgatorio* in which Dante the pilgrim tells Bonagiunta da Lucca that the success of his *dolce stil novo* resulted from his careful noting down of what love spoke in his heart (24.52–54).

cado d'Amor nei volontari inganni.
    Ed a morir per voi sono anco accinta,   145
se d'utile e d'onor esser vi puote
che per voi resti la mia vita estinta.
    Grato suono a l'orecchie mie percuote
che non sosterrà un uom sí valoroso
d'effetto far le mie speranze vuote.   150
    Da l'aspetto sí dolce ed amoroso
non debbo sospettar di morte o pena,
né d'altro incontro a me grave e noioso.
    Ma chi, fuor d'uso, a ben sperar mi mena?
Lassa, e pur so che sorge 'l nembo e nasce   155
sovente in mezzo a l'aria piú serena;
    e cosí sotto un bel volto si pasce
spesso un cor empio degli altrui martíri,
qual che tra' fior vedersi angue non lasce.
    Ma se 'n voi non han forza i miei sospiri,   160
a la nobiltà vostra, a la virtute,
volgete con giudicio i lenti giri.
    Non debbo disperar di mia salute,
s'ai costumi gentil vostri ho rispetto,
ed a le mie profonde aspre ferute;   165
    ma poi di quel che m'incontra, l'effetto
di tormento maggior, di maggior doglia,
mi dà certezza ognor, non pur sospetto:
    benché d'umil trïonfo indegna spoglia
fia la mia vita, se, per troppo amarvi,   170
dal vostro orgoglio avien che mi si toglia.
    Ma s'al mio mal non puote altro piegarvi,
l'esser io tutta vostra mi conceda
ch'io possa almeno in tanto duol pregarvi:
    forse fia che l'orecchie e 'l cor vi fieda   175
il mio cordoglio, assai minore espresso
di quel ch'al ver perfetto si richieda.
    Tanto a me di vigor non è concesso,
ch'esprimer di quel colpo il dolor vaglia,
ch'io porto ne le mie viscere impresso: 180

that I fall so deeply into Love's wily traps.

    And I'm ready and even willing to die for you   145
if you should find it of use or an honor
that my life be cut short on your behalf.

    The news, reassuring, reaches my ears   148
that a man of such valor will not allow
all my hopes to come to nothing.

    From a face so sweet and loving   151
I should not fear death or torment
or any other dire, harsh encounter.

    But who, against habit, makes me hope for good?   154
I know too well, alas, that rainclouds
appear and grow amid the fairest skies;

    and thus beneath a handsome face   157
feeds a heart greedy for another's pain,
just as a serpent hides from sight among flowers.

    But if my sighs have no power over you,   160
turn your eyes, in careful judgment,
to your own nobility and virtue.

    I need not despair of my salvation   163
if I consider your gentle ways
and my own deep, piercing wounds.

    But then the reality that I confront   166
makes me know for certain, not only suspect,
greater torment and greater pain.

    My life would be the worthless token   169
of a low triumph, if, by loving you too much,
it should be taken from me through your pride.

    But if nothing else can bend you to my pain,   172
may my being yours entirely allow me,
in such great woe, to plead with you, at least.

    If perhaps your ear and heart   175
confide my sorrow to you, they express it
far less well than the whole truth requires.

    I have not been granted strength enough   178
to say how much I'm wounded by this blow,
which I carry imprinted in my deepest core.

in dir sí com'Amor empio m'assaglia,
sí come oscura la mia vita ei renda,
lo stil debile a l'opra non s'agguaglia.

Da voi 'l mio mal nel mio amor si comprenda,
ch'è tanto quanto amabile voi sète;   185
e pia la vostra man ver' me si stenda:

quella, in aiuto, man non mi si viete,
che 'l nodo seppe ordire al duro laccio
de la gravosa mia tenace rete;

e 'l volto, onde qual neve al sol mi sfaccio,   190
che m'invaghío di sua bella figura,
soccorra a quel dolor ch'amando taccio.

D'alta virtú la divina fattura,
che 'n voi s'annida come in dolce stanza,
il cui splendor m'accende oltra misura,   195

l'animo di piegarvi abbia possanza,
sí che in tanto penar mi concediate
alcun sostegno di gentil speranza.

Non dico che di me v'innamoriate,
né che, com'io per voi son tutta fiamma,   200
d'un amor cambïevole m'amiate:

del vostro foco ben picciola dramma
ristorar può quell'incendio crudele,
che s'io cerco ammorzarlo, e piú m'infiamma.

Amor, s'ho con voi merto, vi rivele;   205
e le parti, c'ho in me di voi non degne,
agli occhi vostri dolce offuschi e cele,

sí che prima ch'a morte amando io vegne,
quella mercé da voi mi si conceda,
che sgombri 'l pianto ond'ho le luci pregne.   210

Lassa, che s'un nemico a l'altro chieda
al suo bisogno aiuto, ei gli vien dato,
ché la virtú convien che gli odii ecceda;

ed io creder devrò ch'aspro ed ingrato
esser mi debba il mio signor diletto,   215
perch'ei sia forse d'altra innamorato?

Oimè! che, d'altra standosi nel letto,

My feeble style is unequal to the task   181
of saying how cruelly Love assaults me,
and how he casts darkness over all my life.
   Please understand my suffering in love,   184
which is as great as you are worthy of love,
and reach out your kindly hand to me.
   Do not deny me your helping hand,   187
that well knew how to tie the knot
that closed tight my cruel, entrapping net;
   and may the face that melts me like snow in the sun,   190
that made me fall in love with your handsome appearance,
ease the pain I suffer in silence for love.
   May the divine creation of lofty virtue   193
that dwells in you as in a lovely room,
whose splendor inflames me past all measure,
   have the power to soften your spirit   196
so that, in such suffering, you grant to me
some reason to comfort myself with hope.
   I am not saying that you should fall in love with me, 199
or that, because I am all aflame for you,
you should love me in the same way;
   even a tiny measure of your fire   202
can relieve this searing conflagration
which, if I try to quench it, only burns deeper.
   Love, if I deserve anything from you, come forth;   205
and those parts of me that are unworthy of you,
dim and conceal sweetly from your sight,
   so that, before I come to die for love,   208
you grant to me sufficient mercy
to dry the tears that now drench my eyes.
   Alas, if an enemy in need asks help   211
from another, it comes to be granted to him,
for it's right that virtue should overcome hatred.
   And should I believe that my cherished lord   214
must be cruel and heartless to me
because, perhaps, he loves another?
   Ah! how his presence in another woman's bed   217

me lascia raffreddar sola e scontenta,
colma d'affanni e piena di dispetto:
    altra ei fa del suo amor lieta e contenta,   220
e del mio mal con lei fors'ancor ride,
che vanaglorïosa ne diventa.
    Quanto per me si lagrima e si stride,
dolce concento è de le loro orecchie,
da cui 'l mio amor negletto si deride.   225
    Cosí convien che sempre m'apparecchie
a soffrir nuovi di fortuna colpi,
e che 'n novello strazio alfin m'invecchie.
    Né però avien che del mio affanno incolpi
chi piú devrei; ned in mercé mi valse   230
quanto in ciò piú credei che piú 'l discolpi.
    Oimè, che troppo duro Amor m'assalse,
poi che per farmi di miseria essempio,
m'insidia ancor con sue speranze false.
    Da un canto il certo mio danno contempio;   235
e perché 'l duol piú nuoccia meno atteso,
di speme al van desio conforme m'empio.
    Non fosse almen da voi medesmo offeso
l'affetto uman del gentil vostro seno
ne l'essermi il soccorso, oimè, conteso.   240
    D'ogni mia avversità mi duol via meno,
che di veder ch'a voi s'ascriva il fallo
di quanto in amar voi languisco e peno.
    Ben sapete, crudel, che 'l mondo udràllo,
e con mia dolce ed amara vendetta   245
d'ogn'intorno la fama porteràllo.
    Né cosí vola fuor d'arco saetta,
com'al mio essempio mosse fuggiranno
d'amarvi a gara l'altre donne in fretta;
    e quanto del mio mal pietate avranno,   250
tanto, dal vostro orgoglio empio a schivarsi,
caute a l'esperïenzia mia saranno.
    Oh che pregiata e nobil virtú, farsi
anco amar in paese sconosciuto

leaves me cold, alone, and discontent,
overwhelmed by grief and full of spite!

He delights another woman, happy in his love,   220
and perhaps, with her, he jeers at my pain,
so that she feels overweening pride.

Whatever weeping and wailing I do   223
is sweet harmony to both their ears,
who make fun of my neglected love.

So I must constantly ready myself   226
to endure new blows of fortune
and finally to grow old in new distress.

Nor can I blame my pain on him whom most   229
I should. Never has he granted me mercy;
yet the more I think he will, the more I forgive him.

Alas! how cruelly heartless Love has struck me,   232
for to make me a living example of misery,
he still deceives me with misleading hope.

On one side I see my certain loss,   235
and, since least expected pain hurts most,
I fill myself with hope befitting vain desire.

If only you yourself did not wound   238
the human feeling in your noble breast,
or, alas, withhold all comfort from me!

I regret far less my own adversity   241
than seeing that the blame belongs to you
for all my languishing and pain in love.

Know well, cruel man, the world will hear of it,   244
and, along with my sweet and bitter revenge,
will carry the news of it to every place on earth.

And no arrow takes flight from the bow   247
as fast as women, warned by my example,
vying with one another, will flee from loving you;

and the more pity they feel for my pain,   250
the more eagerly will they avoid your cruel pride,
made cautious by my experience with you.

Oh, what a precious and noble virtue—   253
to make yourself loved even in a new land

col benigno e pietoso altrui mostrarsi!   255
   E quante volte è in tal caso avenuto
che de' meriti altrui senz'altro il grido
d'uom ignoto ave 'l cor arder potuto!
   Ond'io, che di mie doti non mi fido,
pensando che voi sète uom degno e chiaro,   260
da me la speme in tutto non divido;
   anzi, nel colmo del mio stato amaro
lusingando me stessa, attender voglio
al mio dolor da voi schermo e riparo,
   poi che di grand'onor il mio cordoglio   265
esser vi può, se pronto a sovenirmi
sarete, mentre a voi di voi mi doglio:
   se non, vedrete misera morirmi.

by seeming kind and pitiful to someone else!

    And how often has it happened in such a case   256
that someone's reputation alone
has had the power to set a heart on fire!

    So though I lack confidence in my own gifts,   259
considering that you are a fine and famous man,
I don't abandon hope entirely.

    Rather, even at the height of my bitterness,   262
flattering myself, I persist in expecting
shelter and refuge from you for my pain,

    for my sorrow could bring you great honor,   265
if you are quick to come to my aid,
even as I complain about you to yourself.

    If not, you'll see me, in misery, die.   268

Capitolo 21

৵

Io dicea: — Mio cor, se ciò mi fanno
l'armi mie proprie, quelle, onde mi punge
la fortuna crudel, che mi faranno? —
    S'io stessa, col fuggir dal mio ben lunge,
sento che 'l duol via piú mi s'avvicina,   5
che la partenza mia mel ricongiunge;
    al mio languir contraria medicina
certo avrò preso al vaneggiar del core,
che per misera strada m'incamina.
    Lassa, or mi pento del commesso errore,   10
anzi non mossi cosí tosto il passo
dal dolce loco ov'abita 'l mio amore,
    ch'io dissi: — Oimè! dunque è pur ver ch'io lasso
quella terra e quell'acque, ove 'l mio sole
di splendor rende ogni altro lume casso? —   15
    E se ridir potessi le parole,
che volgendomi indietro al caro suolo
dissi, qual chi lasciar ciò ch'ama suole,
    vedrei gli augelli ancor con lento volo
seguirmi ad ascoltar il mio lamento,   20
alternando in pia voce il mio gran duolo;
    vedrei qual già fermarsi a udirmi 'l vento,
e quetar le procelle, e i boschi e i sassi
moversi a la pietà del mio tormento.
    Ma per troppo gridar afflitti e lassi   25
sono i miei spirti, onde già i pesci e l'onde
le mie miserie a meco pianger trassi.
    Tanta rena non han d'Adria le sponde,
quante volte il suo nome allor chiamai,
com'or qui 'l chiamo, ov'Eco sol risponde.   30
    Co' sospiri arsi e col pianto bagnai
l'amate spoglie, e di lui in vece accolte

Capitolo 21

FRANCO, MEDITATING ON A LOVER FROM WHOM
SHE IS SEPARATED

I said: "My heart, if my own weapons
do this to me, what will those do
with which cruel fortune pierces me?"
    If I myself feel, having fled far from my love,   4
that pain closes in on me ever more,
that my leaving brings it closer to me,
    I must surely have taken medicine opposed   7
to my languid state and to my heart's raving,
which sends me down a miserable path.
    Alas, I repent now the error I made,   10
or rather, no sooner had I left behind
the cherished place where my love dwells,
    than I said: "Woe is me! Can it really be true   13
that I am leaving this city and these seas
where my sun in his splendor dims all other lights?"
    And if I could repeat the words that I said,   16
turning back to look at my beloved land,
as anyone leaving what she loves is bound to say,
    I would see again the birds following me   19
in their slow flight to hear my lament,
answering my pain with their tender voices;
    I would see the wind almost stop to listen,   22
and the storms die down and the woods and stones
moved to compassion for my torment.
    But my spirits, from wailing too much,   25
are sad and weary, so that now I have moved
the fish and the waves to lament my woes with me.
    Adria's shores have fewer grains of sand   28
than the number of times I then called his name,
just as now I call it here, where only Echo responds.
    With sighs I burned and with tears I bathed   31
his dear garments, and in his place

al seno me le strinsi e le basciai,
dicendo: — O spoglie, che già foste avvolte
intorno a quelle membra, che da Marte   35
sembrano in forma di Narciso tolte,
se 'l ciel mi riconduce in quella parte
onde stolta partí', non sarà mai
che quinci 'l fermo piè volga in disparte. —
Non fu pietra né pianta, ov'io passai,   40
che non piangesse meco, e forse allora
non mi dicesse: — Folle! ove ne vai? —
Dal cerchio estremo, ove fan lor dimora
scintillando le stelle, certamente
meco pianger mostrâr la notte ancora.   45
Ben vidi 'l sol levar chiaro e lucente;
ma perché gli occhi ad abbagliarmi e 'l core
un piú bel lume impresso avea la mente,
scarso del sol mi parve lo splendore;
o fu, forse, ch'udendo 'l mio gran pianto,   50
anch'ei si scolorí del mio dolore.
Oh com'è privo d'intelletto, e quanto
colui s'inganna, che nel patrio nido
viver può lieto col suo bene a canto,
e va cercando or l'uno or l'altro lido,   55
pensando forse che la lontananza
ai colpi sia d'Amor rifugio fido!
Fugga pur l'uom, se sa: la rimembranza
del caro obbietto sempre gli è d'intorno,
anzi porta in cor viva la sembianza.   60
S'io veggo l'alba a noi menar il giorno,
mirando i fiori e le vermiglie rose,
che le cingon la fronte e 'l crin adorno,
— Tal — dico, — è 'l mio bel viso, in cui ripose
tutti i suoi doni il cielo, e la natura   65
la sua eccellenza piú ch'altrove espose. —
Poi, quando scorgo per la notte oscura
accendersi là su cotante stelle,
Amor, ch'è meco, sí m'afferma e giura

I held them to my breast and hugged and kissed them,
 saying, "Oh, garments that were once   34
wrapped around those limbs of his,
limbs that were taken from Narcissus by Mars,[34]
 if heaven ever leads me back to that place   37
from which I foolishly took my leave,
never will I turn my firm step to depart."
 There was neither stone nor plant, wherever I went, 40
that did not weep for me and perhaps say,
"Madwoman! Where are you going?"
 From the farthest circle where the stars   43
make their sparkling abode, they clearly revealed
that even the night was weeping with me.
 I did see the sun rise, shining and bright,   46
but since a more beautiful light was impressed
on my heart and mind to dazzle my eyes,
 the sun seemed to lack its usual splendor,   49
or perhaps on hearing my bitter lament,
even it turned pale in response to my grief.
 Oh, how mindless and how self-deceptive   52
is the man who, though he could happily live
in the heart of his country, his beloved at his side,
 goes on a search from one shore to another, 55
thinking perhaps that distance can be
a safe refuge from the blows of love!
 Let a man flee, if he knows how;   58
the memory of his beloved always surrounds him;
indeed, he carries her image alive in his heart.
 If I see dawn leading the day to us,   61
looking at the flowers and the vermilion roses
that circle her forehead and her lovely hair,
 "Such," I say, "is my love's handsome face, 64
where heaven bestowed all of its gifts,
and nature most reveals her perfection."
 Then when I see through the dark night   67
so many stars light up in the sky,
Love, who is with me, assures me and swears

34. Franco here claims that her Mars-like, that is, military, beloved, also has the physical beauty of Narcissus, the beautiful boy who died of self-love (*Metamorphoses*, 3.407–510).

che quelle luci in cielo eterne e belle   70
tante non son, quante virtú in colui
che poi crudo del sen l'alma mi svelle.
    E per far i miei dí piú tristi e bui,
dal mio raggio lontan, sempre al cor vivo
ho 'l sole ardente, onde pria accesa fui: 75
    al qual piangendo e sospirando scrivo.

that those lights in the sky, fair and everlasting,   70
are not as numerous as the virtues of the man
who ruthlessly tears the soul from my breast.

    And to make my days even sadder and darker,   73
far from my light, I always carry alive in my heart
the burning sun from which I once caught fire,

    to whom, weeping and sighing, I write.   76

Capitolo 22

ᴑ

Poi ch'altrove il destino andar mi sforza
con quel duol di lasciarti, o mio bel nido,
ch'in me piú sempre poggia e si rinforza,
 con quel duol che nel cor piangendo annido,
con la memoria sempre a te ritorno,   5
o mio patrio ricetto amico e fido:
 e maledico l'infelice giorno,
che di lasciarti avennemi; e sospiro
la lentezza del pigro mio ritorno.
 Dovunque gli occhi lagrimando giro,   10
lunge da te, mi sembra orror di morte
qualunque oggetto ancor ch'allegro miro.
 Tutto quel che ristoro e gioia apporte,
per questi campi e per le piagge amene,
reca a me affanno e duol gravoso e forte.   15
 L'apriche valli, d'aura e d'odor piene,
l'erbe, i rami, gli augei, le fresche fonti,
ch'escon da cristalline e pure vene,
 l'ombrose selve, e i coltivati monti,
che da salir son dilettosi e piani,   20
e piú facili quant'uom piú su monti,
 e tutto quel che con industri mani
qui l'arte e la natura e 'l ciel opráro,
sono per me deserti alpestri e strani.
 Non può temprar alcun dolce l'amaro   25
ch'io sento de l'acerba dipartita,
ch'io fei dal natío suolo amato e caro:
 quivi lasciai nel mio partir la vita,
ch'ai piè negletta del mio crudo amante
da me giace divisa e disunita.   30
 E pur tra questi fiori e queste piante
la vo cercando, e di quell'empio l'orme,

Capitolo 22

FRANCO AGAIN, TO VENICE AND HER DISTANT LOVER

Since destiny forces me to go elsewhere,
oh, my beautiful home, with regret at leaving you,
which constantly grows and weighs me down
    with sorrow that I harbor, weeping, in my heart,   4
in memory I constantly come back to you,
oh, friendly and faithful refuge of my birth:
    and I curse the unhappy day   7
when I first left you behind; and I sigh
over the long delay of my slow return.
    Wherever, weeping, I turn my eyes,   10
far from you, whatever I see, however gay,
seems to me the horror of death.
    Everything that brings solace and joy   13
throughout these fields and lovely shores
causes me pain and heavy, dismal grief.
    The sunny valleys, full of breezes and scents,   16
the grasses, the branches, the birds, the cool springs
that pour from crystalline, pure streams,
    the shady groves and cultivated hills,   19
so delightful and so welcoming to climb,
and easier the farther up one goes,
    and all the things that art, nature, and heaven   22
with industrious hands have created here
are savage and foreign deserts to me.
    No sweetness can assuage the bitterness I feel   25
because of the painful departure I took
from my dearly beloved native soil:
    leaving, I left my life behind,   28
which, lying ignored at my cruel lover's feet,
lies torn asunder and parted from me.
    And yet among these flowers and plants   31
I go seeking it, and the tracks of that vile man

ch'ovunque io vada ognor mi sta davante.
   E par ch'io 'l vegga, e poi ch'ei si trasforme
or d'un abete, or d'un faggio, or d'un pino,   35
or d'un lauro, or d'un mirto in varie forme;
   parmelo aver negli occhi da vicino,
e le mani a pigliarlo avide stendo,
e la bocca a basciarlo gli avicino:
   in questo lo mio error veggio e comprendo,   40
ché, da l'imaginar e da la speme
delusa, un tronco o un sasso abbraccio e prendo.
   Se cantando posar gioiosi insieme
duo augelletti sopra un ramo veggo,
con quel desio ch'Amor dolce al cor preme,   45
   del mio misero stato, e piú m'aveggo
che col rimedio de la lontananza,
dov'altri non m'aita, invan proveggo.
   Stan pur duo uccelli in lieta dilettanza,
godendo di quel bene unitamente,   50
ch'al lor desire agguaglia la speranza;
   ne le selve e nei boschi Amor si sente,
dal consorzio degli uomini sbandito,
tra i bruti, i quai pur s'aman parimente;
   un concorde voler al dolce invito   55
de la gioia d'amor le fiere tragge,
con affetto in duo cori egual partito;
   per monti e valli e selve e lidi e piagge,
quinci e quindi congiunta in modo stretto
coppia sen va di due bestie selvagge: 60
   e l'uom, dal cielo a dominar eletto
tutti gli altri animali de la terra,
dotato di ragione e d'intelletto;
   l'uom che, se non vuol, rado o mai non erra,
fa, nei desir d'amor dolci, a se stesso   65
cosí continua abominosa guerra,
   sí ch'a lui poi d'amar non è concesso,
senza trovar di repugnanti voglie
de la persona amata il core impresso.

who stands before me wherever I go.
    And I seem to see him, transforming himself   34
now into a beech tree, now a fir, now a pine,
now a laurel, now a myrtle, into all sorts of shapes.
    It seems to me that I can see him close by,   37
and I reach out with eager hands to seize him,
and try to bring my lips close, to kiss him.
    In this confusion I see and understand   40
that, deluded by imagination and hope,
I embrace and hold a tree trunk or a rock.
    If I see two little singing birds   43
land together in joy on a branch,
with the desire Love gently imprints in the heart,
    I realize that I count in vain   46
on distance as a cure for my misery,
in a place where no one assists me.
    And then two birds share sweet delight,   49
coming together to enjoy that good
that fulfills their desire and hope as one;
    in the groves and woods, one senses Love,   52
driven from the company of men, among
the animals, which love each other equally;
    mutual desire draws wild creatures   55
to the sweet invitation of love's delights,
with feeling shared equally between two hearts;
    in mountains, valleys, groves, banks, and shores,   58
here and there, joined in tight embrace,
pairs of wild beasts wander in twos,
    and man, chosen by heaven to be lord   61
over all the other beasts of the earth,
endowed with reason and with intellect,
    man, who by choice errs rarely or never,   64
desiring sweet love, wages against himself
such a continuous and abominable war
    that in the end it is impossible for him   67
to love without finding his beloved's heart
marked with desires that resist his own.

In ciò contrario a le donne si voglie   70
piú ch'agli uomini 'l ciel; ch'amano senza
sentir quasi in amor altro che doglie.
    Far non può de le donne resistenza
la natura sí molle ed imbecilla,
di Venere del figlio a la potenza;   75
    picciol'aura conturba la tranquilla
feminil mente, e di tepido foco
l'alma semplice nostra arde e sfavilla.
    E quanto avem di libertà piú poco,
tanto 'l cieco desir, che ne desvía,   80
di penetrarne al cor ritrova loco:
    sí che ne muor la donna, o fuor di via
esce de la comun nostra strettezza,
e per picciolo error forte travía.
    Quanto a la libertate è manco avezza,   85
tanto in furia maggior l'avien che saglia,
s'Amor quei nodi vïolento spezza;
    né per poco vien mai che donna assaglia
per tirar il suo amante al suo desio,
ma ciascun mezzo prova quant'ei vaglia.   90
    Cosí sforzata son di far anch'io,
d'amor ne la difficile mia impresa,
per ottener il ben ch'amo e desío;
    e se ben fatt'a me vien grande offesa,
nullo argomento usato in espugnarti,   95
amante ingrato, mi rincresce o pesa.
    Per darti luogo, venni in queste parti,
ed al tuo arbitrio di te cassa vivo,
sperando in tal maniera d'acquistarti.
    Qui, dov'è 'l prato verde e chiaro il rivo,   100
venni, e de le dolci onde al roco suono,
e degli uccelli al canto, e parlo e scrivo.
    In luogo ameno e dilettevol sono,
ma non è quivi l'allegrezza mia,
se non quanto di te penso e ragiono;   105
    anzi 'l pensar di te dagli occhi invia

In this, heaven opposes women   70
more than men, for women feel
almost nothing in love except pain.
　　Women's nature, weak and yielding,   73
is not able to maintain resistance
against the power of Venus's son;
　　　the slightest breeze stirs the female mind,   76
and our simple souls are set ablaze
and filled with sparks by even a tepid fire.
　　And the less freedom we possess,   79
the more blind desire, leading us astray,
will find a way to penetrate our hearts.
　　So a woman either dies of love,   82
or escapes from our shared constraint
and goes far astray for a slight mistake.
　　The less she has the habit of freedom,   85
the greater heights of fury she'll reach
if Love once violently breaks those bonds;
　　　so it is never for a small cause that a woman   88
assails her lover, to bend him to her desire,
but every means she uses proves how she values him.
　　I too am forced to behave in this way   91
in my difficult pursuit of love
to win the bliss I love and long for;
　　　and even if I must suffer great injury,   94
no argument used to fight against you,
thankless lover, discourages me or weighs me down.
　　To satisfy you I came to these parts,   97
and I live shattered, obeying your will,
hoping to win your favor in this way.
　　Here I have come, where the meadow is green   100
and the brook is clear, and I speak and write
of the sweet waves' roar and the singing birds.
　　I am in a serene and beautiful place,   103
but there's no happiness for me here
except when I think and speak of you;
　　　rather, the thought of you brings bitter tears 106

lagrime amare, e de l'altrui piacere
sento piú farsi la mia sorte ria.
   L'altrui gioie d'amor tante vedere
a le fiere, agli augelli, ai pesci darsi   110
mi fa nel mio dolor piú doglia avere:
   non può l'invidia mia dentro celarsi,
ma con sospiri e pianto, e con lamenti,
vien per la bocca e gli occhi a disfogarsi.
   Ben piú che degli altrui dolci contenti,   115
allargo 'l pianto e senza fin mi doglio
de l'acerba cagion de' miei tormenti;
   ma poi d'ammollir tento un aspro scoglio,
che piú s'indura e piú s'impietra, quanto
piú mostro il sospiroso mio cordoglio,   120
   e poi che 'l mio dolor ti giova tanto,
io mi vivrò, tra queste selve ombrose,
sol de la tua memoria e del mio pianto.
   Qui farà l'ore mie liete e gioiose
veder che 'l prato, il poggio, il bosco e 'l fiume   125
dían ricetto a l'altrui gioie amorose;
   veder per natural dolce costume
gli augei, le fiere e i pesci insieme amarsi
in modo che da l'uom non si costume;
   e senza alcun sospetto insieme andarsi   130
liberamente ovunque Amor gli guide,
e l'uno in grembo a l'altro riposarsi.
   Nulla il gran lor piacer toglie o divide,
ma sempre il sommo lor diletto cresce;
di che me, con duol mista, invidia uccide.   135
   Ecco che fuor d'un antro, or ch'io parlo, esce
coppia felice di due dame snelle,
cui sempre star in un sol luogo incresce;
   e là due rondinette unirsi anch'elle
veggo in un ramo verde. Ahi del mio amante   140
voglie contrarie al mio desir rubelle!
   Dove parlan d'amor l'erbe e le piante,
dove i desir d'ognun sono concordi,

to my eyes, and I feel others' pleasure
making my fate more cruel still.
   To see so many joys of love   109
given to the beasts, the birds, and the fish
makes my pain more painful still:
   I cannot conceal the envy I feel,   112
for through sighs, tears, and cries
it finds relief through my mouth and eyes.
   Far exceeding the joy of others,   115
I increase my weeping and grieve without end
over the bitter cause of my suffering;
   but then I try to melt a stern rock,   118
which hardens and turns more stony still
the more I reveal my heartfelt pain,
   and since my suffering pleases you so,   121
here I shall live, among shady groves,
only on the memory of you and my tears.
   Seeing the meadow, hill, wood, and stream   124
here shelter others' loving joys
will make my hours happy and full of joy,
   seeing, through sweet habit, inborn,   127
the birds, beasts, and fish loving each other
in a way not usual for humankind,
   and going freely together without any fear   130
wherever Love leads them on,
each one resting in the other's embrace.
   Nothing deprives them of their joy   133
but their highest delight grows ever greater;
so I am slain by envy, mixed with grief.
   Look! Just as I speak, a loving pair   136
of two slender deer comes forth from a cave,
weary of remaining in the same place;
   and further off, too, I see two swallows mating   139
on a green bough. Alas, that my lover's wishes
should be so opposed and contrary to mine!
   Where the grasses and flowers speak of love,   142
where all creatures' yearnings are in accord,

in quest'almo paese circostante
m'addusse Amor, perch'io piú mi ricordi,   145
ne la dolcezza de l'altrui venture,
dei pensieri d'uom crudel dai miei discordi.
    Né questo accresce sol le mie sventure,
per prova intender dai boschi e dai sassi
quanto sian meco acerbe le sue cure: 150
    ché sempre avanti a la memoria stassi
quanto, per fuggir l'odio di colui,
da la patria gentil mi dilungassi;
    da quell'Adria tranquilla e vaga, a cui
di ciò che in terra un paradiso adorni   155
non si pareggi alcun diletto altrui:
    da quei d'intagli e marmo aurei soggiorni,
sopra de l'acque edificati in guisa,
ch'a tal mirar beltà queto il mar torni;
    e perciò l'onda dal furor divisa   160
quivi manda a irrigar l'alma cittade
del mar reina, in mezzo 'l mar assisa,
    a' cui piè l'acqua giunta umile cade,
e per diverso e tortüoso calle
s'insinua a lei per infinite strade.   165
    Quivi tributo il padre Ocean dàlle
d'ogni ricco tesoro, e 'l cielo amico
ciascun'altra a lei pon dopo le spalle:
    sí che nel tempo novo o ne l'antico
non fu mai chi tentasse vïolarla,   170
ch'al pensar sol confuse ogni nemico.
    Tutto 'l mondo concorre a contemplarla,
come miracol unico in natura,
piú bella a chi si ferma piú a mirarla,
    e senza circondata esser di mura,   175
piú d'ogni forte innaccessibil parte,
senza munizïon forte e sicura.
    Quanto per l'universo si comparte
d'utile e necessario a l'uman vitto,
da tutto l'universo si diparte;   180

into this lovely surrounding countryside,
    Love led me, to recall all the more,   145
in the sweetness of others' good fortune,
that cruel man's thoughts, jarring with mine.
    Nor do my misfortunes increase   148
only because I hear from the woods and the stones
proof of how harsh his feelings toward me are;
    for it is always present to my mind   151
that I left my gentle homeland behind
in order to escape the hatred of that man:
    from that tranquil and beautiful Adria,   154
unequaled by any other land
in whatever adorns a heaven on earth:
    from those gold, marble mansions and sculptured stones,   157
so raised on the waters that the quiet sea
turns back to contemplate such beauty;
    so that the waves, purged of their fury,   160
flow here to bathe the blessed city,
queen of the sea, ensconced on the sea,
    and the water humbly subsides at her feet,   163
and by various and twisting channels
winds its way through her along countless paths.
    Here father Ocean brings tribute to her[35]   166
of opulent treasure, and the benevolent sky
sets her before every other city;
    so that neither in recent nor ancient times   169
has anyone ever tried to invade her,
for simply the thought of it has confounded every foe.
    All the world comes to admire her   172
as the one and only miracle of nature,
more lovely the longer one lingers to look,
    and, though undefended by an outer wall,   175
a site less accessible than any fortress,
even without ramparts, strong and secure.
    Everything the universe contains   178
that is useful and needed for human life
is transported here from the whole universe;

---

35. In Homer, Ocean is the son of Uranus and Gaia, and the husband of the sea goddess Thetis.

ed a render recato a lei 'l suo dritto,
di quel che in lei non nasce, ella piú abonda
d'ogni loco al produr atto e prescritto,
    sí ch'eterna abondanzia la circonda,
e di tutti i paesi fruttüosi   185
piú ricca è d'Adria l'arenosa sponda.
    Altro che valli amene e colli ombrosi
sembrano d'Adria placida e tranquilla
i palagi ricchissimi e pomposi.
    Il mar e 'l lito quivi arde e sfavilla   190
d'amor, che tra nereidi e semidei
quell'acque salse di dolcezza instilla.
    Venere in cerchio ancor degli altri dèi
scende dal ciel su questa bella riva,
con l'alme Grazie in compagnia di lei.   195
    E senza che piú avanti io la descriva,
per fortuna noïosa e violenta,
gran tempo son di lei rimasta priva:
    per far la voglia altrui paga e contenta
io dipartí', sperando alfin quell'ira,   200
se non estinguer, far tepida e lenta.
    Or che quanto si piange e si sospira
per me infelice è tutto sparso al vento,
ché 'l mio amante la vista altrove gira;
    poi che 'l crudele ad altro oggetto è intento,   205
perché lontan da la mia patria amata
vo facendo piú grave il mio tormento?
    Ma se t'ho follemente, Adria, lasciata,
del cor l'arsura alleviar pensando,
dal mio danno veder allontanata,   210
    l'ardor piú tosto è in ciò gito avanzando,
e con la gelosïa e col sospetto
s'è venuto piú sempre riscaldando.
    L'altrui d'amor goduto a pien diletto
per questi campi, e 'l temer che compagna   215
l'empio, a me, non faccia altra del suo letto,
    e de la patria mia celebre e magna

and to render her what is due,   181
she abounds in territories fit and ordained
to produce whatever is not born within her,
   so that eternal abundance surrounds her,   184
and Adria's sandy shore is the richest
among all other fertile lands.
   Far beyond fair valleys and shadowy groves,   187
Adria's rich and splendid palaces
make a serene and peaceful sight.
   There the sea and the shore burn and sparkle   190
with love, who, among Nereids and sea gods,
instills sweetness into those briny waters.
   Venus, encircled by other gods still,   193
descends from heaven to this beautiful shore,
in the company of the noble Graces.
   And without describing her in more detail,   196
because of my adverse, hostile fate,
I have been deprived of her too long;
   to fulfill and appease the will of another,   199
I took my leave, hoping if not to end at last
at least to cool and slow his anger down.
   Now, in spite of all my tears and sighs,   202
unhappy me, everything's cast to the wind,
for my lover turns his gaze elsewhere;
   since the cruel man now pursues another,   205
why, far away from my cherished home,
do I make my suffering even worse?
   But if I left you, Adria, in folly,   208
thinking to lessen the burning of my heart
by seeing myself at a distance from my pain,
   my ardor has been heightened by it instead,   211
and through my jealousy and suspicion
it has constantly burned hotter still.
   The love that others enjoy to the full   214
in these fields, and the fear that the vile man
may take a partner other than me to his bed,
   and the lofty ornaments and undying splendor   217

gli alti ornamenti e lo splendor superno,
qui 'l bosco odiar mi fanno e la campagna:
   ad Adria col pensier devoto interno   220
ritorno e, lagrimando, espressamente
a prova del martír l'error mio scerno.
   Ma se 'l suo fallo scema chi si pente,
d'esser da te partita mi pentisco,
o mio bel nido, e me ne sto dolente;   225
   e da poi che non cessa il mio gran risco
per lontananza, il meglio è ch'io mi mora
del gran dolor che per amar soffrisco,
   senz'a miei danni aggiunger questo ancora,
di far da le mie cose a me piú care   230
per tanto spazio sí lunga dimora.
   Perch'alfin mi risolvo di tornare,
e se non m'è contraria a pien la sorte,
se ben un'ora un secolo mi pare,
   spero tornar in spazio d'ore corte.   235

of my famous and magnificent homeland
make me hate these woods and this countryside:
   To Adria I return, in deep, loyal thought,   220
and weeping, to offer proof of my regret,
I clearly perceive the mistake that I made.
   But if she who repents diminishes her fault,   223
I do repent of departing from you,
oh, lovely shelter, and grief overwhelms me;
   and since my great danger does not end through distance, 226
it is best that I should die
of the great sorrow I suffer for love,
   without adding this further woe to my woes—   229
of making such a lengthy stay
so far from the things that I cherish the most.
   So at last I resolve to return,   232
and if fate doesn't stand in my way,
even though an hour seems like a century,
   in a few short hours I hope to return.   235

Capitolo 23

჻

Lungamente in gran dubbio sono stata
di quel che far a me s'appartenea,
da un certo uomo indiscreto provocata.
   Nel pensier vane cose rivolgea
del far e del non far la mia vendetta,   5
né a qual partito accostarmi sapea;
   alfin, la propria mia ragion negletta,
che 'l buon camin non sa prender né puote,
da la soverchia passïon costretta,
   vengo a voi per consiglio, a cui son note   10
le forme del düello e de l'onore,
per cui s'uccide il mondo e si percuote.
   A voi, che guerrier sète di valore,
e ch'oltre a l'esser de la guerra esperto,
vostra mercede, mi portate amore,   15
   per consiglio ricorro; e ben m'accerto
che mi sareste ancor non men d'aita,
per grazia vostra piú che per mio merto.
   Ma io non voglio a quel dove m'invita
de la vendetta il gran desio voltarmi,   20
benché la via mi sia piana e spedita:
   voglio, prima ch'io giunga al trar de l'armi,
il mio parer communicar con voi,
e con voi primamente consigliarmi;
   e se determinato fia tra noi   25
che con gli effetti io debba risentirmi,
non sarò pigra a pigliar l'armi poi.
   Ma saría forse un espresso avvilirmi,
far soggetto capace del mio sdegno
chi non merta in pensier pur mai venirmi: 30
   un uom da nulla, e non sol vile, e indegno
che da seder si mova a lui pensando

Capitolo 23

FRANCO, TO A FRIEND EXPERT IN DUELING

For a long time I've remained in doubt
about what is proper for me to do,
provoked by a certain indiscreet man.

In my mind, I turned over vain questions,   4
as to whether or not to take revenge,
and I did not know which side to choose;

finally, leaving my reason aside,   7
which neither knows nor can take the proper path,
driven, as it is, by overwhelming pain,

I now come for advice to you,   10
to whom the forms of duels and honor are known,
according to which the world is stricken and slain.

To you, because you're a gallant warrior,   13
and not only an expert in war,
but through your kindness you bear me love,

I turn for advice; and I am sure   16
that you will not be of slight help to me,
more from your graciousness than for my merit.

But I do not want to turn at once   19
to what my longing for revenge invites me,
although the way to it is simple and clear;

I want before I come to pull out weapons,   22
to communicate my opinion to you
and above all to ask you for counsel,

and if between us we should decide   25
that I should express my resentment in deeds,
then I won't hesitate to take up arms.

But perhaps I would, in an obvious way,   28
debase myself by honoring with my scorn
a man who deserves not even a thought,

a man worth nothing, and not only vile,   31
but unworthy to trouble, at the thought of him,

qualunque ancor che pigro e rozzo ingegno.
    E pur d'ira m'infiammo, rimembrando
la villania da lui fatta a se stesso,   35
di doverla a me far forse stimando.
    Inescusabil fallo vien commesso
da chi dice d'alcun mal in sua assenza,
s'anco ver sia quel che vien detto espresso:
    perché in ciò l'uom dimostra gran temenza,   40
e par che 'n quella vece non ardisca
dir il medesmo ne l'altrui presenza.
    Ma poi, se di menzogne si fornisca
e nel contaminar l'onore altrui,
con frode e infamia contra 'l ver supplisca,   45
    ben certamente merita costui
cancellarsi del libro de' viventi,
sí che 'l suo nome ad un pèra con lui.
    Oh, se le rane avesser unghia e denti,
come sarían, se drittamente addocchio,   50
talor piú de' leon fiere e mordenti!
    Ma poi, per gracidar d'alcun ranocchio,
di gir non lascia a ber l'asino al fosso,
anzi drizza a quel suon l'orecchio e l'occhio.
    Se un ser grillo, a dir mal per uso mosso,   55
de la sua buca standosi al riparo,
m'ha biasmato in mia assenzia, io che ne posso?
    E se tratte a quel suon, quivi n'andâro
molte vespe e tafani, e per tenore
di quel suon roco in compagnia ruzzâro,   60
    non patisce alcun danno in ciò 'l mio onore,
e quanto aspetta a me, piú tosto rido;
ma de l'altrui sciocchezza ho poi dolore.
    D'una brutta cornacchia a l'aspro grido
trassero altri uccellacci da carogne,   65
e di sterco l'empiêr la strozza e 'l nido.
    Quest'è proprïetà de le menzogne,
che quelli ancor che son malvagi e tristi
versan sopra l'autor biasmi e vergogne.

even an indolent and vulgar mind.
 And yet I burn with fury as I recall   34
the villainy that he dealt to himself,
thinking perhaps he should aim it at me.
 An inexcusable wrong is committed   37
by a man who defames a woman in her absence,
even if what he says is obviously true,
 because by so doing, he reveals great fear   40
and it seems, from this state, that he does not dare
to say the same thing in that person's presence.
 But if he should arm himself with lies   43
and, while befouling another's honor,
he replaces the truth with fraud and with infamy,
 it is most certain that man deserves   46
to be struck clean out of the book of the living,
so that his name perishes with him.
 Oh, if frogs had claws and teeth,   49
often they would, if I see correctly,
be fiercer than lions and bite more sharply!
 But in response to the croak of a frog,   52
an ass doesn't cease to drink at the ditch;
his ears and eyes, rather, perk up at the sound.
 If a certain Sir Cricket, concealed in his hole, 55
as his habit is, was moved to speak ill of me
in my absence, what can I do about it?
 And if, attracted by the sound,   58
many wasps and horseflies came rushing up
and buzzed in chorus with his rough voice,
 my honor suffers no harm from this,   61
and as far as I'm concerned, I laugh instead;
but then I am wounded by others' stupidity.
 At the harsh cry of an ugly crow,   64
other birds rose up from their prey,
and filled their throats and nests with dung.
 And this is a characteristic of lies—   67
that even people who are evil and mean
pour contempt and shame on the author of lies.

Del mio avversario fûr primieri acquisti   70
sparger detti, in mia assenza, di me falsi,
da nulla verità coperti o misti.

Ad ira contra lui perciò non salsi,
ma m'allegrai, quando contra 'l suo dire
tacendo col mio ver chiaro prevalsi.   75

Ben poi via piú insolente divenire
nel mio silenzio il vidi; e quasi ch'io
d'averlo fatto tale posso dire.

Ma qual era in quel caso officio mio,
se non quel dirmi mal dopo le spalle   80
non curar punto, da un uom vile e rio?

Troppo al giudicio mio vien che s'avvalle
il pensier di chi segue tai diffetti,
c'hanno precipitoso e tetro il calle.

Raffrena, uom valoroso, i ciechi affetti,   85
e non voler opporti a ciascun'orma
de la malignitate ai falsi detti:

segui de la virtú la dritta norma,
che, di se stessa paga, agli altrui errori
generosa non guarda, e par che dorma.   90

Cosí fec'io, che, d'ogni dritto fuori
infamiata e biasmata da un uom vile,
mi confortai co' miei pensier migliori:

e farei piú che mai ora il simíle,
se per la mia pazienzia quel villano   95
non discendesse a via peggiore stile.

Ma con armata e minacciosa mano
m'importuna, e mi sfida, e quasi sforza
il pensier di star queta a render vano.

Con l'acqua alfin ogni foco si smorza;   100
cosí la costui rabbia e l'arroganza
a quel ch'io men vorrei mi spinge a forza.

So ch'egli per natura e per usanza
è pessimo e vilissimo a volere
pugnar con una donna, di possanza.   105

E quasi che non porta anco il devere,

And one advantage my opponent used 70
was to spread rumors while I was away,
false tales untouched and unmixed with truth.

And yet for all this I did not rise in anger 73
but rather rejoiced when, by keeping silent,
my truth prevailed over what he had said.

Then indeed in my silence I saw him 76
grow more and more insolent, and I'd almost say
that it was I who made him that way.

But in that case, what was it my duty to do 79
if not to ignore the talk sent around
behind my back by a wicked, vile man?

In my view a man's thought sinks too low 82
if he's bent on committing this kind of misdeed,
which runs a dark and dangerous course.

Restrain your blind passions, valorous man, 85
and do not continually try to resist
the lying rumors invented by malice;

follow instead the right rule of virtue, 88
sufficient to itself, which generously
ignores others' faults and seems to lie sleeping.

This is what I did, for most unfairly 91
defamed and blamed by a cowardly man,
I consoled myself with higher thoughts;

and now more than ever I'd do the same thing, 94
if, through my patience, that villainous man
did not descend to behavior worse still.

But with an armed and menacing hand 97
he pursues and defies me and does all he can
to frustrate my intent to stay calm.

With water every fire is finally quenched; 100
just so, that man's fury and arrogant ways
force me to do what I least desire.

I know that he, by nature and custom, 103
is thoroughly vile and so great a coward
that he wants to fight with a woman by force.

And as if I don't have the duty 106

ch'al provocar de l'armi io gli risponda,
non usa il ferro ignudo in man tenere.

Ma tanto piú d'audacia ei soprabonda,
quanto farmi paura piú si crede,   110
e con nuove insolenzie mi circonda.

Non so quel che in tal caso si richiede:
il parer vostro non mi sia negato,
ch'a lui son per prestar assenso e fede.

Io sono stata in procinto, da un lato,   115
di disfidarlo a singolar battaglia,
comunque piú gli piace, in campo armato.

Ma dubitai che di piastra e di maglia
ei proponesse grave vestimento,
e ferro che non punge e che non taglia.   120

So ch'egli è un asinaccio a questo intento
d'assicurarsi contra i colpi crudi,
dove vi sia di sangue spargimento:

del resto sovra 'l dorso se gli studi,
s'altri volesse ben con un martello,   125
come s'usa di far sopra le incudi.

Questo m'ha messo a partito il cervello,
ch'io non vorrei con sferza o con bastone
prender a castigar un uom sí fello.

Non so se in ciò potessi con ragione   130
rifiutar armi non micidïali,
ma solamente a bastonarsi buone:

so ch'ei diría ch'a lui si dènno tali,
e ch'io non debbo ricusarle, quando
d'ogni lato le cose vanno eguali.   135

Io sono andata a questo assai pensando,
ed ho discorso che s'io 'l disfidassi,
da l'insultar s'andría forse arretrando:

forse ch'ei volgerebbe altrove i passi,
e meco fuggiría d'entrar in prova,   140
perch'ancor col baston non l'amazzassi.

Ma s'ei temprate ha l'ossa a tutta prova
contra ogni copia di gran bastonate,

to respond to him and his call to arms,
he fails to carry a bare blade in his hand.
    But the more his audacity overflows,   109
the more he believes that he's frightening me,
and on all sides he attacks me with new affronts.
    I don't know what such a case requires;   112
don't deny me your view, for I am prepared
to assent and to have faith in it.
    On one hand, I have been on the point   115
of challenging him to single combat,
however he prefers, on the field of battle.
    But I suspected that he would propose   118
heavy armor of breastplate and mail,
and swords that neither stab nor wound.
    I know that he is a foolish ass,   121
set in this case on protecting himself
against bare blows, when blood comes to be shed;
    for the rest, let him watch out for his back   124
in case someone wants to do with a hammer
what's usually done to the anvil instead.
    This has made me change my mind;   127
I wouldn't like to try to punish
such a wicked man with a whip or a club.
    I don't know whether I could in fairness   130
refuse to use weapons that do not kill
but are only good for giving a beating;
    I know he will say such weapons are due him   133
and that I should not refuse them,
provided that everything else is equal.
    I have thought about this at length   136
and have said that if I were to defy him,
he might retreat, taking back his insults;
    he might turn his steps in another direction   139
and flee from meeting me in combat,
for fear that I'd even club him to death.
    But if he has bones that withstand every test   142
and any number of heavy club strokes,

sí ch'altri a dargli stanco alfin si trova;
    senz'aver le devute sue derrate,   145
rendermi stanca in guisa alfin potrebbe,
che l'armi avessi in mio affanno pigliate.
    E poi di me qual cosa si direbbe?
Ch'io non sia buona per un uom codardo,
cui con la verga un fanciul vincerebbe: 150
    un che fa l'invincibile e 'l gagliardo
contra una donna che sopporta e tace,
senza pur minacciarlo con lo sguardo.
    Dunque 'l debbo lasciar seguir in pace,
e sommettermi in guisa al suo talento,   155
ch'egli m'offenda come piú gli piace?
    Quest'è strana maniera di tormento,
e tal ch'offese a non sopportar usa,
a questa men ch'ad altra atta mi sento.
    Dunque sarò da sí vil uom delusa,   160
senza prender vendetta in parte alcuna
di quanto egli m'offende e sí m'accusa?
    In questo punto il mio pensier s'aduna,
e per incaminarmi a buona strada
trovo scarsa e contraria la fortuna.   165
    Ma s'io sto queta, e, come avien ch'accada
un giorno che passar quindi gli avenga,
incontra armata a ucciderlo gli vada?
    Forse la sete fia che 'n tutto io spenga
di quel sangue maligno, e con diletto   170
senza contrasto alcun vittoria ottenga.
    Dunque commetterò sí gran diffetto
di bruttar di quel sangue queste mani,
ch'è di malizia e di viltate infetto?
    Cessin da me pensieri cosí strani.   175
Ma che farò? S'io taccio, mal; e poi
s'io faccio, peggio. Oh miei discorsi vani!
    Datemi, signor mio, consiglio voi.

so his opponent finally tires of hitting him
    without having gotten what he deserves,   145
at last he might possibly so tire me out
that I'd have armed myself for my despair.
    And what would then be said about me?   148
That I cannot handle a cowardly man,
whom a mere child could defeat with a switch,
    a man who pretends to be strong and unbeatable   151
in battle with a woman who endures and is silent,
without even threatening him with a look.
    Must I, then, let him carry on unstopped,   154
and so submit myself to his whim
that he insults me just as he likes?
    This is indeed a strange kind of torture,   157
and for someone, like me, not used to abuse,
it suits me far less than any other.
    Shall I be mocked, then, by such a villain,   160
without seeking any revenge at all
for how much he insults and accuses me?
    My thought centers on this one point,   163
and to lead my steps onto the right path
I find Fortune tight-fisted and stubborn.
    But what if I hold my peace, and some day   166
it happens that I cross his path
and go to meet him armed for the kill?
    Perhaps I shall slake my thirst completely   169
on his malignant blood, and with pleasure
win a victory without any battle.
    Shall I really commit the foul error   172
of soiling these hands of mine with that blood,
infected with malice and cowardice both?
    Enough of thoughts so alien to me!   175
But what shall I do? Silence is bad,
but action is worse. Oh, useless words of mine!
    Give me, my lord, your advice.   178

Capitolo 24

～

Sovente occorre ch'altri il suo parere
dice, stimando fatte alcune cose,
che non successer, né fûr punto vere.
    Di queste, che pur son dubbie e nascose,
in noi un certo instinto la natura,   5
che tende al peggio ed al biasmarle, pose;
    benché null'opra è di qua giú sicura,
e di quel che men par ch'avvenir possa
stíasi con piú sospetto e con paura.
    Del mondo ingannator quest'è la possa,   10
che quel ch'è piú contrario al ver succeda,
per cagion torta, occoltamente mossa.
    La ragion vuol ch'ogni ben di voi creda,
ma poi del verisimile l'effetto
fa che quel ch'io credei prima discreda.   15
    Comunque sia, egli m'è stato detto:
se falso o ver, non importa ch'io dica
s'io son risolta o se n'ho alcun sospetto:
    basta che mi tegniate per amica,
come infatti vi son, sí che in giovarvi   20
non sarei scarsa d'opra o di fatica.
    Ed or ch'io mi conduco a ragionarvi
di quanto intenderete, a quel m'accosto,
che dè' chi fa professïon d'amarvi.
    Dunque a la mia presenza vi fu opposto   25
ch'una donna innocente abbiate offesa
con lingua acuta e con cor mal disposto;
    e che, moltiplicando ne l'offesa,
quant'è colei piú stata pazïente,
in voi l'ira si sia tanto piú accesa,   30
    sí che, spinto da sdegno, impazïente
le man posto l'avreste adosso ancora,

Capitolo 24

FRANCO, TO A MAN WHO HAS INSULTED A WOMAN

It often happens that a person declares
his opinion, assuming things were done
that never happened at all or were true.
    About such acts, which are doubtful and hidden,   4
nature puts into us a certain instinct
that tends to the worst, and to laying blame,
    although on this earth no action is certain,   7
and of those that seem least likely to happen
we feel the greatest suspicion and fear.
    This is the power of the deceptive world—   10
that what's most contrary to the truth prevails,
led through false logic for motives kept secret.
    Reason requires that I think the best of you,   13
but then the effect of what seems most likely
makes me disbelieve what I thought at first.
    Whatever the case, this is what I've been told: 16
false or true, it matters little
whether I say I'm sure or only suspicious.
    It is enough that you esteem me your friend,   19
as indeed I am, so that I would not spare
any action or effort to please you.
    And now that I'm about to discuss with you   22
the matter I'm coming to, you'll understand
how someone who claims to love you should act.
    So in my presence you were accused   25
of having offended an innocent woman
with your sharp tongue and ill-disposed heart;
    and, multiplying what you did wrong,   28
the more patient she remained,
the more intensely your fury burned,
    so that, driven by scorn, and impatient,   31
you'd have laid hands upon her, as well,

se nol vietava alcun ch'era presente;
  ma voi la minacciaste forte allora,
e giuraste voler tagliarle il viso,   35
osservando del farlo il tempo e l'ora.
  Strano mi parve udir, d'un uom diviso
dai fecciosi costumi del vil volgo,
un cotal nuovo inaspettato aviso;
  e mentre col pensiero a voi mi volgo,   40
de la virtute amico e de l'onesto,
la fede a quel che mi fu detto tolgo.
  Da l'altra parte so quanto è molesto
lo spron de l'ira, e come spesso ei mena
a quel ch'è vergognoso ed inonesto;   45
  né sempre la ragion, che i sensi affrena,
a stringer pronto in man si trova il morso,
e 'l gran soverchio rompe ogni catena.
  Se per impeto d'ira il fallo è occorso,
non durate nel mal, ma conoscete   50
quanto fuor del dever siate trascorso.
  Gli occhi del vostro senno rivolgete,
e quanto ingiurïar donne vi sia
disdicevole, voi stesso vedete.
  Povero sesso, con fortuna ria   55
sempre prodotto, perch'ognor soggetto
e senza libertà sempre si stia!
  Né però di noi fu certo il diffetto,
che se ben come l'uom non sem forzute,
come l'uom mente avemo ed intelletto.   60
  Né in forza corporal sta la virtute,
ma nel vigor de l'alma e de l'ingegno,
da cui tutte le cose son sapute;
  e certa son che in ciò loco men degno
non han le donne, ma d'esser maggiori   65
degli uomini dato hanno piú d'un segno.
  Ma se di voi si reputiam minori,
fors'è perché in modestia ed in sapere
di voi siamo piú facili e migliori.

if someone present had not prevented it;
 but after that you threatened her mightily   34
and swore that you would slash her face,[36]
naming the day and the hour you'd do it.
 It seemed strange to me to hear   37
such a strange and surprising report
of a man set apart from the rabble's low habits;
 and as I turn in my thought to you,   40
the friend of virtue and of honorable deeds,
I cease to believe what I was told.
 On the other hand, I know how harmful   43
the spur of anger is, and how often
it leads to shameful and unjust acts;
 nor is reason, which reins in the senses,   46
always quick enough to pull on the bit,
and great excess breaks every chain.
 If the fault occurred through a fit of anger,   49
don't go on doing wrong, but admit
how far you overstepped the bounds of duty.
 Look with the eyes of your good sense   52
and see for yourself how unworthy of you
it is to insult and injure women.
 Unfortunate sex, always led about   55
by cruel fortune, because you are always
subjected and without freedom!
 But this has certainly been no fault of ours,   58
because, if we are not as strong as men,
like men we have a mind and intellect.
 And virtue does not lie in bodily strength   61
but in the vigor of the soul and mind,
through which all things come to be known;
 and I am certain that in this respect   64
women lack nothing, but, rather, have given
more than one sign of being greater than men.
 But if you think us inferior to you,   67
perhaps it's because in modesty and wisdom
we are more adept and better than you.

---

36. This expression, colloquially stated as *dare la sfregia* (to give the scar), was used to describe the vengeful act through which jealous clients disfigured courtesans who they thought had betrayed them.

E che sia 'l ver, voletelo vedere?   70
Che 'l piú savio ancor sia piú pazïente
par ch'a la ragion quadri ed al devere:
del pazzo è proprio l'esser insolente,
ma quel sasso del pozzo il savio tragge,
ch'altri a gettarlo fu vano e imprudente.   75
E cosí noi che siam di voi piú sagge,
per non contender vi portamo in spalla,
com'anco chi ha buon piè porta chi cagge.
Ma la copia degli uomini in ciò falla;
e la donna, perché non segua il male,   80
s'accomoda e sostien d'esser vassalla.
Ché se mostrar volesse quanto vale
in quanto a la ragion, de l'uom saría
di gran lunga maggiore, e non che eguale.
Ma l'umana progenie mancheria,   85
se la donna, ostinata in sul düello,
foss'a l'uom, com'ei merta, acerba e ria.
Per non guastar il mondo, ch'è sí bello
per la specie di noi, la donna tace,
e si sommette a l'uom tiranno e fello,   90
che poi del regnar tanto si compiace,
sí come fanno 'l piú quei che non sanno
(ché 'l mondan peso a chi piú sa piú spiace)
che gli uomini perciò grand'onor fanno
a le donne, perché cessero a loro   95
l'imperio, e sempre a lor serbato l'hanno.
Quinci sete, ricami, argento ed oro,
gemme, porpora, e qual è di piú pregio
si pon in adornarne alto tesoro;
e qual conviensi al nostro senno egregio,   100
non sol son ricchi i nostri adornamenti
d'ogni pomposo e piú prezzato fregio,
ma gli uomini a noi vengon riverenti,
e ne cedono 'l luogo in casa e in strada,
in ciò non punto tardi o negligenti.   105
Per questo anco è ch'a lor portar accada

And do you want to know what the truth is?   70
That the wisest person should be the most patient
squares with reason and with what is right;
    insolence is the mark of the madman,   73
but the stone that the wise man draws from the well
was thrown in by a foolish, imprudent man.
    And so we women, who are wiser than you,   76
to avoid contention, carry you on our backs,
as the surest of foot carry those prone to fall.
    But most men do wrong in this matter;   79
and woman, to avoid pursuing wrongdoing,
adapts and endures being a vassal.
    Yet if, as far as reason's concerned,   82
she wanted to show what she is worth,
she'd not only be man's equal but surpass him by far.
    But human offspring would cease to exist   85
if woman, determined to prevail in the duel,
were as harsh and cruel as man deserves.
    To not ruin the world, which our species   88
makes so beautiful, woman is silent
and submits to tyrannical, wicked man,
    who then so enjoys having power to rule,   91
as those do most who know the least
(for the wise care least for worldly things),
    that on this account men do honor to women,   94
so that they will yield all power to them,
and men have always preserved it for them.
    So silk and embroidery, silver and gold,   97
gems, crimson cloth, and all that's most precious
men use to embellish their highly placed treasure;
    and, as befits our excellent wisdom,   100
not only are our adornments rich
with every splendid and most prized trim,
    but men approach us with reverence   103
and make way for us at home and in the street,
neither slow nor remiss to do so.
    This is also why their role is to wear   106

berretta in testa, per trarla di noi
a qualunque dinanzi ei se ne vada;
   e s'ancor son tra lor nimici poi,
non lascian d'onorar, sempre ch'occorre,   110
l'istesse donne de' nemici suoi.
   Da questo argumentando si discorre
quanto l'offesa fatta al nostro sesso
la civiltà de l'uom gentile aborre.
   Né ch'io parli cosí crediate adesso   115
con altro fin che di mostrarvi quanto
l'offender donne sia peccato espresso.
   Informata ancor son da l'altro canto
chi sia colei di cui mi fu affermato
che ingiurïaste e minacciaste tanto: 120
   certo questo non merita il suo stato,
e l'avervi 'l suo amore a tanti segni
in tante occasïon manifestato.
   Cessin l'offese omai, cessin gli sdegni,
e tanto piú che d'uom nato gentile   125
questi non sono portamenti degni;
   ma è professïon d'uom basso e vile
pugnar con chi non ha diffesa o schermo,
se non di ciance e d'ingegno sottile.
   Perdonatemi in ciò, ch'io troppo affermo   130
le colpe vostre; poi ch'io non intendo
comprender voi, piú d'alcun altro, al fermo.
   Ma quel ch'adesso vado discorrendo
è quanto ad onta sua colui s'inganni,
che vada con le donne contendendo;   135
   perch'al sicur di lui son tutti i danni:
s'ei vince, mal; e peggio, se vien vinto;
il rischio è certo, e infiniti gli affanni.
   Col viso di rossore infuso e tinto,
d'essere stato ogni uom d'onor s'accorge   140
di far ingiuria a donne unqua in procinto;
   e quanto piú 'l valor viril risorge,
tanto piú l'armi fuor da l'ira tratte

hats on their heads, so they can doff them
when they meet one of us face to face;
    and even if they're enemies to one another, 109
whatever happens, they do not fail
to honor the women related to their enemies.
    Arguing on this basis, it is well known 112
how much the civility of a gentleman
detests an offense made to our sex.
    And don't believe that I speak this way now 115
with any purpose except to show you
how much attacking women is an obvious sin.
    On the other hand, I am also informed 118
who the woman is whom, others have claimed,
you insulted and threatened so much:
    certainly her status does not call for this, 121
nor does the fact that she's shown she loves you
by so many signs on so many occasions.
    Cease your offenses from now on, 124
cease your disdain, and all the more
since this is behavior unfit for a nobleman,
    but it is the act of a low and vile man 127
to fight with a woman lacking defense or shield,
except for gossip and a clever mind.
    Forgive me if in this I insist too much 130
on your faults; for I certainly don't claim
to understand you better than anyone else;
    but what I am now about to explain 133
is how much to his shame a man is deluded
who enters into contention with women;
    for certainly all the damage is his: 136
if he wins, it's bad, and worse if he's vanquished;
the risk is certain and the suffering infinite.
    With a face stained and blushing with red, 139
every man of honor sees that he was close
to dealing any insult to women;
    and the more his manly courage prevails, 142
the more another, ashamed in his turn,

vergognando al suo loco altri riporge,
  e si pentisce de le cose fatte   145
in via che se potesse frastornarle,
le ridurría da l'esser primo intatte.
  Ma poi che non può adietro ritornarle,
con dolci modi a l'offese ripara,
e quanto può, si sforza d'annullarle: 150
  ritorna ancor l'amata al doppio cara
nel rifar de la pace; e per turbarsi,
piú d'ogni parte l'alma si rischiara.
  Cosí nel ben vien a moltiplicarsi,
e cosí certa son che voi farete,   155
sí come suol da ogni par vostro farsi:
  e colei certo offesa o non avete,
o se vinto da sdegno trascorreste,
l'error di voi non degno emenderete.
  Ed io di ciò vi prego in fin di queste.   160

puts aside the weapons he drew in anger,
    and he repents of his actions so much   145
that if he were able to cancel them out,
he'd return them undone to their prior state.
    But since he can't put them behind him,   148
he redresses his wrongs with endearing manners
and, as much as he can, tries to undo them;
    his beloved becomes twice as dear to him   151
when they make peace, and though once perturbed,
her soul, above all, turns serene again.
    And so he increases greatly in goodness,   153
and so I am certain that you will behave
just as your peers are accustomed to do:
    and either you have not truly offended her   157
or, if you transgressed, overcome by scorn,
you will amend the error unworthy of you.
    And I end by entreating you to do this.   160

Capitolo 25

IN LODE DI FUMANE, LUOGO DELL'ILLUSTRISSIMO
SIGNOR CONTE MARC'ANTONIO DELLA TORRE,
PREPOSTO DI VERONA

Non vorrei da l'un canto esser mai stata
a quel bel loco, per dover partire,
come fei, non ben quivi anco arrivata.
    Cosí gravoso il ben suol divenire,
che quant'egli è maggior, via maggior duolo   5
col dilungarsi in noi suol partorire:
    tosto ne va 'l piacer trascorso a volo,
né ponendo in ragion l'util passato,
a la perdita mesti attendem solo.
    E non vorrei però da l'altro lato   10
sí vago nido non aver veduto,
a la tranquillità soave e grato.
    E se pari al desio non l'ho goduto,
quanto gustato piú, tanto piú caro,
il lasciarlo mi fôra dispiaciuto.   15
    E pur, formando un pensier dolce amaro,
con la memoria a quei diletti torno,
che infiniti a me quivi si mostrâro:
    sempre davanti gli occhi ho 'l bel soggiorno,
da cui lontan col corpo, con la mente,   20
senza da me partirlo unqua, soggiorno;
    ricrear tutta in me l'alma si sente,
mentre qua giú sí lieto paradiso
da dover contemplar le sta presente.
    Da questo lo mio spirto non diviso   25
va ripetendo le bellezze eterne,
dal soverchio piacer vinto e conquiso.
    E mentre le delizie avido scerne,
nel gioir di se stesso, afflige i sensi,

Capitolo 25

IN PRAISE OF FUMANE, THE VILLA BELONGING TO
COUNT MARCANTONIO DELLA TORRE,
CANON OF VERONA

On one hand, I'd prefer never to have been
in that beautiful place only to leave,
as I did, before I'd properly arrived.

How burdensome a good thing can become,   4
given that the greater it is, the more grief
is born in us when we must leave it behind:

the pleasure we enjoyed flies quickly away;   7
and giving no thought to past benefit,
we sadly remember only what we've lost.

And yet on the other hand I wouldn't want   10
not to have seen such a beautiful dwelling,
gracious and beloved to tranquillity.

And, though I have not enjoyed it to the full,   13
the more I had, the more I'd have cherished it,
and the more leaving it would have brought me regret.

Even so, forming a bittersweet thought,   16
I return in memory to the infinite delights
that were there revealed to me:

I have that fair site always before my eyes,   19
and though absent from it in body,
in my mind I still dwell there, never departing.

Within me my soul feels wholly reborn   22
when such a joyful heaven on earth
presents itself for her contemplation.

My spirit, never quitting this place,   25
recalls its endless beauties again and again,
vanquished and conquered by the highest pleasure.

And while my eager spirit perceives these delights,   28
in its own joy it brings pain to my senses,

che non puon separati ancor goderne: 30
    così, quando m'avien ch'amando pensi
a l'abitazïon vaga e gentile,
tra gioia e duol convien che 'l cor dispensi.
    In questo piglio in man pronta lo stile;
e per gradir al sentimento, fingo   35
quel loco quanto possi al ver simíle:
    e se ben so ch'a impresa alta m'accingo,
tirata da la mia propria vaghezza,
senz'arte quel ch'io so disegno e pingo.
    Oh che fiorita e feconda bellezza   40
quivi mostra e dispiega la natura,
raro altrove o non mai mostrarla avezza!
    Certo è questa quell'unica fattura,
in cui, vinta se stessa, a tutte prove
ripose ogni sua industria, ogni sua cura.   45
    Di tutto quel che piaccia al mondo e giove,
favorevole il cielo a cotal opra, .
il maggior vanto eternamente piove.
    Quivi 'l ciel manda il suo favor di sopra,
né men la terra in adornar tal parte   50
con gli altri, a gara, elementi s'adopra.
    Vince l'imaginar d'ogni umana arte
la disposizïon di tutto 'l bene,
ch'unito quivi intorno si comparte:
    e pur di quell'altezza, ove perviene   55
l'eccellenza de l'arte in cose belle,
vestigie espresse il bel luogo ritiene.
    Così determinarono le stelle
far quivi in dolci modi altrui palese
quanto puon destinar ed influir elle.   60
    In questo avventuroso almo paese
l'ornamento del ciel si mostra in terra,
ch'a farlo un paradiso in lui discese.
    Di lieti colli adorno cerchio serra
l'infinita beltà del vago piano,   65
dove Flora e Pomona alberga ed erra.

which, at this distance, can no longer enjoy them.
So when it happens that I lovingly think   31
about that longed for, kindly home,
my heart must be split between joy and sorrow.
In this state, I take up my pencil in ready hand   34
and to satisfy my longing, I depict
that place as truthfully as I can:
And though I know that I undertake a great task,   37
drawn onward by my own desire,
without art I paint and draw what I know.
Oh, what flowering and joyful beauty   40
nature there displays and unfolds,
which she rarely or never shows anywhere else!
Certainly this is the unique creation   43
into which, surpassing herself in every way,
she put all her effort and all her care.
Heaven, favoring such a work,   46
pours down unendingly the greatest fame
of containing every good and joy in the world.
Here heaven sends down its favor from above,   49
and earth makes no less an effort to compete,
adorning this place with her own elements.
The imagination in every human art   52
is excelled by the arrangement of all the good
that, gathered together, is shared out here:
and yet the beautiful place preserves   55
clear reminders of the height attained
by the great skill of art to make beautiful things.
This is the way the stars resolved here   58
through lovely means to show to men
how much they can shape and influence fate.
In this blessed, loving countryside   61
the ornaments of heaven appear on earth,
and descend to make it a paradise.
A circle adorned by joyful hills enfolds   64
the infinite beauty of the lovely plain,
where Flora and Pomona dwell and roam.[37]

37. Flora and Pomona were the Roman goddesses of spring and summer, and of the flowers and fruits accompanying each season.

Quasi per gradi su di mano in mano
di fuor s'ascende 'l poggio da le spalle,
sempre al salir piú facile e piú piano;
    quinci in giú per soave e destro calle   70
s'arriva a la pianura in pochi passi,
ch'è posta in forma di rotonda valle:
    se non che in guisa rilevata stassi,
ch'è quasi, entro a quei colli, un minor colle,
che 'ntorno a lor si dispiani e s'abbassi,   75
    sí che d'entrarvi a Febo non si tolle,
poco alzatosi fuor de l'orïente,
nel prato d'erbe rugiadoso e molle.
    Entra 'l sol quanto entrar se gli consente
da un bosco d'alti pini e di cipressi,   80
pien d'ombre amiche al dí lungo e fervente;
    e gode di veder quivi con essi
de la sua amata in corpo umano fronde,
già braccia e chiome, or verdi rami spessi,
    tra' quai quanto piú penetra e s'asconde,   85
per la memoria, ch'anco entro 'l cor serba,
de l'amorose sue piaghe profonde.
    De la ninfa la sorte cosí acerba
pietoso Apollo ai grati rami tira,
ed a quivi posar vago tra l'erba: 90
    l'aria d'intorno ancor dolce sospira
di Dafne al caso, e spirto d'odor pieno,
le vaghe foglie ventilando, spira.
    E 'l ciel, là piú ch'altrove mai sereno,
fa che d'ogni stagion la copia vuote   95
in quella terra il corno suo ripieno.
    Quivi con l'urne non mai stanche o vuote
a portar l'acque son le ninfe pronte,
tai che 'l cristal sí chiaro esser non puote:
    queste versando van da piú d'un fonte   100
le succinte e leggiadre abitatrici
di questo e quel vicin ben cólto monte;
    ed a l'altre compagne cacciatrici,

As if mounting a staircase, a step at a time,   67
approaching from behind, you climb the hill,
easier and less steep as you ascend.

    Down from there by a smooth and gentle path   70
in a few steps you reach the plain,
which is set in the curve of a rounded valley,

    but it stands at a certain height,   73
which makes it among these a lesser hill,
which flattens and levels out around them,

    so that Phoebus is not kept from entering,   76
as soon as he has risen from the east,
the dewy and yielding meadow of grass.

    The sun penetrates, as far as he's allowed,   79
a wood of lofty pine and cypress,
full of shadows welcome in the long, hot day,

    and he delights in seeing, among the trees,   82
his beloved, once human, now a mass of leaves,
once arms and hair, now thick green branches,[38]

    where he enters as deeply as he can and hides,   85
moved by the memory, still kept in his heart,
of the deep wounds caused in him by love.

    The nymph's cruel fate draws Apollo,   88
pitiful, to her welcoming branches
and he rests tenderly upon the grass:

    all around, the air sighs softly still   91
over Daphne's sad fate, and a scented breath
stirs, inhaling, the enchanted leaves.

    And the sky, clearer than ever there,   94
makes the abundance of every season
pour its cornucopia over this land.

    There in urns never tiring or empty   97
the nymphs swiftly carry water
so clear that crystal could not be clearer.

    Pouring water from many fountains   100
go these light-footed dwellers, in high-waisted gowns,
in this and the next field-planted mountain;

    and huntresses come to their companions,   103

---

38. Phoebus Apollo's beloved, now composed of leaves and branches, is Daphne, a nymph
who was turned into a laurel tree as she fled from the god (*Metamorphoses*, 1.452 –567).

che, dietro i cervi stanche, a rinfrescarsi
vanno le fronti angeliche beatrici,   105
    co' bei liquidi argenti intorno sparsi
porgon dolce liquor da trar la sete,
e le candide membra da lavarsi.
    Dai freschi rivi e da le fonti liete,
quasi scherzando, l'acque in vario corso   110
declinan verso 'l pian soavi e quete;
    e poi che 'n lenta gara alquanto han corso,
per via diversa si raggiungon tutte
verso un bel prato, a lor dinanzi occorso;
    e da natural arte a far instrutte   115
bello quel sito a maraviglia, vanno
per canali angustissimi ridutte.
    Quivi entrate, a varcar poco spazio hanno,
ch'a un fiorito amenissimo giardino
dolce tributo di se stesse dànno: 120
    con man distesa e passo tardo e chino
dàn di se stesse le piú dolci e chiare
al giardinier ch'a l'uscio sta vicino.
    Questi, com'a lui piace, le fa entrare,
ch'obedïenti a l'arte fan quel tanto   125
ch'altri accorto dispon che debban fare.
    Non cede l'arte a la natura il vanto
ne l'artificio del giardin, ornato
d'alberi cólti e di sempre verde manto;
    sovra 'l qual porge, alquanto rilevato,   130
d'architettura un bel palagio tale,
qual fu di quel del Sol già poetato:
    infinito tesor ben questo vale
per l'edificio proprio, e gli ornamenti,
che 'n ricchezza e in beltà non hanno eguale.   135
    I fini marmi e i porfidi lucenti,
cornici, archi, colonne, intagli e fregi,
figure, prospettive, ori ed argenti,
    quivi son di tal sorte e di tai pregi,
ch'a tal grado non giungono i palagi   140

exhausted in the pursuit of deer,
to cool their angelic maidens' brows;
    with lovely silver waters splashed around them,   106
they offer sweet liquids to quench their thirst
and to bathe their snow-white limbs.

    From the cool banks and the laughing fountains,   109
the waters, as if in play, take different routes,
smooth and calm, down toward the plain;
    and after they have run a slow race,   112
from their diverse paths they all join together,
toward a lovely field lying before them;
    and taught by nature's art to make   115
this site marvelously beautiful,
they flow, bound in by narrowest canals.

    Once arrived, traversing a short space,   118
they offer themselves in sweet tribute
to a blooming, pleasant garden:
    with generous hands and slow, humble step   121
they give their sweetest and clearest waters
to the gardener, standing at the entrance.

    He, as he pleases, lets them inside,   124
for, following art, they do whatever
a talented man designs for them to do.

    Art does not yield to nature   127
the glory of the garden's artifice,
adorned with rare trees and a mantle ever green;
    above it, placed on a slight rise,   130
architecture gives us the sight of a palace
as beautiful as the Sun's, sung in poets' verse.[39]

    This palace is worth an infinite treasure   133
for the building itself, and for its trim,
which has no equal in richness and beauty.

    Fine marbles and polished porphyry,   136
cornices, arches, columns, carvings, and friezes,
figures, perspectives, gold and silver
    are here of such quality and value   139
that they cannot be matched by the palaces built

---

39. Ovid describes the palace of Apollo, the Sun, in *Metamorphoses*, 2.1–18.

che fêr gli antichi imperadori e regi.
    Ma le commodità di dentro e gli agi
son cosí molli, che gli altrui diletti
al par di questi sembrano disagi.
    Per li celati d'òr vaghi ricetti,   145
sul pavimento, che qual gemma splende,
stan sopra aurati piè candidi letti.
    Di sopra da ciascun d'intorno pende
di varia seta e d'òr porpora intesta,
che 'l contegno de' letti abbraccia e prende;   150
    di coltre ricamata o d'altra vesta
di ricca tela ognun s'adorna e copre,
sí ch'a fornirlo ben nulla gli resta.
    Di diversi disegni e diverse opre
su coverte e cortine in tutti i lati   155
vario e lungo artificio si discopre.
    I dèi scender dal cielo innamorati
dietro le ninfe qui si veggon finti,
in diverse figure trasformati;
    e d'amoroso affetto in vista tinti,   160
seguitar ansïosi il lor desio
dove dal caldo incendio son sospinti.
    Qui trasformata in vacca si vede Io,
e cent'occhi serrar il suo custode,
al suon di quel, che poi l'uccise, dio.   165
    Da l'altra parte Danae in sen si gode
vedersi piover Giove in nembo d'oro,
dov'altri piú la chiude e la custode;
    il quale altrove, trasformato in toro,
porta Europa; ed altrove, aquila, piglia   170
Ganimede e 'l rapisce al sommo coro.
    Di Licaon fatta orsa ancor la figlia,
mentre ucciderla il figlio ignota tenta,
assunta in cielo ad orsa s'assomiglia:

by ancient emperors and kings.

But within, the furnishings and comforts   142
are so relaxing that other delights
seem discomforts compared to these.

In chambers lovely with golden hangings,   145
on a floor that shimmers like a gem,
white beds stand on golden feet.

Above and around each one hangs   148
a dark red tapestry of varied silk and gold,
which embraces and copies the shape of the bed;

with embroidered covers or other rich cloth   151
every bed is graced and laid,
so that nothing further remains to adorn it.

Through diverse designs and diverse forms   154
on covers and curtains on every side
varied and sustained artistry is revealed.

Here are depicted enamored gods   157
descending from heaven in pursuit of nymphs
transformed into diverse shapes;

and with faces colored by passionate love,   160
eager, they pursue their desires,
wherever they're driven by the hot fire.

Here is seen Io, turned into a cow,   163
and her guardian blinks his hundred eyes
at the sound of the god who later slew him.[40]

In another place Danae delights, seeing Jove,   166
in a golden cloud, pour into her lap,
in the room where she's kept under lock and key.[41]

Elsewhere Jove, changed into a bull,   169
carries off Europa, and elsewhere, as an eagle,[42]
he grabs and lifts Ganymede up to heaven's choir.

And Lycaon's daughter, turned into a bear,[43]   172
while her son tries to kill her, not knowing who she is,
raised to the sky, still resembles a bear.

---

40. Io, loved by Jove, was changed through Juno's jealousy from a woman into a cow and given Argus, a hundred-eyed monster later slain by Mercury, to watch over her (*Metamorphoses*, 1.583–721).

41. *Metamorphoses*, 4.610–1; 6.113; 11.116–7.

42. Europa, the daughter of the Phoenician king Agenor, was carried off by Jove to Crete, where she gave birth to Minos (*Metamorphoses*, 2.836–75; 3.1–25). Ganymede, a beautiful boy, was snatched away by Jove and taken to Mount Olympus to be the cupbearer of the gods (*Metamorphoses*, 10.155–161).

43. Lycaon's daughter, the nymph Callisto, was transformed into a bear by Juno out of

né pur orsa celeste ella diventa,   175
figurata di stelle in cotal segno,
ma 'l figlio in ciel l'altr'orsa rappresenta.
    Quanto è possente il nostro umano ingegno,
che vive fa parer le cose finte
per forza di colori e di disegno!   180
    Di seta e d'oro e varie lane tinte,
nei tapeti ch'adornan quelle stanze,
da l'imitar le cose vere èn vinte.
    E perché nulla a desïar avanze,
ch'orni di Giove un'alta regia degna,   185
dove, lasciato 'l ciel, qua giuso ei stanze,
    qualunque ebbe tra noi la sacra insegna,
ch'a quei con le sue man Dio stesso porge,
che d'esser suoi vicari in terra ei degna,
    qualunque di pastor al grado sorge   190
de la chiesa divina, in espresso atto
nobilmente dipinto ivi si scorge:
    quivi ciascun pontefice ritratto
piú che dal natural vivo si vede,
di tela, di colori e d'ombre fatto;   195
    e com'a tanta maestà richiede,
da l'altre in parte eccelsa e separata
sí reverende imagini han lor sede.
    Similmente, in maniera accomodata,
di quei l'effigie ancor son quivi, i quali   200
del ciel sostengon la felice entrata:
    quanti mai fûr nel mondo cardinali
quivi entro stan co' papi in compagnia,
e vescovi, e prelati altri assai tali.
    Perché conforme al paradiso sia   205
quell'albergo divino, in sé ritiene
di gente i volti cosí santa e pia.
    Di quel ch'al sacerdozio si conviene,
da l'essempio di molti espressi quivi,
in perfetta notizia si perviene: 210
    questi, ancor morti, insegnar pònno ai vivi,
anzi in ciel vivon sí, che 'l loro nome
in terra sempre glorïoso arrivi.
    E perch'alcun io non distingua o nome,

Nor has she become a celestial bear alone,   175
mapping out this figure in stars,
but the sky's other bear represents her son.

How powerful is our human invention,   178
which can bring depicted things to life
by means of color and design!

In the tapestries that adorn those rooms,   181
made of silk and gold and multicolored wool,
imitation surpasses things that really exist.

And so that nothing more should be desired   184
that could embellish a realm worthy of Jove,
where, having left heaven, he could stay here below,

whoever among us held the sacred sign   187
that God himself places in the hands
of those he deems worthy to be his vicars on earth,

whoever is rising to the level of pastor   190
of the divine church, in action suited to him
can be seen nobly painted there.

Here each pope can be seen portrayed,   193
more alive to the eye than he was while he lived,
of canvas, colors, and shading composed;

and, as such great majesty requires,   196
in a higher place distinguished from others
such reverend images have their seat.

Similarly, in a style that befits them,   199
there are also the portraits of those
who sustain the blessed entrance to heaven;

as many cardinals as ever existed in the world   202
are there, in the company of popes and bishops,
and many other churchmen like them.

So that this heavenly residence   205
may resemble paradise, it contains
the faces of people so saintly and pious.

From the many examples of men shown there   208
one can come to a perfect understanding
of what is fitting for the priesthood:

though dead, these men can still teach the living—   211
indeed, they live in such a way in heaven
that their names will always be famous on earth.

And though some I cannot recognize or name,   214

---

vengeance for her relationship with Jove; she was changed into the constellation Ursa Major, and her son, Arcas, into Ursa Minor (*Metamorphoses*, 2.409–507).

di quelli intendo che fûro innocenti,   215
e del demonio fêr le forze dome.
   Le costor fronti a mirar riverenti,
cosí pinte, ne fanno, e in noi pensieri
destano de le cose piú eccellenti:
   seguendo l'orme lor, fan ch'altri speri,   220
che tien lo scettro de la casa vaga,
d'alzarsi al ciel per quei gradi primieri.
   Questa de la sua vista ognuno appaga,
e sol de la memoria al cor m'imprime
colpi che 'nnaspran la già fatta piaga.   225
   Di que' be' colli a le frondute cime
alzo 'l pensier, che, dal duol vinto e stanco,
fa che gli occhi piangendo a terra adime.
   Standomi sul verron del marmo bianco,
dove 'l palagio alzato agguaglia il monte,   230
ricreata posava il braccio e 'l fianco:
   qui piagner Filomena le triste onte
con la sorella sua dolce sentía,
da lor non cosí chiare altrove cónte:
   da le fontane ad ascoltar venía   235
questo e quel ruscelletto, e mormorando
quasi con lor piangeva in compagnia.
   Ben poscia a quel tenor dolce cantando
givan gli augelli per li verdi rami,
del loro amor le passïon mostrando.   240
   Oh che liete querele, oh che richiami
formavan contra 'l ciel, sí come suole
chi, benché ridamato, altrui forte ami!
   Con voce piú che d'umane parole
par che sappian parlar quelli augelletti,   245
sí ch'ad udirli ancor fermano il sole.
   Talor narrano poi gli alti diletti,
che spesso dagli amati abbracciamenti
prendon, de le lor vaghe al fianco stretti.
   Di gran dolcezza il cielo e gli elementi,   250
per tal piacere e per molti altri assai,

I know that they were pure of spirit,
and that they defeated the devil's power.

Thus portrayed, their brows inspire us   217
to admire them reverently and awaken in us
thoughts of the most lofty things:

they make the man who holds the scepter   220
of this gracious house hope, by following them,
to rise to heaven by the steps they have taken.

The sight of this villa delights all who see it,   223
and its memory alone strikes blows to my heart,
which increase the pain of my previous wound.

To those beautiful hills with their leafy treetops,   226
I lift my thought, conquered and worn by grief,
which forces my weeping eyes to look down.

Lingering on the white marble balcony,   229
where the high-set palace is level with the hill,
resting, I used to lean on my arm and side.

Here I heard Philomela with her sweet sister[44]   232
lament, recounting her sorrowful shames,
more audible here than anywhere else;

from the fountains this and that little brook   235
came to listen, and, murmuring,
seemed to accompany them in their weeping.

Soon after, singing in high, sweet harmony,   238
the birds fluttered in the green branches,
revealing the power of their love.

Oh, what happy complaints, oh, what laments   241
they addressed to heaven, as does the person
who, loved by one, strongly loves another!

These little birds seem able to speak words   243
in a voice more than human, so that they could
stop even the sun, hearing them, in its course.

Sometimes they tell of the great delight   247
they often take in loving embraces,
tightly bound to the sides of those they love.

With great sweetness, in serenity and calm,   250
the sky and the elements there rejoice,

44. Philomela is the nightingale, Procne the swallow. See the note to *Capitolo* 3, line 25.

quivi gioiscon placidi e contenti;
    e rischiarando ognor piú Febo i rai,
la fiorita stagion vago rimena
di molti, non che d'un, perpetui mai.   255
    D'arabi odor la terra e l'aria piena,
l'una piú sempre si rinverde e infiora,
l'altra ognor piú si tempra e rasserena.
    Oh che grata e dolcissima dimora,
dove quanto di vago ognor piú miri,   260
tanto piú da veder ti resta ancora!
    Dovunque altri la vista a mirar giri,
ne la beltà veduta oggetto trova,
che piú intente a guardar le luci tiri;
    e nondimen, perch'ognor cosa nova   265
d'intorno appar, che l'animo desvía,
ad altra parte vien ch'indi le mova.
    La bellezza del sito, alma, natía,
gli occhi fuor del palazzo a veder piega
quanto ivi ricca la natura sia;   270
    ma poi di dentro tal lavor dispiega
l'arte, che la natura agguaglia e passa,
ch'ivi l'occhio, a mirar vòlto, s'impiega;
    e mentre da un oggetto a l'altro passa,
l'un non gustato ben, da nòve brame   275
tirato, impazïente il preso lassa.
    Cosí non trae, ma piú cresce la fame
d'assai vivande un prodigo convito,
che de l'una al pigliar l'altra si brame:
    cosí ne la virtú de l'infinito,   280
senza mai sazïarne, ci stanchiamo,
s'al sommo bene è 'l pensier nostro unito.
    Questa insazïetà grande proviamo
espressamente, allor che l'intelletto
divin, filosofando, contempliamo.   285
    Lascia sempre di sé piú caldo affetto,
ne l'affannata mente, il ver supremo,
ond'ha perfezzïon l'uom da l'oggetto;

delighting in this pleasure and many others more;
    and Phoebus, always brightening his rays,   253
handsome, brings back the flowery season
of not merely one but many endless Mays.

    The earth and air are full of exotic scents,   256
one constantly renews her greenery and blossom,
the other becomes ever more temperate and clear.

    Oh, what a gracious and lovely home,   259
where the more you gaze with a roving eye,
the more remains for you to see!

    Wherever one turns to admire the view,   262
in the beauty seen an object is found
that draws the eyes to look more closely;

    and yet, even though something new appears   265
at every moment and leads the soul one way,
the eyes are soon drawn to another place.

    The gentle, native beauty of the site   268
leads the eyes outside the palace to see
how rich nature is in these surroundings;

    but then, inside, art displays such skill   271
that it equals and outdoes nature,
so that the eye, drawn to wonder, rests here;

    and, while it moves from one object to another,   274
without completely enjoying the first, drawn
by new desires, impatient, it leaves what it's seen.

    So a prodigious banquet of foods   277
does not dispel but increases hunger,
so that one dish is longed for while another is eaten:

    so, though never satisfied entirely,   280
we find repose in the power of the infinite,
if our thought is united with the highest good.

    We feel this great lack of satisfaction   283
for a particular reason: that, by philosophizing,
we may contemplate the divine intellect.

    Divine truth leaves in the struggling mind   286
an ever stronger love for itself,
through which man draws perfection from physical things,

benché l'affanno è tal, ch'ognor più scemo
del mortal fango il nostro spirto face,   290
e d'ir al ciel gli dà penne a l'estremo.
    Felice affanno, che ristora e piace
ne l'unir di quest'anima a quel vero,
che gli umani desir pon tutti in pace:
    a quel che del suo eccelso magistero   295
mostrò grand'arte in queste alme contrade,
feconde del piacer celeste intiero.
    Qui di là su tal grazia e favor cade,
ch'abonda al compartirsi in copia molta
la gioia in ogni parte e la beltade: 300
    sí che mentre ad un lato ancor sol vòlta
gode la vista, in quel più sempre scorge
nova maniera di vaghezza accolta,
    né de l'una ben tosto ancor s'accorge,
che s'offre l'altra e, quasi pur mo' nata,   305
meraviglia e diletto insieme porge.
    Del giardin vago è la sembianza grata,
e mentre in lui la maniera risguardi
d'ogni parte ben cólta e ben piantata,
    lepri e conigli andar pronti e gagliardi   310
nel corso vedi; e mentre che t'incresce
d'esserti di tal vista accorto tardi,
    ecco ch'altronde ancor vaga schiera esce
di cervi e capri e dame e d'altri tali,
onde la maraviglia e 'l piacer cresce.   315
    Ma poi tra quelle schiere d'animali
scopri distinto del giardino il piano
d'acque in angusti e limpidi canali,
    e splender su per l'onde di lontano
vedi i pesci guizzando, che d'argento   320
sembra che nuotin d'una e d'altra mano.
    E mentre l'occhio a vagheggiar è intento
il piacer vario del fiorito suolo,
più sempre di mirar vago e contento,
    di questo ramo in quel cantando a volo   325

though the struggle is such that at every moment   289
it frees our spirit further from earthly mire,
and gives it wings, at last, to fly to heaven.

    Blessed struggle, which rests and delights   292
in the union of this soul to that truth
that brings peace to all human desires:

    that truth that, through its lofty power,   295
revealed its great art in these gentle lands,
fertile in all the delight of heaven.

    Here from on high fall such grace and favor   298
that in great and abundant supply
joy and beauty are shared out everywhere;

    so that while vision finds delight turned   301
in one direction, in some other one
it discovers another sort of beauty,

    and no sooner has this beauty been perceived   304
than the other comes into view, and, as if
newborn, mixes wonder with delight.

    The lovely garden's appearance gives pleasure,   307
and as you admire the elegance there
of every well-kept and neatly planted part,

    you see hares and rabbits, darting swiftly and boldly; 310
and while you regret that such a scene
did not sooner catch your eye,

    now from another side come forth   313
roaming herds of deer, goats, buck, and other game,
which increase your wonder and delight.

    But then among these animals in herds   316
you see, set apart from the garden,
the water meadow with narrow, clear canals,

    and you see, in the far-off waves, the shimmer   319
of darting fish, which seem to be silver
as they swim from side to side.

    And while the eye is intent on enjoying   322
the varied delights of the flowering ground,
ever more eager and contented to look,

    from this branch to that, singing as they fly,   325

gir vede copia d'augelletti snelli,
quai molti insieme, e qual vagando solo.
    Quinci s'accorge che di fior novelli
e frutti antichi son quei rami carchi,
non pur di nidi d'infiniti augelli.   330
    Senza che 'l guardo quinci e quindi varchi,
l'incontran d'ogni parte i piacer tutti,
in quest'officio non mai stanchi o parchi.
    E se nel giardin visti in un ridutti
fiere, augei, pesci, rivi, arbori e foglie,   335
fior sempre novi, e d'ogni stagion frutti,
    a mirar in disparte altri s'accoglie,
e come nel guardar talvolta occorre,
da la pianura a l'alto a mirar toglie,
    ne la beltà de' vaghi colli incorre,   340
ch'a la vista, che s'alza, umili e piani
lietamente si vengono ad opporre.
    Questi, dal bel palazzo non lontani,
sembra che per raccôrlo in mezzo 'l seno
si stringan verso lui d'ambe le mani;   345
    e 'ntanto spiegan tutto aperto e pieno
il grembo lor di dolcezze infinite,
che la vista bear possono a pieno.
    Le pecorelle, a pascer l'erbe uscite,
biancheggian per li poggi, a cansar lievi,   350
per poco d'ombra timide e smarrite;
    di questi monti son queste le nevi:
ché quindi 'l verno standosi ognor lunge
non vien giamai che 'l bel terreno aggrevi.
    Quindi letizia e molto utile giunge   355
de le gregge bianchissime ai signori,
di quel che se ne tonde, e uccide, e munge.
    Sparsi per l'ombre, siedono i pastori,
e le canne dispari a sonar posti,
cantan de' loro boscarecci amori;   360
    e se i greggi talvolta erran discosti,
col fischio il caprar sorto gli richiama,

many tiny, nimble birds are seen,
many in a group, one wandering alone.

    There one notices that these branches are laden   328
with new blossoms and ripened fruit,
not only with countless nests of birds.

    No need for the gaze to cross back and forth,   331
for pleasures come on their own to meet it
from every path, never worn out or meager.

    And if in the garden are seen, grouped together,   334
wild beasts, fish, riverbanks, trees, and leaves,
flowers always blooming and fruits of every season,

    to look far away attracts someone else,   337
and when, as sometimes happens when looking,
the gaze shifts up from low to higher places,

    it encounters the beauty of these graceful hills,   340
which, low and smooth, as sight moves upward,
joyfully come to present a contrast.

    They appear, not far from the noble house,   343
to reach out both their hands toward it
in order to gather it to their breast;

    meanwhile they spread their lap   346
wide open, filled with innumerable delights,
to give full pleasure to the gaze.

    Lambs let out to graze in the pastures   349
whiten the hills, glad to wander afar,
but timid and misled by even a small shadow;

    they are the snows upon these hills,   352
so even though winter here lasts a long time,
it never weighs down the lovely landscape.

    Here joy meets great usefulness   355
in the pure white flocks' benefit to the men
who shear and slaughter and feed upon them.

    The shepherds sit scattered in shady spots   358
and, intent on playing their uneven pipes,
they sing about their sylvan loves.

    And if the flocks sometimes roam in the distance,   361
the goatherd stands and whistles to call them back,

poi torna de la musa ai suoi proposti.
    Talor la pastorella ivi, ch'egli ama,
de la fistola al suon mossa ne viene,   365
in modo che di lui cresce la brama:
    fisse le luci avidamente ei tiene
ne le braccia e nel sen nudi, e nel viso,
e d'abbracciarla a pena si ritiene.
    Ma poi quindi a guardar l'occhio diviso   370
tira l'udito suon d'un corno roco,
quando piú in quei pastori egli era fiso;
    ed ecco, da color lontano un poco,
cani co' cacciator disposti in caccia,
ciascuno intento al suo ufficio e 'l suo loco.   375
    Per folti arbusti un can quivi si caccia,
e per terra latrando un altro fiuta,
e de l'orme seguendo va la traccia,
    e tanto corre in fretta e 'l luogo muta,
che d'una macchia fuor la lepre salta: 380
il bracco geme e in seguirla s'aiuta;
    gridan le genti, e intorno ognun l'assalta:
chi le spinge da tergo il veltro in fretta,
qual corre a la via bassa, e quale a l'alta.
    E mentre qua e là ciascun s'affretta,   385
il tuo sguardo, ch'a lor dietro s'aggira,
s'incontra in piacer novo che 'l diletta:
    però ch'altrove d'improviso mira
gente ch'al visco ed a le reti stese
schiera d'augelli accortamente tira.   390
    In queste e quelle insidie non comprese
di quei c'han maggior prezzo a le gran mense
vengon tutte le sorti in copia prese.
    A chi stender piú franco il volo pense,
piú facilmente incontra d'esser còlto   395
ne le non viste reti, ancor che dense.
    Ma 'l tuo sguardo, che va d'intorno sciolto
da questa novità de l'uccellare,
vien da un altro piacer piú novo tolto:

and then returns his attention to the muse.
 Sometimes the shepherdess he loves arrives,   364
attracted by the sound of his panpipe,
in a way that increases his desire:
 he keeps his eyes fixed avidly   367
on her arms and bare breast and beautiful face,
and he can barely refrain from embracing her.
 But then the sound of a raucous horn   370
distracts the shepherd's eye the more,
the more it was absorbed in looking;
 and look! at a little distance away   373
hounds and hunters arranged for the chase,
each intent on his task and position.
 Through thick bushes a dog runs here in pursuit,   376
and on the ground, barking, he sniffs out new prey,
and following its footsteps, tracks it down,
 and he runs so fast and covers so much ground   379
that the hare leaps straight out of a bush:
the hound gives a howl and strains to catch it;
 the people shout and each one attacks it;   382
one man drives the greyhound speeding on its tail,
one takes the low path, another the high one.
 And while each man rushes here and there,   385
your gaze, which follows close behind them,
meets with new pleasures that delight it:
 but then in another place it suddenly sees   388
people using birdlime and outstretched nets
skillfully catching flocks of birds.
 Into this and that unsuspected trap   391
come all species of birds, caught in abundance,
of the kind most valued at great feasts.
 For those birds that try to fly free,   394
it is all the easier to be caught
in nets, which though thick, they do not see.
 But your gaze, moving freely about,   397
drawn from this novelty of catching birds,
shifts, attracted to a newer delight;

perché dinanzi ad abbagliarlo appare   400
del sol un raggio, il qual mandan reflesso
l'acque d'un fonte cristalline e chiare.
    E l'occhio, alquanto chiusosi in se stesso,
dopo quel vacillar s'apre, e ritorna
a guardar quivi dentro l'ombra presso;   405
    e di smeraldi in fresca riva adorna,
di liquido cristal sopra un ruscello,
vede ch'altri a pescar lento soggiorna:
    l'amo innescato tien sospeso in quello,
e con la canna in man fermato attende   410
che 'l pesce cada al morso acuto e fello.
    Altri con reti in varia guisa il prende,
e con piè nudi da la sponda sceso,
frugando per le buche il laccio stende:
    si lancia e scuote il pesce vivo e preso,   415
né cessa di saltar per fin che more,
tratto del fonte in un pratel disteso.
    Vince di questo il soave sapore
quel di quant'altro mai stagno o palude
alberghi, o fondo salso o dolce umore.   420
    Nulla di quel che in sé beato chiude
un terren paradiso, un ciel terrestre,
dal paese amenissimo s'esclude.
    Di semicapri dèi turba silvestre
il fertile terren pianta e coltiva,   425
sotto influsso di stelle amiche e destre;
    e quella che del capo al padre viva
uscío, de' boschi e de le cacce dea,
di questi monti ha in custodia l'oliva.
    Quel che vivo nel ventre infante avea   430
la madre allor che 'l consiglio l'estinse
di Giunon fella, a lei contraria e rea,
    che Giove tolto al proprio lato il cinse,
né fin che nove mesi fûr finiti,
dal fianco, onde 'l nudriva, unqua il discinse,   435
    qui gli olmi guarda, e le ben cólte viti;

for a ray of sun appears before it   400
to dazzle it, reflected from
a fountain's crystalline, bright waters.
     And the eye, for a moment closed in on itself,   403
after this shift opens and returns
to look deep into the shadow nearby;
     and on a cool bank adorned with emeralds   406
above a stream of liquid crystal,
it sees a man slowly passing time fishing:
     he suspends the baited hook in the stream,   409
and with the pole held firmly in his hand,
waits to catch the fish with his sharp, fierce hook.
     Another man nets fish in various ways,   412
and, having climbed barefoot down from the bank,
stretches out the trap, testing it for tears:
     the fish, caught but still living, leap and turn,   415
and keep on jumping until they die,
taken from the water and laid out in the meadow.
     This catch surpasses in delicate flavor   418
fish that dwell in any pool or marsh,
on a salty bottom or in fresh water.
     Nothing of what an earthly paradise,   421
a terrestrial heaven, blessedly contains,
is lacking from this most delightful land.
     A sylvan band, half gods, half men,[45]   424
plant and cultivate the fertile soil,
under the influence of fond and lucky stars:
     and she who sprang full-grown from her father's head,   427
the goddess of woods and of the hunt,[46]
protects the olive tree among these hills.
     The god whom his mother bore as an infant,[47]   430
alive in her womb when she was killed
through fierce Juno's jealous and cruel advice,
     whom Jove bound into his own side,   433
and did not, until nine months had passed,
unloose from his nurturing thigh,
     here oversees the elms and the well-tended vines,   436

45. These are satyrs, demigods half men, half goats, said to live in ancient woods.

46. Athena, the Roman Minerva, was said to have been born from the head of her father, Zeus. But Franco may mean Diana, the goddess of the hunt.

47. Bacchus (the Greek Dionysus) was the son of Semele by Zeus. Juno advised Semele to ask Jove to appear to her in full godly glory, which he granted, so dazzling her that she died. Jove then carried his son in his thigh until he was ready to be born (*Metamorphoses*, 3.312).

le biade di Proserpina la madre,
Vertunno e Flora gli arbori graditi.
    Mille, scese dal ciel, benigne squadre
d'eletti spirti infiorano il bel nido,   440
e 'l guardan da le cose infeste ed adre.
    Dolce de' miei pensieri albergo fido,
pien d'aranci e di cedri, e lieto in guisa
che vince ogni concetto, ogni uman grido,
    resta la mente mia vinta e conquisa,   445
che 'l ben in te con larga mano infuso
dal celeste Motor forma e divisa;
    e come tu sei bel fuor d'uman uso,
cosí ne l'opra de l'imaginarti
riman l'ingegno inutile e confuso;   450
    e se vaga pur vengo di lodarti,
come confusa son dentro, confondo
de le tue lodi l'ordine e le parti.
    Ben quanto in questo assai mal corrispondo,
tanto ne la prontezza del desire   455
con grata rispondenza sovrabondo.
    Vorrei, ma in parte non so alcuna, dire
le lodi del signor che ti possiede,
né stil uman poría tant'alto gire.
    Com'ogni loco è cielo, ove Dio siede,   460
ma poi nel ciel, ch'è adorno a maraviglia,
espressamente ferma la sua sede,
    cosí gran lode ogni soggiorno piglia
da quel signor, dovunque mai perviene,
che regge 'l mio voler con le sue ciglia;   465
    ma pur il seggio suo proprio ei ritiene
in voi, perciò sommamente beate,
contrade soavissime ed amene:
    per lui tante beltà vi furon date,
e senza lui de' vostri pregi intieri   470
sareste senza dubbio alcun private.
    Gitene, colli, assai per questo alteri,
ch'avete grazia di servir a lui,

these the harvest of Proserpina's mother,[48]
those the trees dear to Vertumnus and Flora.[49]

    A thousand kind squadrons of chosen spirits,   439
descended from heaven, deck the fair nest with flowers
and protect it against hostile and threatening things.

    Sweet and faithful shelter for my thoughts,   442
full of orange trees and cedars, and joyous
in a way that exceeds all human grasp and fame,

    my mind remains overwhelmed and stunned,   445
for it recalls the good poured into you
with a generous hand by the celestial Mover;

    and since your beauty exceeds any human norm,   448
so in the effort of imagining you,
the intellect remains inept and confused;

    and if, in my longing, I try to praise you,   451
because I'm confused within, I confuse
the order and the elements of your praise.

    As badly as my words match my will in this,   454
I abound as far in eager desire
to write with a grace that measures up to you.

    I would like, although I hardly know how,   457
to speak in praise of the lord who owns you,
but no human style can rise so high.

    Just as any place where God resides is heaven,   460
yet in heaven, which is marvelously adorned,
he deliberately establishes his seat,

    so every spot acquires great praise   463
from this lord, wherever he may go,
who rules my will with a blink of his eyes.

    And yet he maintains his true seat here   466
in you, so that you are most highly blessed,
most serene and agreeable countryside:

    by him you were granted so much beauty   469
that without him, you would doubtless be
deprived of everything that gives you value.

    Go forth, hills, most proud on this account—   472
that you enjoy the favor of serving a man

---

48. Proserpina was the daughter of Ceres, the Roman goddess of agricultural fertility.

49. Vertumnus was the god of autumn and late-season fruits, Flora the goddess of spring.

degno di mille mitre e mille imperi.
   Quest'è il buon vostro regnator, per cui   475
vincon le vostre inusitate forme
tutto 'l diletto de' paesi altrui.
   Per farsi incontra a le sue gentili orme
crescon l'erbette e i fior, ch'al suo toccarli
vien che nova beltà gli orni e riforme;   480
   e l'onorate man presta a lavarli
dentro la stanza l'acqua dolce arriva,
e dietro vaga ognor par brame andarli.
   Da questa una fontana si deriva,
che d'ogn'intorno puro argento stilla   485
da vena di cristal corrente e viva.
   Dentro 'l terren fecondo il cielo instilla
virtú che fa produr soavi frutti,
e l'aria salutifera e tranquilla:
   il piacer sommo e 'l vero fin di tutti   490
è che 'l signor gli goda e gli divida,
ch'ad arbitrio di lui furon produtti.
   Qualunque in verde ramo augel s'annida,
a lui canta, a lui vive, e s'a lui piace,
lieto sostien ancor ch'altri l'uccida;   495
   qualunque in monte o in piano animal giace,
selvaggio errante, liberale dono
di se stesso a costui contento face;
   e le mandre, che quivi in copia sono,
e tutto quel che la terra produce,   500
son di lui molto piú ch'io non ragiono.
   Qui la natura carca si riduce,
per dar del suo tesoro a lui tributo,
che da l'Indo e 'l Sabeo quivi traduce:
   non fosse questo ben da lui goduto,   505
certo è che in tanta copia mai dal cielo
non fôra ad alcun altro pervenuto.
   A costui cede il gran signor di Delo,
piú del suo chiaro, del valor il lume,
cui nube non offusca od altro velo;   510

worth a thousand miters and a thousand kingdoms.

    This is your good ruler, through whom   475
your extraordinary beauties excel
everything that gives delight in other lands.

    To encounter his noble footsteps,   478
the little grasses and flowers grow high,
for at his touch new beauty adorns and renews them;

    and, ready to wash his honored hands,   481
fresh water enters his room and seems
always to long to follow close behind him.

    From this water a fountain is formed,   484
which pours forth pure silver everywhere
from a fast-running, fresh stream of crystal.

    Into the fertile land heaven instills   487
a power that brings forth sweet fruit
and makes the air healthful and serene;

    the supreme joy and true goal of all these things   490
is that their lord enjoys and shares them out,
for they were produced according to his will.

    Whatever bird nests in a green bough   493
sings to him, lives for him, and, if it pleases him,
it remains happy even if a man kills it;

    whatever creature dwells on the hill or in the plain,   496
wandering in the wild, freely offers itself
as a gift to him, content to do so;

    and the herds, which are so numerous there,   499
and everything that the earth brings forth
belong to him more than I can say.

    Here, heavy with riches, nature lightens her load   502
in order to add tribute to his treasure,
which arrives here from the Indus and Sheba;[50]

    if all this wealth did not bring him pleasure,   505
certainly such abundance never before
would have come from heaven for any other man.

    To this man the great lord of Delos[51]   508
gives not only the brightness but the power of his light,
which no cloud or other veil obscures;

---

50. The Indus is a river in India, Sheba a southern region of Arabia. Both countries were famous for their wealth of natural resources.

51. The god of the island Delos is Apollo.

  e di dolce eloquenzia il puro fiume
a lui dona di Giove il fedel messo,
ch'al cappello ed ai piè porta le piume.
  A questo, a cui comandar è concesso
agli elementi che in quel suo soggiorno   515
oprano quanto è piú gradito ad esso,
  andai, dal gran desio tirata, un giorno:
non per error di via, né ch'io passassi
quindi avante d'altronde al mio ritorno;
  ma d'Adria mossi a quest'effetto i passi,   520
né interromper giamai vòlsi il vïaggio,
perch'a l'andar via pessima trovassi.
  Di questo mio signor cortese e saggio,
nel sentier aspro, mi fu grata scorta
de la virtute il sempiterno raggio: 525
  da cosí chiaro e dolce lume scorta,
la strada, ch'al desio lunga sembrava,
al disagio parea commoda e corta.
  La difficoltà grande superava
d'ogni altra cosa sol con la speranza,   530
che di veder uom sí gentil portava.
  Alfin pur giunsi a la bramata stanza,
né potrei giamai dir sí com'io fossi
raccolta con gratissima sembianza.
  A sí dolce spettacolo rimossi   535
tutti i miei gravi e torbidi pensieri,
che venner meco, allor che d'Adria mossi,
  e tra mille gratissimi piaceri,
ristoro presi e mi riconfortai,
qual fa chi 'l suo ben gode e 'l meglio speri.   540
  Ma poco al mio talento mi fermai
al loco da me dianzi raccontato,
di cui piú bello non si vide mai,
  né con piú vago e splendido apparato
di vasi, e di famiglia bene instrutta,   545
che pronta al signor serve d'ogni lato,
  e intorno a lui con ordine ridutta,

and the pure river of sweet eloquence   511
is given him by the faithful messenger of Jove,[52]
who wears feathered wings at his head and his feet.

   To him, who has been given command   514
over the elements, which, on his estate,
perform as much as he requires,

   I went one day, drawn by strong desire,   517
not because I took the wrong road
or once passed by, returning from elsewhere;

   I left Adria precisely for this purpose,   520
and I refused to interrupt my journey
just because the road that led there was so bad.

   On the rough path I was kindly accompanied   523
by the eternally shining beacon
of the virtue of my wise and courteous lord:

   and, escorted by that bright, sweet light,   526
the road, which seemed so long to my desire,
to my discomfort appeared smooth and short.

   Obstacles of every other kind   529
were overcome only through my hope
of seeing such a noble man.

   Yet at last I reached the place I longed for,   532
and I will never be able to describe
with what a gracious manner I was received.

   At such a welcome sight, I shed   535
all the grave and troubled thoughts
that came with me when I left Adria;

   and amid a thousand delightful pleasures   538
I was comforted and restored,
as one enjoys bounty and hopes for the best.

   But I stayed a short time, compared to my wish,   541
in the place that I have just described,
more beautiful than anyone has ever seen,

   and a fairer and more splendid display of wares   544
and a household of well-trained servants,
ready to wait on their lord from all sides,

   and around him, lined up in good order,   547

---

52. Mercury (the Greek Hermes), Jove's messenger, was associated with eloquent human speech.

di varia età, di vario pelo mista,
vestita a un modo, corrisponde tutta.

Questa tra l'altre è ancor nobile vista,   550
veder d'intorno a sé ben divisata
d'onesta gente vaga e doppia lista.

Dunque, de le Fumane unica, amata
terra, ov'albergan le delizie, quante
ogni stanza real pòn far beata,   555

cedano Baie, e Pozzuol non si vante,
ch'unite in loro han le vaghe Fumane
le grazie di là suso tutte quante.

Cose tutte eccellenti e sopraumane,
dolci a la vista, al gusto, e gli altri sensi,   560
le piagge han grate agli occhi, al varcar piane.

E perch'al loco internamente io pensi,
quanto piú di lui parlo, e manco il lodo,
e i miei desir di lui si fan piú intensi.

Volando col pensier, la lingua annodo.   565

of various ages and shades of hair
yet, dressed alike, they obey him as one.

    This among others is another noble sight,   550
to have before one's eyes, in handsome livery,
a double row of honest, good-looking folk.

    So, unique and beloved land of Fumane,   553
where enough delights abide to make
every royal seat a place of bliss,

    let Baia and Pozzuoli cease to boast,[53]   556
for lovely Fumane contains within
all the heavenly graces attributed to them.

    Excellent, superhuman even, sweet   559
to the eyes, to the taste, and all the other senses,
the hills are lovely to look at and easy to climb.

    And because I think, deep inside, of that place,   562
the more I speak of it, the less I praise it,
and my desires for it grow more intense.

    Flying in thought, I tie my tongue into a knot.   565

---

53. Baia and Pozzuoli were Neapolitan villas praised in the poetry of Luigi Tansillo (Favretti, "Rime," 371).

BIBLIOGRAPHY

PRIMARY TEXTS

Agrippa, Henricus Cornelius. *Declamation on the Nobility and Preeminence of the Female Sex* (1509). Trans. Albert Rabil. Chicago: University of Chicago Press, 1996.

Alberti, Leon Battista. *The Family in Renaissance Florence*. Trans. Renée Neu Watkins. Columbia: University of South Carolina Press, 1969.

Aretino, Pietro. *Lettere, il primo e secondo libro*. In *Tutte le Opere*, ed. Francesco Flora and Alessandro del Vita. Milan: Mondadori, 1960.

———. *Dialogues*. Trans. Raymond Rosenthal. New York: Marsilio, 1994.

Ariosto, Ludovico. *Orlando Furioso*. Trans. Barbara Reynolds. 2 vols. 2d ed. New York: Penguin Books, 1977.

Astell, Mary. *The First English Feminist: Reflections on Marriage and Other Writings*. Ed. Bridget Hill. New York: St. Martin's Press, 1986.

Barbaro, Francesco. *On Wifely Duties*. Trans. Benjamin Kohl. In *The Earthly Republic*, ed. Kohl and R. G. Witt, 179–228. Philadelphia: University of Pennsylvania Press, 1978.

Boccaccio, Giovanni. *Concerning Famous Women*. Trans. Guido A. Guarino. New Brunswick, N.J.: Rutgers University Press, 1963.

———. *Corbaccio or the Labyrinth of Love*. Trans. Anthony K. Cassell. 2d rev. ed. Binghamton, N.Y.: Medieval and Renaissance Texts and Studies, 1993.

———. *Il Decamerone*. In *Tutte le opere di Giovanni Boccaccio*, vol. 4, ed. Vittore Branca. Milan: Mondadori, 1976.

———. *The Decameron*. Trans. Guido Waldman. Oxford: Oxford University Press, 1993.

Bruni, Leonardo. "On the Study of Literature, to Lady Battista Malatesta of Montefeltro" (1405). In *The Humanism of Leonardo Bruni: Selected Texts*. Trans. Gordon Griffiths, James Hankins, and David Thompson, 240–51. Binghamton: Medieval and Renaissance Texts and Studies, 1987.

Calza, Carlo. *Documenti inediti sulla prostituzione tratti dagli archivi della repubblica veneta.* Milan: Tipografia della Società Cooperativa, 1869.

Castiglione, Baldassare. *The Courtier.* Trans. George Bull. New York: Viking Penguin, 1967.

Il Catalogo di tutte le principali et più honorate cortigiane di Venezia (1575). In Rita Casagrande di Villaviera, Le cortigiane veneziane del Cinquecento. Milan: Longanesi, 1968.

Cicero, Marcus Tullius. *Letters to Atticus.* Trans. E. D. Winstedt. Cambridge: Harvard University Press, 1928.

Dazzi, Manlio. *Il fiore della lirica veneziana: Il libro segreto (chiuso),* vol. 2. Vicenza: Neri Pozza, 1956.

De Lorenzi, G. Batta. *Leggi e memorie venete sulla prostituzione fino alla caduta della Repubblica.* Venice: Privately published for Lord Orford,1870–72.

Elyot, Thomas. *Defence of Good Women: The Feminist Controversy of the Renaissance.* Ed. Diane Bornstein. Facsimile Reproductions. New York: Delmar, 1980.

Erasmus, Desiderius. "Courtship," "The Girl with No Interest in Marriage," "The Repentant Girl," "Marriage," "The Abbot and the Learned Lady," "The New Mother." In *The Colloquies of Erasmus,* trans. Craig R. Thomas. Chicago: University of Chicago Press, 1965.

Fonte, Moderata (Modesta Pozzo-Zorzi). *Il merito delle donne.* Venice: Domenico Umberti, 1600. Ed. Adriana Chemello. Mirano: Eidos, 1988.

———. *Tredici canti del Floridoro.* Venice: Rampazetti, 1581.

———. *The Worth of Women: Wherein Is Clearly Revealed Their Nobility and Their Superiority to Men.* Ed. and trans. Virginia Cox. Chicago: University of Chicago Press, 1997.

Franco, Veronica. *Lettere familiari a diversi.* Venice: n.p., 1580.

———. *Lettere dall'unica edizione del MDLXXX con Proemio e nota iconografica.* Venice, 1580. Ed. Benedetto Croce. Naples: Ricciardi, 1949.

———. *Terze rime.* Venice: n.p., 1575.

———. *Rime: Gaspara Stampa e Veronica Franco.* Ed. Abdelkader Salza. Scrittori d'Italia, vol. 52. Bari: Laterza, 1913.

———. *Veronica Franco: Rime.* Ed. Stefano Bianchi. Milan: Mursia, 1995.

Kempe. Margery. *The Book of Margery Kempe.* Trans. Barry Windeatt. New York: Viking Penguin, 1986.

King, Margaret L., and Albert Rabil, Jr., eds. *Her Immaculate Hand: Selected Works by and about the Women Humanists of Renaissance Italy.* Binghamton: Medieval and Renaissance Texts and Studies, 1983; 2d rev. ed., 1991.

Klein, Joan Larsen, ed. *Daughters, Wives, and Widows: Writings by Men about Women and Marriage in England, 1500–1640.* Urbana: University of Illinois Press, 1992.

Knox, John. *The Political Writings of John Knox: The First Blast of the Trumpet against the Monstruous Regiment of Women and Other Selected Works.* Ed. Marvin Breslow. Washington, D.C.: Folger Shakespeare Library, 1985.

Kors, Alan C., and Edward Peters, eds. *Witchcraft in Europe, 1100–1700: A Documentary History.* Philadelphia: University of Pennsylvania Press, 1972.

Kræmer, Heinrich, and Jacob Sprenger. *Malleus Malificarum* (ca. 1487). Trans. Montague Summers. London: Pushkin Press, 1928; reprinted New York: Dover, 1971.

de Lorris, Guillaume, and Jean de Meun. *The Romance of the Rose.* Trans. Charles Dahlbert. Princeton: Princeton University Press, 1971; reprinted University Press of New England, 1983.

Marinella, Lucrezia. *La nobiltà e l'eccellenza delle donne.* Venice: Giovanni Battista Ciotti, 1600; 2d ed., 1601.

de Navarre, Marguerite. *The Heptameron.* Trans. P. A. Chilton. New York: Viking Penguin, 1984.

de Pizan, Christine. *The Book of the City of Ladies.* Trans. Earl Jeffrey Richards. Forward Marina Warner. New York: Persea Books, 1982.

Spenser, Edmund. *The Faerie Queene.* Ed. Thomas P. Roche, Jr.,with C. Patrick O'Donnell, Jr. New Haven: Yale University Press, 1978.

Teresa d'Avila, Saint. *The Life of Saint Teresa of Avila by Herself.* Trans. J. M. Cohen. New York: Viking Penguin, 1957.

Toderini, Teodoro. *Genealogie delle famiglie venete ascritte alla cittadinanza originaria.* 4 vols. Miscellanea codici, I.

Vecellio, Cesare. *Degli habiti antichi et moderni di diverse parti del mondo.* 2 vols. Venice: D. Zenaro, 1590.

Venier, Domenico. *Rime di Domenico Venier.* Ed. Pierantonio Serassi. Bergamo: Lancelotti, 1751.

Vives, Juan Luis. *The Instruction of the Christian Woman.* 2d ed. Trans. Rycharde Hyrde. London, 1557. Originally published 1524.

Weyer, Johann. *Witches, Devils, and Demons in the Renaissance: Johann Meyer, De Praestigiis daemonum.* Ed. George Mora with Benjamin G. Kohl, Erik Midelfort, and Helen Bacon. Trans. John Shea. Binghamton: Medieval and Renaissance Texts and Studies, 1991.

Wilson, Katharina M., ed. *Medieval Women Writers.* Athens: University of Georgia Press, 1984.

———, ed. *Women Writers of the Renaissance and Reformation.* Athens: University of Georgia Press, 1987.

Wilson, Katharina M., and Frank Warnke, eds. *Women Writers of the Seventeenth Century.* Athens: University of Georgia Press, 1989.

SECONDARY TEXTS

Adler, Sara Maria. "Veronica Franco's Petrarchan *Terze Rime:* Subverting the Master's Plan." *Italica* 65, no. 3 (1988): 213–33.

Aguzzi-Barbagli, Danilo. "Dialettica femminista di Veronica Franco." *Proceedings*: *Pacific Northwest Council on Foreign Languages, Twenty-eighth Annual Meeting (1977)*, 84–7.

Balduino, Armando. "Restauri e recuperi per Maffio Venier." In *Medioevo e Rinascimento veneto: Con altri studi in onore di Lino Lazzarini*, 2: 231–63. 2 vols. Padua: Antenore, 1979.

Barzaghi, Antonio. *Donne o cortigiane? La prostituzione a Venezia: Documenti di costume dal XVI al XVIII secolo.* Verona: Bertani, 1980.

Bassanese, Fiora A. "Private Lives and Public Lies: Texts by Courtesans of the Italian Renaissance." *Texas Studies in Language and Literature* 30, no. 3 (1988): 295–319.

———. "What's In a Name? Self-Naming and Renaissance Women Poets." *Annali d'Italianistica* 7 (1989): 104–15.

———. "Selling the Self; or, the Epistolary Production of Courtesans." In *Italian Women Writers from the Renaissance to the Present*, ed. Maria Ornella Marotti, 69–82. University Park: Pennsylvania State University Press, 1996.

Beilin, Elaine V. *Redeeming Eve: Women Writers of the English Renaissance.* Princeton: Princeton University Press, 1987.

Benson, Pamela. *The Invention of Renaissance Woman: The Challenge of Female Independence in the Literature and Thought of Italy and England.* University Park: Pennsylvania State University Press, 1992.

Bianchi, Stefano. "Petrarchismo liminare, tradizione letteraria e 'gioco d'amore' nella poesia di Veronica Franco." In *Passare il tempo: La letteratura del gioco e dell'intrattenimento dal XII al XVI secolo,* 2: 721–37. Rome: Salerno, 1993.

Bistort, Giulio. *Il Magistrato alle Pompe nella Repubblica di Venezia.* Venice: Emiliana, 1912; reprinted Bologna: Forni, 1969.

Bloch, R. Howard. *Medieval Misogyny and the Invention of Western Romantic Love.* Chicago: University of Chicago Press, 1991.

Casagrande di Villaviera, Rita. *Le cortigiane veneziane del Cinquecento.* Milan: Longanesi, 1968.

Chemello, Adrianna. "Donna di palazzo, moglie, cortigiana: Ruoli e funzioni sociali della donna in alcuni trattati del Cinquecento." In *La corte e il 'Cortegiano,'* ed. Amedeo Quondam. Rome: Bulzoni, 1980.

Chojnacka, Monica. "Women, Charity, and Community in Early Modern Venice: The Casa delle Zitelle." *Renaissance Quarterly* 51 (Spring 1998): 68–91.

Chojnacki, Stanley. "'The Most Serious Duty': Motherhood, Gender, and Patrician Culture in Renaissance Venice." In *Refiguring Woman: Perspectives on Gender and the Italian Renaissance*, ed. Marilyn Migiel and Juliana Schiesari, 133–54. Ithaca: Cornell University Press, 1991.

———. "La posizione della donna a Venezia nel Cinquecento." In *Tiziano e Venezia*, 65–70. Vicenza: Neri Pozza, 1980.

Cohen, Elizabeth. "'Courtesans' and 'Whores': Words and Behavior in Roman Streets." *Women's Studies* 19, no. 2 (1991): 201–8.

Costa, Pietro. *Les Courtisanes et la police des moeurs à Venise.* Sauveterre: Imprimerie Chollet, 1886.

Crescimbeni, Giovan Mario. *L'istoria della volgar poesia.* 6 vols. Venice: L. Basegio, 1730–31.

Croce, Benedetto. "La lirica cinquecentesca" in *Poesia popolare e poesia d'arte: Studi sulla poesia italiana dal Tre al Cinquecento,* 414–9. Bari: Laterza, 1933.

———. "Veronica Franco." In *Poeti e scrittori del pieno e tardo Rinascimento,* 3: 218–34. Bari: Laterza, 1952.

———. "Sulla iconografia di Veronica Franco." In *Anedotti di varia letteratura,* 2: 1–11. Bari: Laterza, 1953.

Davis, Natalie Zemon. *Society and Culture in Early Modern France,* chaps. 3 and 5. Stanford: Stanford University Press, 1975.

De Nolhac, Pierre, and Angelo Solerti. *Il viaggio in Italia di Enrico III Re di Francia e le feste a Venezia, Ferrara, Mantova e Torino.* Turin: 1890.

Derosas, Renzo."Moralità e giustizia a Venezia nel '500–'600: Gli esecutori contro la bestemmia." In *Stato, società e giustizia nella Repubblica Veneta,* ed. Gaetano Cozzi. Rome: Jouvence, 1980.

Diberti Leigh, Marcella. *Veronica Franco: Donna, poetessa e cortigiana del Rinascimento.* Ivrea: Priuli and Verlucca, 1988.

Doglio, M. L. "Scrittura e 'offizio di parole' nelle *Lettere familiari* di Veronica Franco." In *Lettere e donna: Scrittura epistolare al femminile tra Quattro e Cinquecento,* 33–48. Rome: Bulzoni, 1996.

Ellero, Giuseppe. *Archivio I.R.E.: Inventari di fondi antichi degli ospedali e luoghi pii di Venezia: Istituzioni di Ricovero e di Educazione.* Venice: 1984–87.

Favretti, Elena. "Rime e Lettere di Veronica Franco." *Giornale storico della letteratura italiana* 163, no. 523 (1986): 355–82.

Feldman, Martha. "The Academy of Domenico Venier, Music's Literary Muse in Mid- *Cinquecento* Venice." *Renaissance Quarterly* 44, no. 3 (1991): 475–510.

———. *City Culture and the Madrigal at Venice.* Berkeley: University of California Press, 1995.

Ferguson, Margaret W., Maureen Quilligan, and Nancy J. Vickers, eds. *Rewriting the Renaissance: The Discourses of Gender Difference in Early Modern Europe.* Chicago: University of Chicago Press, 1986.

Finlay, Robert. *Politics in Renaissance Venice.* New Brunswick: Rutgers University Press, 1980.

Frugoni, A. Giovanni. "I capitoli della cortigiana Veronica Franco." *Belfagor* 3 (1948): 44–59.

Garner, Jane F. *Women in Roman Law and Society.* Bloomington: Indiana University Press, 1992.

Il gioco dell'amore: Le cortigiane di Venezia dal Trecento al Settecento. Exhibition catalogue, Casinò Municipale, Ca' Vendramin Calergi, 1990. Venice: Berenice, 1990.

Graf, Arturo. "Una cortigiana fra mille: Veronica Franco." In *Attraverso il Cinquecento,* 215–351. Turin: Chiantore, 1888.

Grendler, Paul F. *Schooling in Renaissance Italy: Literacy and Learning, 1300–1600.* Baltimore: Johns Hopkins University Press, 1989.

A History of Women in the West. Vol. 1, *From Ancient Goddesses to Christian Saints,* ed. Pauline Schmitt Pantel. Cambridge: Harvard University Press, 1992. Vol. 2, *Silences of the Middle Ages,* ed. Christiane Klapisch-Zuber. Cambridge: Harvard University Press, 1992. Vol. 3, *Renaissance and Enlightenment Paradoxes,* ed. Natalie Zemon Davis and Arlette Farge. Cambridge: Harvard University Press, 1993.

Herlihy, David. "Did Women Have a Renaissance? A Reconsideration." *Medievalia et Humanistica,* n.s. 13 (1985): 1–22.

Horowitz, Maryanne Cline. "Aristotle and Woman." *Journal of the History of Biology* 9 (1976): 183–213.

Hull, Suzanne. *Chaste, Silent, and Obedient: English Books for Women, 1475–1640.* San Marino, Calif.: Huntington Library, 1982.

Jones, Ann Rosalind. "Assimilation with a Difference: Renaissance Women Poets and Literary Influence." *Yale French Studies* 62 (1981): 135–53.

———. "City Women and Their Audiences: Louise Labé and Veronica Franco." In *Rewriting the Renaissance: The Discourses of Gender Difference in Early Modern Europe,* ed. Margaret W. Ferguson, Maureen Quilligan, and Nancy J. Vickers, 299–316. Chicago: University of Chicago Press, 1986.

———. "Surprising Fame: Renaissance Gender Ideologies and Women's Lyric." In *The Poetics of Gender,* ed. Nancy K. Miller, 74–95. New York: Columbia University Press, 1986.

———. *The Currency of Eros: Women's Love Lyric in Europe, 1540–1620.* Bloomington: Indiana University Press, 1990.

Jordan, Constance. *Renaissance Feminism: Literary Texts and Political Models.* Ithaca: Cornell University Press, 1990.

Kelly, Joan. "Did Women Have a Renaissance?" In her *Women, History, and Theory.* Chicago: University of Chicago Press, 1984. Also in *Becoming Visible: Women in European History,* ed. Renate Bridenthal, Claudia Koonz, and Susan M. Stuard, 175–202. 2d ed. Boston: Houghton Mifflin, 1987.

———. "Early Feminist Theory and the *Querelle des Femmes, 1400–1789.*" In *Women, History and Theory,* 65–109. Chicago: University of Chicago Press, 1984. Also in *Signs* 8 (1982): 4–28.

Kelso, Ruth. *Doctrine for the Lady of the Renaissance.* 2d ed. Foreword by Katharine M. Rogers. Urbana: University of Illinois Press, 1978. Originally published 1956.

King, Margaret. *Women of the Renaissance.* Foreword by Catharine R. Stimpson. Chicago: University of Chicago Press, 1991.

Laqueur, Thomas. *Making Sex: Body and Gender from the Greeks to Freud.* Cambridge: Harvard University Press, 1990.

Larivaille, Paul. *La vita quotidiana delle cortigiane nell'Italia del Rinascimento: Roma e Venezia nei secoli XV e XVI.* Paris: Hachette, 1975.

Lawner, Lynn. *Lives of the Courtesans.* Milan: Rizzoli, 1985.

Lerner, Gerda. *Creation of Feminist Consciousness, 1000–1870.* New York: Oxford University Press, 1994.

Lichtenstein, Jacqueline. "Making Up Representation: The Risks of Femininity." *Representations* 20 (1987): 77–87.

Lochrie, Karma. *Margery Kempe and Translations of the Flesh.* Philadelphia: University of Pennsylvania Press, 1992.

Maclean, Ian. *The Renaissance Notion of Woman: A Study of the Fortunes of Scholasticism and Medical Science in European Intellectual Life.* Cambridge: Cambridge University Press, 1980.

———. *Woman Triumphant: Feminism in French Literature*, 1612–1652. Oxford: Clarendon Press, 1977.

Martin, Ruth. *Witchcraft and the Inquisition in Venice, 1550–1650.* Oxford: Basil Blackwell, 1989.

Masetti Zannini, Gian Ludovico. "Veronica Franco a Roma: Una pellegrina 'tra mille.'" *Strenna dei romanisti* (1982): 322–31.

Masson, Georgina. *The Courtesans of the Italian Renaissance.* London: Secker and Warburg, 1975.

Matter, E. Ann, and John Coakley, eds. *Creative Women in Medieval and Early Modern Italy.* Philadelphia: University of Pennsylvania Press, 1994.

Menetto, L., and G. Zennaro, eds. *Storia del malcostume a Venezia nei secoli XVI e XVII.* Abano Terme: Piovan, 1987.

Migiel, Marilyn. "Gender Studies and the Italian Renaissance." In *Interpreting the Italian Renaissance: Literary Perspectives*, ed. Antonio Toscano, 29–41. Stony Brook, N.Y.: Forum Italicum, 1991.

———. "Veronica Franco (1546–1591)." In *Italian Women Writers: A Bio-bibliographic Sourcebook,* ed. Rinaldina Russell, 138–44. Westport, Conn.: Greenwood Press, 1994.

Migiel, Marilyn, and Juliana Schiesari, eds. *Refiguring Woman: Perspectives on Gender in the Italian Renaissance.* Ithaca: Cornell University Press, 1991.

Milani, Marisa. "L'incanto' di Veronica Franco." *Giornale storico della letteratura italiana* 262: no. 518 (1985): 250–63.

Molmenti, Pietro. *La storia di Venezia nella vita privata dalle origini alla caduta della repubblica.* 3 vols. 7th ed. Bergamo: Istituto italiano d'arti grafiche, 1928.

Monson, Craig A., ed. *The Crannied Wall: Women, Religion, and the Arts in Early Modern Europe.* Ann Arbor: University of Michigan Press, 1992.

Muir, Edward. *Civic Ritual in Renaissance Venice.* Princeton: Princeton University Press, 1981.

Musatti, Eugenio. *La donna in Venezia.* Padua: Arnaldo Forni, 1892.

Nordio, Tiziana Agostini. "Rime dialettali attribuite a Maffio Venier: Primo regesto." *Quaderni veneti* (1985): 7–23.

Okin, Susan Moller. *Women in Western Political Thought*. Princeton: Princeton University Press, 1979.

Olivieri, Achillo. "Erotisme et groupes sociaux à Venise au XVIe siècle: La Courtisane." *Communications* 35 (1982): 85–91.

Padoan, Giorgio. "Il mondo delle cortigiane nella letteratura rinascimentale." In *Le cortigiane di Venezia dal Trecento al Settecento*. Exhibition catalogue, Casino Municipale, 1990. Milan: Berenice, 1990.

Pagan, Pier. "Sulla Accademia 'Venetiana' o della 'Fama.'" *Atti dell'Istituto Veneto di Scienze, Lettere ed Arti* 132 (1973–74): 359–92.

Pagels, Elaine. *Adam, Eve, and the Serpent*. New York: HarperCollins, 1988.

Pancrazi, P. "Lettere di cortigiana onesta." In *Nel giardino di Candido,* 109–16. Florence: Monnier, 1950.

Phillipy, Patricia. "'Altera Dido': The Model of Ovid's *Heroides* in the Poems of Gaspara Stampa and Veronica Franco." *Italica* 69 (1992): 1–18.

Piseztsky, Rosita Levi. *Storia del costume in Italia*. 5 vols. Turin: Einaudi, 1964–69.

Poli, Doretta D. "La moda nella Venezia del Palladio, 1550–1580." In *Architettura e utopia nella Venezia del Cinquecento*, ed. Lionello Puppi. Milan: Electa, 1980.

Pomeroy, Sarah. *Goddesses, Whores, Wives, and Slaves: Women in Classical Antiquity*. New York: Schocken Books, 1976.

Pullan, Brian. *Rich and Poor in Renaissance Venice: The Social Institution of a Catholic State, 1580 to 1620*. Cambridge: Harvard University Press, 1971.

Quondam, Amedeo. *Le 'carte messaggiere': Retorica e modelli di communicazione epistolare per un indice dei libri di lettere del Cinquecento*. Rome: Bulzoni, 1981.

Rose, Mary Beth. *Women in the Middle Ages and the Renaissance: Literary and Historical Perspectives*. Syracuse: Syracuse University Press, 1986.

Rosenthal, Margaret F. "A Courtesan's Voice: Epistolary Self-Portraiture in Veronica Franco's *Terze Rime* (1575)." In *Writing the Female Voice: Essays on Epistolary Literature*, ed. Elizabeth Goldsmith, 3–23. Boston: Northeastern University Press, 1989.

———. "Veronica Franco's *Terze Rime*: The Venetian Courtesan's Defense." *Renaissance Quarterly* 42, no. 2 (1989): 227–57.

———. "Venetian Women Citizens and Their Discontents." In *Sexuality and Gender in Early Modern Europe: Institutions, Texts, Images*, ed. James Grantham Turner, 107–32. Cambridge: Cambridge University Press, 1992.

———. *The Honest Courtesan: Veronica Franco, Citizen and Writer in Sixteenth-Century Venice*. Chicago: University of Chicago Press, 1992.

Rossi, Paola. "I ritratti femminili di Domenico Tintoretto." *Arte illustrata* 30 (1970): 92–9.

Ruggieri, Nicola. *Maffio Venier: Arcivescovo e letterato veneziano del Cinquecento*. Udine: Tipografia Bosetti, 1909.

Ruggiero, Guido. *The Boundaries of Eros: Sex Crime and Sexuality in Renaissance Venice.* New York: Oxford University Press, 1985.

Schiavon, Alessandra. "Per la biografia di Veronica Franco: Nuovi documenti." *Atti dell'Istituto Veneto di Scienze, Lettere ed Arti* 137 (1978–79): 243–56.

Stortoni, Laura Anna, ed. *Women Poets of the Italian Renaissance: Courtly Ladies and Courtesans.* Trans. Laura Anna Stortoni and Mary Prentice Lillie. New York: Italica Press, 1997.

Stuard, Susan M. "The Dominion of Gender: Women's Fortunes in the High Middle Ages." In *Becoming Visible: Women in European History*, ed. Renate Bridenthal, Claudia Kooonz, and Susan M. Stuard, 153–72. 2d ed. Boston: Houghton Mifflin, 1987,

Taddeo, Edoardo. *Il manierismo letterario e i lirici veneziani del tardo Cinquecento.* Rome: Bulzoni, 1974.

Tassini, Giuseppe. *Veronica Franco: Celebre poetessa e cortigiana del secolo XVI.* Venice: Fontana, 1874; reprinted Venice: Alfieri, 1969.

Tetel, Marcel. *Marguerite de Navarre's Heptameron: Themes, Language, and Structure.* Durham, N.C.: Duke University Press, 1973.

Treggiari, Susan. *Roman Marriage: Iusti Conjuges from the Time of Cicero to the Time of Ulpian.* Oxford: Oxford University Press, 1991.

Ulvioni, Paola. "Accademie e cultura in Italia dalla Controriforma all'Arcadia: Il caso Veneziano." In *Libri e documenti: Archivio storico civico e Biblioteca Trivulziana.* Milan: Archivio Storico Civico e Biblioteca Trivulziana, 1979.

Urgnani, Elena. " Veronica Franco: Tracce di dantismi in una scrittura femminile." *Canadian Journal of Italian Studies* 14, nos. 42–3 (1991): 1–10.

Walsh, William T. *St. Teresa of Avila: A Biography.* Rockford, Ill.: TAN Books and Publications, 1987.

Warner, Marina. *Alone of All Her Sex: The Myth and the Cult of the Virgin Mary.* New York: Knopf, 1976.

Weisner, Merry E. *Women and Gender in Early Modern Europe.* Cambridge: Cambridge University Press, 1993.

Willard, Charity Cannon. *Christine de Pizan: Her Life and Works.* New York: Persea Books, 1984.

Wilson, Katharina, ed. *An Encyclopedia of Continental Women Writers.* New York: Garland, 1991.

Zorzi, Alvise. *Cortigiana veneziana: Veronica Franco e i suoi poeti.* Milan: Camunia, 1986.

INDEX